# Amid a Warring World

**Issues in the History of American Foreign Relations**

*Series Editor:* Robert J. McMahon, Ohio State University



***Previously published titles in this series:***

*Crisis and Crossfire:*
*The United States and the Middle East since 1945* (2005)
Peter L. Hahn, Ohio State University

*The Color of Empire: Race and American Foreign Relations* (2006)
Michael L. Krenn, Appalachian State University

*Intimate Ties, Bitter Struggles:*
*The United States and Latin America since 1945* (2006)
Alan McPherson, Howard University

*The Triumph of Internationalism:*
*Franklin D. Roosevelt and a World in Crisis, 1933–1941* (2007)
David Schmitz, Whitman College

*John F. Kennedy: World Leader* (2010)
Stephen G. Rabe, University of Texas at Dallas

*How the Cold War Ended: Debating and Doing History* (2011)
John Prados, National Security Archive

# Amid a Warring World

## *American Foreign Relations, 1775–1815*

**Robert W. Smith**

**Potomac Books**
*Washington, D.C.*

**Library of Congress Cataloging-in-Publication Data**

Smith, Robert W., 1967–

Amid a warring world : American foreign relations, 1775–1815 / Robert W. Smith.

p. cm. — (Issues in the history of American foreign relations)

Includes bibliographical references and index.

ISBN 978-1-59797-521-6 (hardcover : alk. paper)

ISBN 978-1-59797-522-3 (pbk. : alk. paper)

ISBN 978-1-61234-132-3 (electronic)

1. United States—Foreign relations—1775–1783. 2. United States—Foreign relations—1783–1815. I. Title.

E249.S65 2012

327.73009'033—dc23

2012018890

Printed in the United States of America on acid-free paper that meets the American National Standards Institute Z39-48 Standard.

Potomac Books
22841 Quicksilver Drive
Dulles, Virginia 20166

First Edition

10 9 8 7 6 5 4 3 2 1

*In memory of my aunt,*
*Barbara Gordon*
*A reader*

# Contents

# Series Editor's Note

From the birth of the American republic in the late eighteenth century to the emergence of the United States as a fledgling world power at the end of the nineteenth century, the place of the United States within the broader international system of nation-states posed fundamental challenges to American and foreign statesmen alike. What role would—and could—a non-European power play in a Eurocentric world order? The combination of America's stunning economic transformation and two devastating world wars helped shatter the old European order, catapulting the country into a position of global preeminence by the middle decades of the twentieth century. Since the mid-1940s, it has become common to refer to the United States as a superpower. Since the collapse of the Soviet Union, America's only serious rival, and the concomitant end of the Cold War, it has become common to label the United States as the world's lone superpower—or "hyperpower," as a French diplomat labeled it in the late 1990s.

By any standard of measurement, the United States has long been, as it remains today, the dominant force in world affairs—economically, politically, militarily, and culturally.

The United States has placed, and continues to place, its own indelible stamp on the international system while shaping the aspirations, mores, tastes, living standards, and sometimes resentments and hatreds of hundreds of millions of ordinary people across the globe. Few subjects, consequently, loom larger in the history of the modern world than the often uneasy encounter between the United States and the nations and peoples beyond its shores.

This series, *Issues in the History of American Foreign Relations*, aims to provide students and general readers alike with a wide range of books, written by some of the outstanding scholarly experts of this generation, that elucidate key issues, themes, topics, and individuals in the nearly 240-year history of U.S. foreign relations. The series covers an array of diverse subjects spanning from the era of the founding fathers to the present. Each book offers a concise, accessible narrative based upon the latest scholarship, followed by a careful selection of relevant primary documents. Primary sources enable readers to immerse themselves in the raw material of history, thereby facilitating the formation of informed, independent judgments about the subject at hand. To capitalize upon the unprecedented amount of non-American archival sources and materials currently available, most books feature foreign as well as American material in the documentary section. A broad, international perspective on the external behavior of the United States, one of the major trends of recent scholarship, is a prominent feature of the books in this series.

It is my fondest hope that this series will contribute to a greater engagement with and understanding of the complexities of this fascinating—and critical—subject.

ROBERT J. MCMAHON
OHIO STATE UNIVERSITY

# Acknowledgments

I would like to thank Don Jacobs, formerly of Potomac Books, for bringing me on board, Hilary Claggett of Potomac for seeing this project through to its conclusion, and Bob McMahon for including me in this series.

I would like to thank my family, particularly my mother, Claire, and brother Matt for their support.

Although this book took about a year to write, it is stacked on top of twenty years of studying early American diplomacy. I was guided along the way by William C. Stinchcombe, Stephen Saunders Webb, James Roger Sharp, and Ralph Ketcham at Syracuse University; the late John Selby, Edward Crapol, Michael McGiffert, and Charles F. Hobson at the College of William and Mary; and Joseph A. Fry of the University of Nevada at Las Vegas.

I would also like to thank my friends Mary Carroll Johansen, Kathy Lisiewicz, and David Rawson for reading drafts and helping remove errors, grammatical and otherwise.

Thomas A. Bailey, *A Diplomatic History of the American People*, 10th ed. (© 1980 by Prentice Hall). Reprinted by permission of Pearson Education, Inc., Upper Saddle River, NJ.

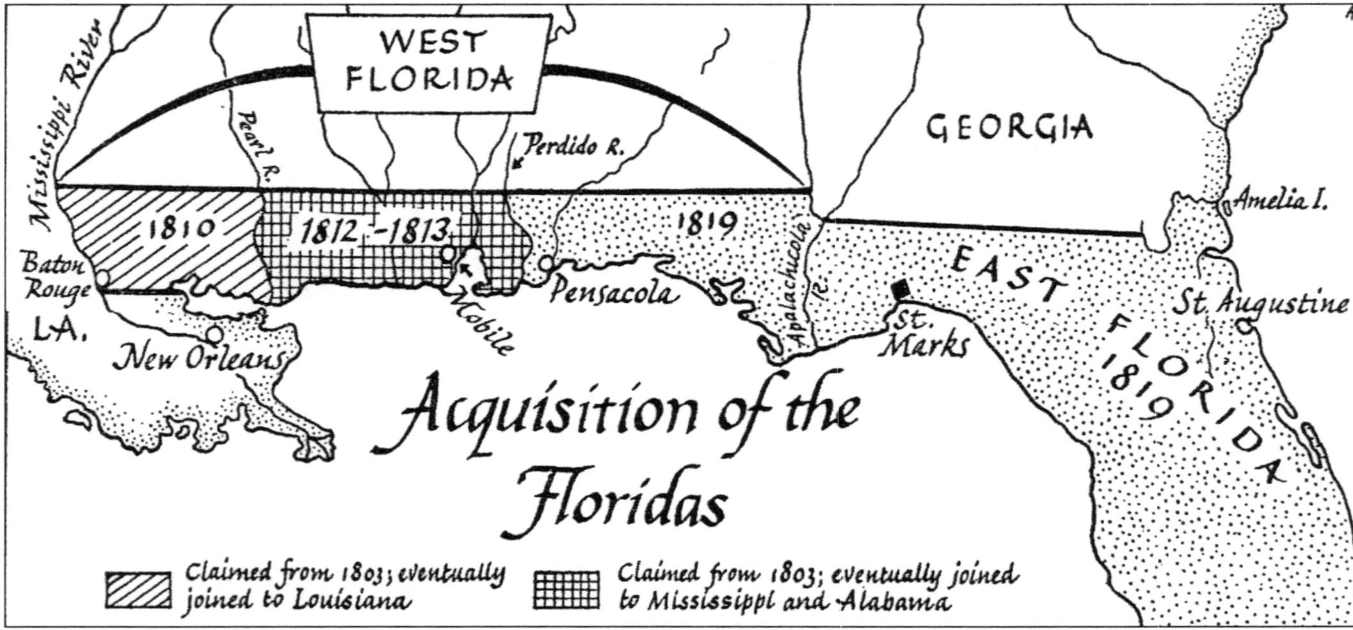


George C. Herring, *From Colony to Superpower: US Foreign Relations since 1776* (© 2011 by Oxford University Press, Inc.), 42. Reprinted by permission of Oxford University Press, Inc.

# Introduction

In 1810 Caesar Rodney described the "critical situation of our country" to President James Madison. "We live in an age without precedent in history," Rodney wrote. "A solitary neutral, amid a warring world." Rodney lamented that "the rules of virtue & morality, which bound together the great families of ma[n]kind, are violated with impunity, as caprice, interest or ambition dictate." Mankind lay at the mercy of French and British cannon. "Grotius and Puffendorf, Vattel and Burlimqui [Burlamaqui] may be laid on the shelf."[1] The intensity of war in 1810 was new, but the idea of an Atlantic world framed by Anglo-French conflict was not. It was the central truth of American diplomacy from the American Revolution to the War of 1812.

The period between 1775 and 1815 might well be called the "critical period" of American foreign relations. At no time in American history was the existence of the republic in greater physical peril from external threats. Questions of American foreign policy dominated American public life in a way unequalled until the period since 1941. From the American Revolution through the War of 1812, the United States was a small military power surrounded by great powers hostile to each other and at times hostile to the United States. Furthermore, the era was dominated by two great revolutions that reshaped the Atlantic world. The problem for American diplomats and foreign policy makers was to preserve the United States, both as an independent nation and a republic, in a decidedly unequal contest with the great powers. Samuel Flagg Bemis framed this process as seeking "America's advantage from Europe's distress," the subtitle of *Pinckney's Treaty*. Many Americans assumed that neutrality and commercial pressure were sufficient tools to exploit Europe's divisions and perceived economic weakness. The first forty years of American diplomacy would demonstrate whether or not these beliefs were valid.

The question of American power lay at the heart of the debate over American independence. The radicals believed that the American spirit and market were enough and favored rapid independence and an aggressive promotion of neutral rights. The moderates doubted American power and were inclined to move slowly, and only with assured French support. By the end of the American Revolution, the moderates had won the debate. The victory masked the defects of the confederation until the diplomatic humiliations of the 1780s forced the United States to create a government that could properly harness American military and economic power.

The French Revolution, and the wars it created, dominated the Atlantic world from 1789 to 1815. American diplomacy was born in a world of great power conflict over limited issues, with room for neutrals to maneuver. After 1789 Americans faced a death struggle between Great Britain and France, with no room for neutrals. The Federalists accommodated themselves to this new reality by forming a policy of naval armament and a diplomacy that sought normal relations with both powers but did not try to resolve the issues the war created. The Republicans, however, clung to the power of the American market as a sufficient lever to change British and French maritime power. The result was the War of 1812.

Americans viewed their diplomacy through the accumulated wisdom of the colonial experience with the wider world. Various colonies, especially Massachusetts, embraced the idea that America was fundamentally separate from Europe. The colonies often had to engage in their own diplomacy with Indian tribes, other colonies, and the mother country itself. Beginning in the 1620s, the colonies sent agents to lobby in London. Edward Winslow of Plymouth was the first career agent. By the middle of the eighteenth century, the agent was an integral part of colonial government. It was not a coincidence that two of the new nation's first diplomats, Benjamin Franklin and Arthur Lee, had been longtime colonial agents.

The colonies were part of the broader Atlantic world, framed by the so-called Westphalia system, beginning with the Peace of Westphalia in 1648. The system assumed a world of sovereign nation-states and was confirmed in the Treaty of Utrecht in 1713, which separated the Spanish and French crowns. Broadly speaking, the wars of the Westphalia system were limited in scope and ambition, owing as much to technological and financial limits as to political thinking. None of the great powers contemplated the complete destruction of the others. This balance of power system gave rise to what contemporaries called "the law of nations." The two most prominent writers on the law of nations were the seventeenth-century Dutch writer Hugo Grotius (author of *The Free Sea* and *The Rights of War and Peace*) and the eighteenth-century Swiss writer Emmerich de Vattel (author of *The Law of Nations*). Grotius offered a legal and diplomatic rationale for a broad definition of neutral rights. Vattel's work, which became a general guide to diplomacy, posited a world in which the balance of power would protect the small powers from the depredations of the great powers. Throughout the eighteenth century, the European powers agreed that there were rules of conduct. They did not necessarily agree on what those rules were, however, and works on the law of nations could be mined for evidence to support almost any policy decision.

The diplomatic world of the eighteenth century was framed by the long conflict between Great Britain and its allies on one side and France (usually allied with Spain) on the other. The colonies became a key part of this contest. During the War of Jenkins's Ear (1739–48) the British undertook significant military operations in the colonies. The French and Indian War (1754–63) was in large part a contest over who would rule the eastern third of North America. The British victory brought an enlarged empire and new imperial policy. Britain's attempt to pay for and more tightly regulate its empire led to the Stamp Act, the Townshend Duties, and the other acts that led the American colonies to rebellion.

During the controversy over British taxation, Americans turned to the English Opposition school, particularly John Trenchard and Thomas Gordon (writing jointly under the pseudonym "Cato"), Lord Bolingbroke, and James Burgh. These writers not only criticized the growth of royal influence in Parliament, but also the course of British foreign policy, which tended toward a greater involvement in continental affairs after the Hanoverian succession. The Opposition writers portrayed Great Britain as an island whose interest lay in promoting the colonial trade and the navy, and avoiding continental entanglements that could lead to creation of a standing army.

If Great Britain's power depended on its navy, and its navy on the colonial trade, then the colonists had a weapon in economic coercion. The Stamp Act triggered the first continental nonimportation agreement. This allowed the colonists to resist without committing treason. It also appealed to colonists' sense of superior virtue, as guardians of British liberty. Very simply, Americans came to believe that economic power could secure any political end. Economic coercion came close enough to working during the Stamp Act crisis to give the idea validity. With each succeeding crisis, however, nonimportation grew weaker. Ultimately, the threat of economic coercion did not prevent or ameliorate the British crackdown on Massachusetts in the wake of the Boston Tea Party. At the first Continental Congress, the delegates advised nonimportation, nonexportation, and the stockpiling of weapons. The radicals favored economic coercion because they believed it was the best weapon. The moderates went along because it fell short of armed revolt or independence.

When resistance became armed rebellion in the spring of 1775, Congress was forced to consider the questions of diplomacy with other nations. The colonial heritage, the law of nations, the idea of a balance of power, British political thought, and the experience of resistance to British taxation formed the framework of American foreign policy.

# CHAPTER 1

# The Diplomacy of Independence

In retrospect, the Battles of Lexington and Concord on April 19, 1775, marked the point where independence became inevitable. When the Continental Congress reconvened on May 10, many members had not yet reached that conclusion. The radicals and moderates both supported the war effort, and both sought to insulate America from European politics. The radicals and moderates split over independence. The radicals, in favoring a rapid declaration of independence, counted on the natural valor of the Americans and a corresponding weakness in British character. They also assumed that the desire for American trade would gain French and Spanish aid on American terms. The moderates did not overrate American valor or assume British weakness. They also did not believe that European powers would grant aid without imposing harsh political conditions. The moderates thus hoped to secure enough aid to maintain the war effort and force the British into a favorable settlement. The radical and moderate dispute over whether or not American power could reorder the world remained the fundamental issue in American foreign policy throughout the founding era. Although the world changed drastically between 1775 and 1815, the core of the radical/moderate dispute did not.

## The Birth of American Diplomacy

Throughout 1775 the moderates held the upper hand. Neither the public mind nor a majority of Congress was prepared for a final break. Foreign policy had to be conducted in a manner that did not preclude reconciliation. Therefore, in July and August 1775, Congress debated and rejected plans to open American ports to the world. On September 18 Congress created a foreign policy machinery by establishing the Secret Committee, charged with directing a clandestine trade to secure war matériel. Congress elected the membership the next day, filling the committee with moderates from the middle colonies and New England merchants. No important radicals were elected.[1] Congress gave the Secret Committee the power to trade agricultural produce for arms and supplies on October 6. Its creation marked a fusion of radical and moderate policy. The moderates for tactical reasons and the radicals for ideological reasons sought to separate commercial from political relations by seeking trade with no political commitments. The division was built into the very foundation of American foreign policy. On November 29, 1775, Congress went further and created the first body formally charged with the conduct of foreign relations, the Committee of Secret Correspondence, renamed the Committee on Foreign Affairs in 1777. This committee's official purpose was to correspond with friends of America in Great Britain, Ireland, and "elsewhere." It was stacked with moderates, including Benjamin Franklin, who was a reluctant supporter of independence. On December 12 the committee appointed Arthur Lee as political agent. Lee, a Virginia radical, had served under Franklin as assistant colonial agent for Massachusetts and had nearly a decade's worth of contacts in pro-American and reformist circles in London. The mention of friends elsewhere gave the opening for the radicals to pursue aid from foreign sources, particularly France, without committing the moderates to independence.

Since the Seven Years' War, France had sought ways to redress the balance of power. During the Stamp Act crisis, French observers reported on the progress of American resistance, and some Americans even talked of seeking French aid. Étienne-François, Duc de Choiseul, the French foreign minister, sent agents to the British colonies but in 1768 decided against intervention, as the Americans were not prepared for rebellion. Charles Gravier, Comte de Vergennes, succeeded Choiseul as foreign minister in 1774. In September 1775 Pierre-Augustin Caron de Beaumarchais—playwright, merchant, and part-time secret agent—urged Vergennes to take action in America. Soon after, Vergennes sent Julien-Alexandre Achard de Bonvouloir to meet informally with Congress. His timing could not have been better. Bonvouloir arrived in December, soon after Lee's appointment as agent. The Committee of Secret Correspondence asked if France would send supplies and engineers. Bonvouloir answered yes. At the end of the month, Bonvouloir reported to Vergennes that Congress was on the verge of declaring independence.

Just as war preceded independence, so did foreign policy. Congress approved an invasion of Canada in July 1775, which should be considered America's first foreign adventure. The radicals argued that the Quebec Act was the worst of all the British acts and assumed that the Canadians would agree. Most Canadians showed little enthusiasm for either side, and the invasion failed at Quebec on December 31. On February 4, 1776, Congress received a letter from an anonymous Canadian who believed that Canada would oppose Great Britain. In response Congress chose the first American diplomatic mission, which would set the template for future missions. Diplomatic missions had to be balanced, usually sectionally or politically. The Canada mission needed a religious balance. The first member was Benjamin Franklin, whose presence was testimony to the mission's importance. The other two official members were Marylanders Charles Carroll of Carrollton, a Catholic, and Samuel Chase, a Protestant. John Carroll, a Catholic priest and Charles Carroll's cousin, accompanied the mission. Congress completed the instructions on March 20, taking great pains to emphasize that Canada's Catholics would enjoy complete freedom of religion. Soon after arriving, however, Franklin determined the mission was hopeless and returned to Philadelphia.

Time ultimately favored the radicals, but in early 1776 the middle colonies resisted independence. Radicals in Congress stayed away from overt support of independence, but those outside were not so confined. On January 10, 1776, Thomas Paine published the first edition of *Common Sense*. Paine's pamphlet was the most effective public argument for independence and the clearest statement of radical foreign policy. Lexington and Concord ended any hope of reconciliation. "The blood of the slain, the weeping voice of nature cries, 'TIS TIME TO PART.'" Paine dismissed as an absurdity the idea that a continent could be "perpetually governed by an island."[2] If America was to be independent, it had to defeat the mightiest power on earth. Paine restated the argument the radicals had made since the Stamp Act—that Great Britain depended on America for its survival. Furthermore, all Europe depended on American trade, which would allow America to gain alliances without political commitments. "The commerce, by which she hath enriched herself are the necessaries of life, and will always have a market while eating is the custom of Europe," Paine argued. "Our plan is commerce, and that, well attended to, will secure to us the peace and friendship of all Europe; because, it is the interest of all Europe to have America a *free port*."[3]

Paine forced a more public and open debate on independence. The momentum shifted from the radicals having to downplay independence to the moderates defending delay. Even though the moderates opposed independence and a formal appeal to foreign power, they were willing to discuss trade as a means of resistance that preserved the chance of reconciliation. Reconciliation depended on an acceptable British offer, which never came. On February 27 Congress learned of the American Prohibitory Act, passed by Parliament on December 23, 1775, which made all ships departing American ports subject to capture. This intensified the discussion of foreign aid. The moderates wanted to send a merchant to France with no official political mission. The radicals wanted to use trade as a substitute for a political alliance. "Is any assistance attainable from F.? What Connection may We safely form with her?" John Adams asked Congress in March 1776. "1st. No Political Connection. Submit to none of her Authority—receive no Governors, or officers from her. 2d. No military Connection—Receive no Troops from her. 3d. Only a Commercial Connection, i.e. make a Treaty, to receive her Ships into our Ports. Let her engage to receive our Ships into her Ports—furnish Us with Arms, Cannon, Salt Petre, Powder, Duck, Steel."[4] On March 3 Congress commissioned Silas Deane, a former delegate from Connecticut, as a commercial agent to France. Officially Deane was to pose as a Bermuda merchant buying provisions for the army. Unofficially he was to determine if France wished a more formal treaty with America.

In retrospect the radicals' expectation that American trade without a political commitment would bring a French alliance was unrealistic. At the time, the radicals and Vergennes were in agreement. In February the foreign minister received Bonvouloir's report. Beaumarchais agreed with Bonvouloir's conclusions and argued that secret aid would preserve the French West Indies without the risk of war with Great Britain. Vergennes forwarded Beaumarchais's advice to the king and asked Geronimo, Marques de Grimaldi, the Spanish foreign minister, to join France in aiding the American rebels. In March Vergennes wrote a memorandum to the king titled "Considérations." Vergennes recommended that both France and Spain make military preparations, while at the same time maintaining friendly relations with Great Britain. France should send secret aid to America, mainly weapons and other war matériel, until the colonies declared their independence.

Sometime in April Vergennes directed his secretary, Joseph-Matthias Gérard (later ennobled as Gérard de Rayneval) to write another report, titled "Réflexions." Having set the policy of aiding the colonists, Vergennes now sought to explain why. The report was informed by the zero-sum logic of mercantilism and the balance of power. The colonies made Great Britain the superior power. If France helped dismember the British Empire, the trade that enriched the British would flow to France, increasing French power. Furthermore, France would be able to recover access to the Newfoundland fisheries and the islands at the mouth of the St. Lawrence River. Rayneval was careful to add that France did not wish to recover Canada, which would drive the Americans back to the British. As long as Americans could perform in the field, France should send munitions. On May 2, 1776, Louis XVI gave one million livres (about $4 million in 1776) to a front, Rodrigue Hortalez & Company, led by Beaumarchais.[5]

Despite the Canada debacle, the military situation was overall favorable. The British army left Boston for Halifax on March 17, 1776, taking the town's loyalists with them. This fostered the idea that the Americans could defeat Great Britain without foreign troops. On April 6 Congress opened American ports to the world. It was not enough for the radicals. John Adams believed that other nations would not aid America until it had declared independence. In May 1776 Congress requested the colonies that had not already done so to form new governments and suppress royal authority. The colonies began to authorize their delegates in Congress to approve independence. Richard Henry Lee of Virginia, Arthur Lee's brother, moved to declare independence on June 7. On July 1 Pennsylvania's John Dickinson gave his final speech against independence, focusing on foreign affairs. He dismissed the idea that a declaration of independence would bring French aid. "When We have bound ourselves to an eternal Quarrel with G.B. by a Declaration of Independence, France has nothing to do but hold back & intimidate G.B. till Canada is put into her Hands, then to intimidate Us into a most disadvantageous Grant of our Trade," he argued. Independence would not bring foreign aid, but lengthen the war. "A *Partition* of these Colonies will take Place if G.B. cant conquer Us."[6] However, Dickinson knew he had lost, and Congress approved independence on July 2.

Now formally established, the United States could treat with France and other powers. In June, in anticipation of independence, Congress had appointed John Adams chairman of a committee to draft the Model Treaty. Adams based his diplomacy on the belief that the United States had the public virtue to defend its independence and needed only matériel from other nations. The Model Treaty embodied the radical program of a commercial alliance with no political or military obligations. The treaty offered "a firm, inviolable, and Universal Peace, and a true and Sincere Friendship," between the United States and the signatory power. If Great Britain declared war on the signatory power, the United States promised not to aid Great Britain, and if any power joined an alliance with the United States, there would be no separate peace. The treaty gave each side most-favored-nation status—that is, each nation would pay the lowest duties charged by the other. It also enshrined the neutral rights doctrines of "free ships make free goods" (enemy goods aboard neutral or allied ships are not subject to capture) and a limited definition of contraband—that is, goods that a neutral power could not trade with a belligerent power and still retain the character of a neutral. Adams, following a broad definition of neutral rights, excluded ships' stores from the contraband list.[7]

As Adams drafted his treaty, France began to send aid to America by way of Rodrigue Hortalez & Company. Beaumarchais worked with Arthur Lee on the matter. Lee considered the aid a gift and begged Beaumarchais not to ask for payment. Deane arrived in Paris on July 7, 1776. Vergennes received him, allowed him to engage in commerce, and then passed him off to Beaumarchais. Deane eclipsed Lee in importance, as Lee had no specific powers to treat, and Deane had authorization to buy munitions and an unofficial mandate to establish political relations. Deane, as part of his cover, became an investor in Rodrigue Hortalez. Deane's rise and commercial activities were a sore point with Lee and provided the source for future controversies.

Even after independence, some moderates hoped for an accommodation. British diplomacy (if that term could be used) failed before 1782 because the British overestimated American loyalism and made offers that were either insufficient or too late. In May 1776 Parliament gave the brothers Adm. Lord Richard Howe and Gen. William Howe (the British commander-in-chief in America) instructions to issue pardons and convene a new congress upon the dissolution of the Continental Congress and the Continental Army. The Howes, who were generally pro-American, first tried to open negotiations with Continental Army commander-in-chief Gen. George Washington. When that failed, they sent Gen. John Sullivan, captured at Brooklyn Heights, as a messenger to Congress. John Adams preferred to ignore the Howes, but Congress voted to send a commission of Adams, Franklin, and Edward Rutledge of South Carolina to meet with the Howes on Staten Island. The Americans would not treat on any basis other than independence, which the Howe brothers had no power or inclination to grant. The meeting broke up on September 13 and extinguished accommodationist sentiment. Congress approved a slightly modified Model Treaty on September 17. A week later Congress appointed its first official overseas diplomatic mission, naming Franklin, Deane, and Thomas Jefferson commissioners to France. Jefferson declined and was replaced by Arthur Lee.

The idea of a limited relationship with France was predicated on a quick American victory. The second half of 1776 was as unfavorable as the first half had been promising. Washington failed to chase the British out of New York and was himself chased headlong through New Jersey. As the British neared Philadelphia, Congress retreated to Baltimore on December 12. By the end of December, Congress abandoned the Model Treaty as the basis for relations with France and authorized the commissioners to do whatever was necessary to bring France into the war.

Franklin arrived in France on December 4, 1776. He was naturally the focal point of the American mission, being already well known to the intellectual circles of Paris. (He is the only American revolutionary who would be known to history without the revolution.) Franklin did not call at Versailles until France extended recognition. Rather, he let France come to him at his residence in Passy, which served as the headquarters of the American mission. Franklin was a pioneer of what later generations would call public diplomacy. The French built him into their ideal of an unspoiled American, and he let them. The French wanted to see a backwoods philosopher. Franklin was the most urban American of his time, but he obliged. He abandoned the powdered wig in favor of a coonskin cap, hardly the outfit he would wear to a meeting of the Royal Society. The French believed Franklin was a Quaker. He played along. His greatest service to the revolution in early 1777 was to let Paris adore him and keep the idea of America alive. His image appeared everywhere: on miniatures, on snuffboxes, on everything the eighteenth century considered collectable. The American mission, however, was a mass of conflicting personalities. Franklin allowed Deane to take the lead in negotiations, but Lee, a volatile personality under the best of circumstances, resented Deane's rise. Lee had already served an unpleasant term as Franklin's deputy and was now convinced Franklin and Deane were working against him.

Franklin's conflict with Lee, like that with Adams later, was as much about policy as personality. The radicals were forced to accept the idea of a close military alliance with France, without which the moderates never believed the United States could prevail. The new split between the radicals and moderates over foreign policy was over soliciting more European powers as allies. Both considered the question in the context of keeping the United States shielded from European politics. The radicals proposed to send ministers across Europe. They believed that most nations desired American trade and that having many allies would prevent a dangerous dependence on France. The moderates believed that an alliance with France would prevent the need for other allies, thus keeping the United States out of European politics. "But I have never yet changed the Opinion I gave in Congress, that a Virgin State should preserve the Virgin Character, and not go about suitering for Alliances, but wait with decent Dignity for the applications of others," Franklin advised Lee.[8]

Lee, however, was anxious to gather more allies as the chief means of victory. Francis Wharton later termed the practice of sending ministers without knowing if they would be received "militia diplomacy," after a phrase in a letter John Adams wrote in 1782.[9] The first target, outside of France, was Spain. Americans presumed that Spain too would be eager to strike a blow against the British Empire. Vergennes planned from the beginning to bring Spain into the war, and in 1776 he convinced Charles III to donate one million livres to the American cause, washed through Rodrigue Hortalez. On February 15, 1777, José Moñino y Redondo, Conde de Floridablanca, replaced Grimaldi as foreign minister. Throughout the course of the war, Floridablanca was the immovable object blocking American diplomatic plans. He was a staunch defender of the Spanish Empire as it was and sought to recover the parts lost to the British during the eighteenth century. Where Vergennes saw opportunity in the American Revolution, Floridablanca saw only danger to the Spanish Empire. Floridablanca saw no reason to encourage Lee or risk trouble with the British. Lee wrote a memorial (an informal state paper) to the Spanish government on March 8, urging Spain to enter the war by the 1777 campaign season. Floridablanca allowed secret aid and, with more caution and less enthusiasm than Vergennes, was willing to keep the war going and see what happened next.

Richard Henry Lee was a key member of the radical faction, often referred to as the Adams-Lee faction. The radicals favored Lee's mission and others like it. In early May 1777 Congress appointed Ralph Izard of South Carolina as commissioner to Tuscany and another Lee brother, William, as commissioner to Prussia and the Holy Roman Empire. On June 5 Congress confirmed Lee as commissioner to Spain. Arthur Lee departed on May 15 in search of allies. He found no takers in Vienna or Berlin and returned to Paris in July. There he nursed his resentment of Franklin and Deane. Lee always considered Deane's commercial character suspect and sent his brother and fellow radicals a steady stream of complaint. Similarly Franklin's willingness to play a subordinate role to France made him an insufficient patriot in Lee's eyes. On November 7, 1777, Congress recalled Deane and replaced him with John Adams. The recall had nothing to do with Lee's complaints, but rather with Deane's enlistment of too many French officers who did not speak English.

Vergennes was increasingly troubled by the unofficial nature of France's participation in the war. The military situation in 1777 was worse than the year before, and Vergennes feared that the opportunity to humble Great Britain would pass. He sent a message to Louis XVI arguing that the time had come to choose war or peace. Secret aid was no longer enough. Vergennes argued for a full and formal alliance with the United States, with Spain joining. Each power would agree not to sign a separate peace. The French navy was nearing full strength and, if combined with the Spanish fleet, would equal the British. The king agreed on the condition that Spain join the coalition. Spain was the weak link in Vergennes's plans. Floridablanca preferred an angry truce between America and Great Britain guaranteed by France and Spain. That would weaken Great Britain and America, and thereby protect Spain's interests in the Caribbean and the Mississippi Valley.

The diplomatic deadlock in Europe was broken in America. The British colonial office rejected William Howe's plan to send a massive army to America in favor of Gen. John Burgoyne's more modest plan to divide the continent.

Burgoyne planned to have three armies converge on Albany—his own from the north, Howe's from the south, and Col. Barry St. Leger's from the west. St. Leger's army, however, fell at Oriskany, New York. Howe had the option of marching on either Albany or Philadelphia and decided to assault Philadelphia, reasoning that taking the capital should end the war. The British victory at Germantown, Pennsylvania, on October 4, 1777, demonstrated that the Continental Army could stand and fight, but Congress still had to flee Philadelphia, where Howe set up winter headquarters. Burgoyne led his army down the Hudson Valley, where he met the Continental Army led by Gen. Horatio Gates. Gen. Benedict Arnold led a victorious charge at Bemis Heights, forcing Burgoyne to surrender at Saratoga on October 17, 1777. For the first time, an American army had captured a British army.

## The French Alliance

News of Saratoga arrived in Paris on December 3 and sent the American, British, and French diplomats scrambling to figure out their next move. Like Vergennes, Deane and Franklin grew frustrated at the covert war, although Franklin was too skilled a diplomat to show it. The British were contemplating a change in policy, and Saratoga strengthened the hand of those who favored granting American autonomy, although the ministry of Frederick Lord North showed no signs of wavering. William Eden, director of British espionage on the continent, sent Paul Wentworth, the former agent for New Hampshire, to meet the Americans in December and January. Wentworth promised everything in general but nothing specific to head off a Franco-American alliance. Franklin and Deane listened but would make no official response unless Great Britain was prepared to recognize American independence.

The Wentworth mission was a potential nightmare for Vergennes. He had cultivated the American war for two years. If Great Britain acted according to what France and the United States thought its interests were, it might offer a deal that would foreclose the possibility of a Franco-American alliance. This fear led Vergennes to act more quickly and unilaterally than he would have preferred. On December 17, 1777, he offered a formal alliance with the United States. Vergennes acted without consulting Spain, which again refused to recognize the United States. Vergennes and Louis XVI abandoned the idea of waiting for Spain. On

January 8, 1778, Vergennes told Franklin and Deane that the king was prepared to offer an alliance.

Did Saratoga cement the French alliance? The traditional answer has been yes. Jonathan Dull has argued to the contrary, that the French naval preparations were ready and France would have entered the war anyway in March 1778. Saratoga merely came at a fortunate time.[10] But France would not have entered the war if the British had won at Saratoga. Vergennes backed the American Revolution on a calculation of French interest and might have backed out for the same reason. Doubtless the British reaction to Saratoga upset Vergennes's plans and pushed him into action before he preferred. Vergennes always counted on the French and Spanish together to match the British navy and still pursued a Spanish alliance.

France and the United States signed two treaties on February 6, 1778: the Treaty of Amity and Commerce and the Treaty of Alliance (*Traité d'Alliance éventuelle et déffensive* in the French text). The former substantially repeated the Model Treaty. The French agreed to most-favored-nation status, the American definition of contraband of war, and the principle that free ships make free goods. Vergennes, like Adams, saw free commerce as a bond of friendship and a weapon against Great Britain. In the Treaty of Alliance, both sides agreed to "make it a common cause" if Great Britain declared war on France and established the independence of the United States as the main purpose of the alliance. The United States reserved the right to annex Canada, Bermuda, or any other part of continental British North America. France renounced any interest in Canada but retained the right to attack and annex any part of the British West Indies. Article 11 promised that each power "from the present time and forever" would guarantee the other's American possessions. A separate and secret article allowed for Spain to enter the war on the terms agreed to by the United States and France.[11] Deane and Franklin signed for the United States. Conrad-Alexandre Gérard, longtime bureau chief in the foreign ministry, signed for France and was appointed minister to the United States. Congress ratified the treaty on May 4. The American Revolution was now a European war.

The alliance helped thwart Great Britain's last peace effort before Yorktown. Lord North proposed a conciliatory plan on February 17, 1778, that would renounce the direct taxation of the colonies and send a commission to America. North chose Eden as an envoy and directed him to choose the other members.

Eden selected Frederick Howard, Earl of Carlisle, to lead the commission and added George Johnstone, the former governor of East Florida. The Carlisle Commission, as it became known, offered almost a complete reversal of British policy since 1774, if not 1763. The commission could promise that the British government would not establish a standing army in time of peace or change colonial charters without consent. North was willing to let Congress remain as an official body and admit American representation in Parliament. Others proposed to go further. On April 7 Charles Lennox, Duke of Richmond, moved to acknowledge American independence. William Pitt opposed the motion with his dying speech, and William Petty, Earl of Shelburne, assumed the lead of the pro-American but anti-independence forces. The commission had counted on a carrot-and-stick appeal, of compromise backed up by a military presence. The commission arrived in America on June 5, only to find the British had evacuated Philadelphia on May 8. Had North's proposal been British policy in 1763, there would have been no resistance movement; had it been in 1774, there would have been no war. If the Howe brothers had been authorized to treat on the basis of North's 1778 proposals, the moderates might have repented of their support for independence. By 1778 it was too late. On June 13 Congress considered the Carlisle proposal. Four days later it rejected any negotiation that did not recognize independence and that was inconsistent with the French alliance.

With the last hopes for reconciliation swept away, there was nothing to prevent the United States from fully embracing the French alliance. Gérard arrived on July 11 and presented himself to Congress the next day. Most members of Congress projected their own goals onto the new ally. The radicals in particular saw France as the shield that would provide cover while the United States acquired Canada, Nova Scotia, and the fisheries off of Newfoundland. William Stinchcombe is correct in arguing that the radicals expected too much from the French and too little from the American side.[12] This was the source for later recriminations against France for betraying American interests. The radicals tended to be of two minds about France—on the one hand expecting great generosity and on the other remaining suspicious of French intentions. The radical attitude was consistent with their belief that American trade was the most valuable prize of the war and that the nations of Europe would line up and bid for it. If the radicals could have read Gérard's instructions, their fears would have been justified.

Gérard pledged France to defend American independence and not sign a separate peace. Gérard was instructed to squelch any such effort to conquer Canada and only agree to it as a last resort. Keeping Canada in British hands would be far better for French interests. Gérard and Vergennes saw the United States as a client state that should always feel the need for French assistance. Gérard was to open the way for Spain to enter the war and gain a share of the fisheries with France. Gérard had no orders to gain American access to the fisheries.

Gérard's first task was to manage Congress. The conflict within the American mission in Paris gave Gérard his opportunity. Deane's removal had done nothing to change matters. John Adams arrived in Paris on April 1, 1778, and discovered the chief object of his mission, an alliance, was already accomplished. At first Adams tried to maintain a neutral position between Franklin and Lee, but his personal inclinations and political beliefs led him to side with the latter. Adams, like Lee, was critical of Franklin's work habits. Adams once observed that Franklin slept through most of the debates in Congress, while Adams worked himself nearly to death. Franklin spoke ungrammatical (if understandable) French, while Adams tortured himself with grammars and dictionaries. Like Lee, Adams was a jealous guardian of his fame and was appalled to be confused with his cousin Samuel or, worse, with Thomas Paine. Adams could not stand to see Franklin as the toast of Paris, when he believed he knew the truth about the "backwoods philosopher."

The conflicts among the present and former envoys exploded in Congress in September 1778. Deane arrived back in the United States at the same time as Gérard and spent the next two months gathering allies among the moderates. Deane believed that he, more than anyone else, was responsible for securing French aid. Deane's chief critic was Richard Henry Lee. On September 11 Congress abolished the unwieldy commission system and on September 14 named Franklin sole minister to France. Adams left for home a few months later. Richard Henry Lee made sure his brother received a commission to Spain. Deane blamed Arthur Lee for his current difficulties in Congress. Lee had spent the last two years accusing Deane of corruption for his role in Rodrigue Hortalez & Company. Deane responded with worse accusations against Lee. On December 5, 1778, Deane published an article in the *Pennsylvania Packet* ridiculing Lee's diplomatic efforts, particularly in Spain and Prussia, and claiming that Lee had to be dragged into the alliance with France. Deane accused Lee of being in secret contact with

British agents and of treason. Thomas Paine leaped to Lee's defense. Paine was secretary to the Foreign Affairs Committee and privy to all the details of French aid. Paine denounced Deane in print on December 15 and revealed that the French had sent secret aid prior to the treaty and that Deane's contributions were minimal. This article caused difficulties with Gérard, who was outraged that Paine revealed what the French had not acknowledged. In January 1779 Henry Laurens, a Lee ally, resigned as president of Congress when it failed to immediately vindicate Lee and censure Deane. He was replaced by John Jay, a leading moderate and Deane supporter.

Congress never got to the bottom of the Silas Deane affair. After months of debate in Congress and the newspapers, Congress allowed Deane to leave before giving a full accounting. His guilt or innocence depended on one's frame of reference. It was common in the eighteenth century for office holders to profit by their offices. The moderates, who did not have an elevated sense of American virtue, accepted Deane's commercial activities as normal. More importantly, Deane helped bring in a flow of French supplies, which the moderates considered indispensable for victory. For the radicals, Deane's actions marked a triumph of personal gain—what John Adams called the "Spirit of Commerce"—over the public good. The radicals expected more self-sacrifice out of their officials and from the public at large. Furthermore, Deane had gone along with Franklin in promoting a policy of subordination to France. The radicals saw France as a partner, not a patron. Corruption and dependence were two of the great political sins of the English Opposition philosophy, and the radicals believed Deane was guilty of both.

The revived radical/moderate split gave Gérard the opportunity to try to make the American Revolution safe for Spain. By 1778 the main goal of French diplomacy was to bring Spain into the war. Floridablanca had a long wish list and had only to wait until Vergennes gave him everything he wanted. Failing that, Floridablanca would approach the British directly. In December 1778 he offered Spanish neutrality in exchange for Gibraltar and Minorca. The British refused, and Spain inclined toward joining the French war against Great Britain as the way to its diplomatic goals. On April 3, 1779, Spain called for a cease-fire between France and Great Britain and offered to mediate. The offer was merely a pretext for war. Before Great Britain could officially respond, Spain signed the secret Convention of Aranjuez with France on April 12, 1779. Under this agreement,

Spain would enter the war as a French ally but at a heavy price. Spain wanted everything it had lost to Great Britain in previous wars. France promised to launch an invasion of Great Britain and to secure Mobile, Pensacola, and Minorca, and eject the British from Honduras. Above all, Spain wanted Gibraltar. France and Spain agreed to sign no peace with Great Britain until Spain recovered Gibraltar.

Even more so than the Franco-American alliance, the Convention of Aranjuez marked a defining point of the war. France now had two allies with conflicting interests. The war for American independence was now to be fought for Spanish objectives. France had overpaid for the Spanish alliance. Vergennes's diplomatic plans called for joint naval action, and Vergennes believed that only a combined Franco-Spanish navy could hold off the British. Spain contributed secret aid to the United States through Oliver Pollock, the American agent in New Orleans. Spanish aid was not negligible. Bernardo de Gálvez's campaign against Pensacola in March 1781 absorbed British resources that might have been used elsewhere. But liabilities outweighed benefits. French efforts to make the United States more acceptable to Spain ultimately backfired and forced France to pursue policies that fed the perception that France betrayed the United States. The Franco-Spanish alliance got off to a disastrous start. A Franco-Spanish fleet gathered in July for an assault on Great Britain and then fell victim to various delays and shipboard illnesses. France and Spain abandoned the effort on September 8, 1779.

The Spanish alliance provided the backdrop for Gérard's mission to the United States. He had three main goals designed to make the United States more manageable and more palatable to Spain: to determine the conditions for a truce with Great Britain, to set American territorial demands (and ideally reduce them), and to have Congress name a peace commission and minister to Spain. At first Congress had a long list of peace ultimatums. On February 23, 1779, a committee created to draft the peace demands listed independence, control of all territory to the Mississippi River, British evacuation of American territory, access to the Newfoundland fisheries, free navigation of the Mississippi to its mouth, and either the cession or independence of Nova Scotia. That was too much for France or Spain to accept, and Gérard prepared to whittle down the demands. Vergennes cautioned Gérard not to become attached to any one faction, but Gérard soon found himself relying on the moderates against the radicals. The idea of a truce was to be a nonstarter. Gérard discussed the idea with three unnamed delegates who approved the idea but did not believe the idea had general support. The majority of delegates feared that discussing the idea of a truce would undercut the demand for unconditional independence. The idea of a truce languished in June and died completely in August.

Gérard was more successful in limiting American territorial and commercial demands. He assured Congress that neither France nor Spain would take territory from the United States but advised Congress that France would not support the cession of territory that the United States did not actually possess at the time of peace negotiations. Gérard's two main targets were the Mississippi and the fisheries. Both could be seen as sectional interests and would seem an opportunity for coalition building along sectional lines. The Adams-Lee faction was a combination of New England and Virginia against New York and Pennsylvania. Virginia separated from New England over the peace ultimatums. Virginia had no interest in the fisheries, and New England had little in the Mississippi. As far as Virginia and other states were concerned, the trans-Appalachian West was already part of the United States; the fisheries would have to be conquered. The southern states all had sea-to-sea charters, and Virginia claimed the entire Ohio territory as well. Of the northern states, only Massachusetts and Connecticut held similar claims, but New England was more oriented toward the Atlantic. For the New Englanders, the fisheries provided an export crop, which they compared to Virginia tobacco or South Carolina rice. As the radicals divided, the moderates opposed both claims. The fisheries proved the easier target. On August 14, 1779, Congress approved independence and possession of territory to the Mississippi north of 31° north as the ultimatums. The fisheries were considered vital to a commercial treaty but were not to be an object of the war.

As Gérard sought to moderate American peace demands, he lobbied Congress to choose a more cooperative diplomatic corps. The French naturally favored Franklin's retention, as did Congress. Encouraged by Gérard, the moderates went after the other American diplomats in Europe. In June Congress recalled William Lee and Ralph Izard. The radicals backed Arthur Lee for the combined post of peace commissioner and minister to Spain. The moderates and Gérard backed Jay. The radicals eventually abandoned Lee as damaged goods, and Congress voted on September 25 not to renew his commission. The next day, the New England delegates nominated Adams as minister to Spain. On September 27, in an unusual Sunday session, Congress voted to divide the two positions and elected Adams peace commissioner. A month later Congress elected Henry Laurens commissioner to the Netherlands, nearly completing the diplomatic establishment.

The moderates began to erode radical strength by 1779, but the radicals still held the upper hand. They thwarted Gérard's attempt to explore a truce and to appoint Jay to the combined post of peace commissioner and minister to Spain. The radicals' position remained secure as long as the military situation allowed. The British gave up on reconquering the North and Gen. Sir Henry Clinton's troops were bottled up in New York City. In the South the British conquered Georgia in 1779, but the massive campaign through the Carolinas lay in the future. As matters stood in 1779, it seemed the United States could afford a policy independent of France.

In August 1779 Gérard announced to Congress that he was retiring to France, just as his replacement, Anne-César, Chevalier de la Luzerne, arrived in Boston. Vergennes warned Luzerne not to attach himself exclusively to one party, as Gérard had done. Gérard's openly promoderate position only fed radical suspicions. Gérard was not trained to deal with a decentralized republic. Eighteenth-century diplomacy was run by men of the same class and social standing who understood the same rules and did their business in secret. American diplomacy seemed to be conducted in the front yard of Independence Hall. It was not unexpected that the first French minister to the United States, like the first American mission to France, would encounter certain difficulties. The main complication to the Gérard mission was the Spanish alliance, which forced Gérard to reconcile two irreconcilable sets of demands.

Vergennes could arrange for an American minister to Spain, but he could not make Floridablanca welcome him. Jay landed at Cadiz at the end of January 1780. He proceeded slowly, sounding out officials in Madrid before heading to the capital. Floridablanca later remarked that Jay's "two chief points were: Spain, recognize our independence; Spain, give us more money."[13] Floridablanca grudgingly gave the latter but would not yield on the former. Although it was no longer a condition of peace, navigation of the Mississippi was listed among Jay's objectives. Jay himself preferred to rely on the French alliance and not seek out others. Floridablanca was willing to talk through back channels. He would be happier if

Jay went home, but while the British held Gibraltar Spain was unwilling to risk a rift with France. Each intermediary informed Jay that the Mississippi was a main obstacle to a treaty. Jay had asked for some leeway, but Congress affirmed the American right to navigate the river on October 4, 1780. Jay received the instructions on January 30, 1781.

Jay might have expected his mission to go better, as it (and he) had France's blessing. The same cannot be said of his rival and colleague, John Adams. A leaky ship had forced Adams to land in Spain and travel overland to Paris, arriving on February 9, 1780. At first Adams hid the nature of his mission for fear that Franklin would undermine him. In 1780, as in 1778, Adams had no patience for Franklin's style of diplomacy. Adams favored the direct approach in diplomacy as in all things and believed that all nations, even Great Britain, eventually would bid for American trade and friendship. Since 1776 the radicals believed that all the United States had to do was announce that it was open for business. Therefore, there was no need for elaborate court ritual and circuitous diplomacy. Franklin defended his approach by arguing that Adams did not understand how Europe worked. "He [Adams] thinks . . . that the United States has been too free in Expressions of Gratitude to France," but Franklin believed "that this Court is to be treated with Decency & Delicacy."[14]

Adams wanted to announce to the British that he was prepared to treat for peace, in order to force the British to reveal their policy. Vergennes thought the measure was more than premature, as the British had made no moves toward peace. Adams failed to convince Vergennes to begin peace negotiations. He also failed to change French military strategy. Adams, like the majority of the radicals, believed that all America needed from France was naval cover and war matériel. The Spanish alliance redirected French resources to Spanish objectives, particularly Gibraltar. Viewing the war as primarily a war for American independence, Adams considered the failed assault on Gibraltar a waste of time and resources. He repeatedly recommended that the French send the bulk of their fleet to the United States, to prevent Great Britain from resupplying its army and force the army to concentrate in New York City. Vergennes viewed the war as primarily between Great Britain and France. Even without Spain, it was unlikely that France would devote itself entirely to American independence when France had continental, African, and Indian interests to consider.

By July 1780 Vergennes desperately wanted to be rid of Adams. Adams had discussed seeking aid from the Netherlands. Vergennes was reluctant to let Adams proceed; as he was not enamored of the idea of an envoy he could not control conducting an independent foreign policy. But he relented in July, and Adams departed for the Netherlands on July 27. On September 16 Adams received authorization from Congress to act until Laurens arrived. However, Laurens had been captured off the coast of Newfoundland on September 3. The British discovered in his possession a 1778 draft treaty between the United States and the Netherlands written by William Lee and Jean de Neufville, neither of whom had any authorization to make an agreement. Laurens spent the next two years in the Tower of London.

Adams was the standard-bearer of radical diplomacy in seeking out allies in some sort of ideological sympathy with the United States, rather than simply relying on France, whose chief intention was to humble Great Britain. Adams targeted the Netherlands as a fellow republic. While in the Netherlands, Adams believed he saw the opportunity to bring in Russia as an ally. Russia, as an absolute monarchy, would have no political sympathy for the United States, but it had assumed the leadership of the Armed Neutrality, which demonstrated a commitment to the same maritime principles of the United States.

Adams described the Armed Neutrality as "one of the most brilliant events which has yet been produced by the American Revolution."[15] Adams was technically correct, but he attributed it to the spread of American principles. The events leading to the formation of the Armed Neutrality began in July 1778, when a ship described as an American privateer attacked eight British ships sailing out of Archangel, Russia. Empress Catherine II proposed a treaty between Russia and Denmark in August, calling for mutual protection of neutral vessels and British ships trading with neutrals in the North Sea. Denmark countered with an offer of mutual protection in all seas, which Russia rejected. The idea of a league of neutrals languished until Spain entered the war in 1779. The Spanish capture of a Dutch ship carrying Russian cargo, followed by the capture of a Russian ship, revived the project. Catherine II issued the Declaration of Armed Neutrality on February 28, 1780. Of the five principles of the Armed Neutrality, the first three—freedom of neutrals to trade with belligerents, free ships make free goods, and a limited definition of contraband—appeared in the Model Treaty. The fourth principle stated that only an effective blockade (that is, with a reasonable certainty of capture) could be considered legal, and the fifth set the first four as the basis for judging the legality of prizes.[16]

To Adams the Armed Neutrality was the fulfillment of the American Revolution in international diplomacy. Adams hoped that a bloc of neutrals would force Great Britain to negotiate with the United States on the basis of independence. On April 13, 1780, the Dutch received an invitation to join. They were at first reluctant. On November 10, Sir Joseph Yorke, the British ambassador, gave the Dutch an ultimatum to break off contact with America. The Netherlands joined the Armed Neutrality on November 20, leading the British to go to war on December 20. Adams wanted the United States to join the Armed Neutrality. Congress agreed and elected Francis Dana, Adams's secretary, minister to Russia on December 19. Congress instructed Dana to seek admission to the Armed Neutrality, hoping that an agreement of maritime principles would trump belligerent status. Russia declined to go to war to defend the Dutch, ending any chance for the Armed Neutrality to have any weight.

Dana's appointment marked the last triumph of the radicals in American diplomacy before the peace treaty. Radical success always depended on military success. The storm clouds that gathered in 1779 rained disaster on the United States in 1780. A Franco-American siege of Savannah failed in October 1779. Then the Continental currency collapsed. In March 1780 Congress devalued Continental paper, sending French merchants begging for help from Paris. The British shifted operations south, where they expected to find more loyalists. Gen. Sir Henry Clinton laid siege to Charleston on March 29, 1780, and took the city after six weeks. From there, Lord Cornwallis ranged throughout the South. The British defeated an army of Continentals and militia under Horatio Gates at Camden, South Carolina, on July 16, 1780. Nathanael Greene replaced Gates as commander of the Southern Department of the Continental Army and adopted a strategy designed to use Cornwallis's own strength against him. Greene led Cornwallis on a chase through the Carolinas, ending at Guilford Court House, North Carolina, on March 15, 1781. Greene inflicted damage on Cornwallis and withdrew, forcing Cornwallis to retreat to Wilmington for supplies before making his final stand in Virginia. Congress clung more tightly to France and tried to remove any obstacles to a treaty with Spain. On November 13, 1780, the Virginia legislature allowed its delegation to drop the issue of the navigation of the Mississippi if that proved necessary to secure a Spanish alliance. Congress issued the new instructions on February 15, 1781. Cornwallis's gains in the Carolinas proved illusory. The loyalists who appeared when Cornwallis arrived disappeared when he left, and the British could not control any southern territory outside the port cities. However, in March 1781 the United States appeared on the verge of defeat, and all of the powers involved in the war sought a way out.

Vergennes led the way. By early 1781 he was the chief diplomat of a coalition fighting an inconclusive and expensive war. Russian chancellor Nikolai Panin had proposed mediation since 1778. In the summer of 1780, he proposed it anew to Olivier de Saint-George, Marquis de Vérac, the French ambassador to Russia. Russia orally proposed mediation to the British in December 1780. Great Britain, to avoid giving offense to Russia, accepted on the condition that Austria joined as comediator. Vergennes was attracted by the idea of a truce and a peace congress. In February 1781 he believed that a long-term truce would allow Great Britain to attend a peace congress without directly acknowledging American independence. His model was the truce between Spain and the Netherlands in 1608. Vergennes was also willing to accept a settlement on the basis of *uti possidetis*, or territory held. Great Britain would have to evacuate New York City but would be allowed to retain Georgia, South Carolina, parts of Maine, and western New York. Luzerne described a rapidly disintegrating situation in America. Despite a solid wall of American opposition to a truce, Vergennes believed, or convinced himself, that the United States could not carry on the war and would have to make a deal.

Adams was the only American authorized to attend a peace conference. That was a further complication for Vergennes. The foreign minister sent Luzerne instructions to have Congress place Adams more directly under French control or to appoint more peace commissioners. Vergennes would prefer to have Adams removed outright, but that was more politically difficult. In May 1781 Russia and Austria issued a call for a peace congress to be held at Vienna. Vergennes reluctantly summoned Adams, who arrived in Paris the first week of July. Vergennes informed Adams that the mediators agreed that Great Britain and the United States should negotiate without preconditions. Adams ultimately concluded that the United States could not negotiate without prior acknowledgment of American independence and left for Amsterdam on July 23. Adams liked to claim credit for killing the conference, but George III refused to send an envoy to any conference that included the United States.

When Adams returned to the Netherlands, his quest for Dutch money and a Dutch alliance made no progress. That was a common experience for American diplomats in Europe. On July 2 Jay officially informed Floridablanca of his new instructions and asked Armand Marc, Comte de Montmorin, the French ambassador, to intercede with the Spanish government. Floridablanca asked Jay to draft a proposed treaty on September 19. Three days later, Jay presented a treaty that combined features of the commercial treaty and alliance with France. It offered most-favored-nation status and would allow Spain to specify the contraband list. Article 6 stated that the "United States shall relinquish to his Catholic majesty, and in future forbear to use, or attempt to use the navigation of the river Mississippi from the thirty-first degree or north latitude—that is, from the part where it leaves the United States—down to the ocean." As he would five years later, Jay avoided language that indicated the United States had abandoned a right to the lower Mississippi. In his explanation of the article, Jay emphasized how large a concession he had made and implied that Charles III should be ready to reciprocate. Jay concluded with a mutual guarantee of American territory, similar to the French treaty. The offer would expire at the end of hostilities. Floridablanca could not accept the idea that the United States would border the Mississippi and refused. Not even news of Yorktown, which arrived in late November, would change Spanish policy.[17]

Dana's mission to Russia was less dramatic. Despite Russian interest in ending the war, the Russian government had no interest in American independence. Dana spoke neither Russian nor French. He might have sought an introduction through Vérac, but the French ambassador spoke no English. Neither Vérac nor Vergennes supported the mission, and Dana later attributed his failure to Vérac's interference. Congress advised Dana to back off negotiations after the peace treaty. After two years in Russia, Dana left for home.

Luzerne had greater luck controlling Congress than Vergennes did controlling American diplomats. Luzerne learned from Gérard's mistakes and did not confine his lobbying efforts to the moderates, understanding that he needed radical allies to promote French interests. Radical strength had also diminished during Luzerne's tenure. By their own political beliefs, the radicals tended to distrust central power and favored rotation in office. A generational shift had occurred by 1780–81. Many of the new members of Congress had entered politics during the American Revolution, rather than during the resistance movement. They had not agonized over independence or experienced the dark days of the end of 1776 and were more prone to panic. The military situation also played a key role in Luzerne's success. In June 1781 the war seemed a disaster, with the British occupying most of the South and threatening Virginia. Southerners who might have been radicals by political inclination became moderates out of necessity. James Madison is a good example. Like the radicals, Madison believed that the value of American trade was sufficient to secure American diplomatic goals. Yet the British invasion of Virginia led Madison to endorse an almost complete reliance on France, agreeing with the moderates.

Luzerne told Congress of the constant friction between Adams and Vergennes, and advised that Adams had become the biggest obstacle to both peace and continued French support. On June 11, 1781, Congress voted to make Adams a member of a three-person peace commission, with Jay as the second member. When Congress could not decide among Franklin, Laurens, and Jefferson as third member, they expanded the commission to five members and added all three. Congress had combined a sectional and political balance, and leaned toward appointing remaining members who were already in Europe. Congress approved the new instructions on June 15, which required the commission to negotiate only with the concurrence and approval of France. The Americans were to consider themselves bound by French advice. Luzerne was not done shaping the American government to his liking. He believed that a strong Congress would be easier to manage than a decentralized confederation and lobbied for Maryland, the last holdout, to ratify the Articles of Confederation. He also advocated the creation of a department of foreign affairs. To ensure a friendly presence, Luzerne's secretary, François Barbé de Marbois, urged Robert R. Livingston, a leading moderate, to accept the nomination. In August 1781 Congress chose Livingston over the hapless Arthur Lee.

Congress could not know that the war was about to end. Luzerne had an idea, or at least he knew that François-Joseph-Paul, Comte de Grasse, would take his fleet from the West Indies to the Chesapeake, but he did not share that information with Congress. Luzerne instead informed Washington and his French counterpart, Jean-Baptiste Donatien de Vimeur, Comte de Rochambeau, in August. Washington abandoned his plans for an assault on New York City, and the two armies marched toward Virginia. De Grasse entered Chesapeake Bay on September 5 and blocked a British relief fleet. The allied army laid siege to Yorktown on October 6. With no prospect of victory or escape, Cornwallis offered parley on October 17, and the British army surrendered on October 19.

## The Treaty of Paris

Yorktown had accomplished what Saratoga could not. It killed the hope that America would be reconquered and rejoined to the empire. On February 22, 1782, Henry Seymour Conway moved in Parliament that the war be ended. It barely failed. Five days later he offered a motion that all those who advocated carrying on the "offensive war" be considered enemies to the king. That motion passed. On March 4 Parliament voted to suspend offensive operations. The North ministry tottered, and North offered his resignation on March 20. The king selected Charles Watson-Wentworth, Marquis of Rockingham, for a new ministry, with Charles James Fox as foreign minister and the Earl of Shelburne as secretary of state for home and colonial affairs. All three had reputations for being pro-American without supporting independence. The first Rockingham ministry had repealed the Stamp Act and passed the Declaratory Act. Shelburne favored American rights but had vigorously opposed the Duke of Richmond's motion for independence.

Franklin too knew that Great Britain now had no choice but to seek peace. In March 1782 he wrote to every contact he had (and he had many) offering to open negotiations. He wrote to Shelburne on March 21, before learning of his appointment. Franklin suggested that Great Britain give as much as possible (by which he meant Canada) in order to end the war quickly and remove any future points of controversy. Franklin's approach matched some of the thinking within the Rockingham ministry, which wanted to liquidate the American conflict and concentrate on France. On April 12, 1782, Adm. George Rodney defeated de Grasse at Îles des Saintes in the Leeward Islands. That battle forced Vergennes to abandon hope of forcing British concessions in Africa or India.

On the same day as Rodney's victory, Richard Oswald met with Franklin at Passy. Oswald was a Scottish merchant whose contacts list was almost as long as Franklin's. He had extensive dealings with America and was sympathetic toward the United States. Oswald arranged for Laurens, his business partner, to be released from the Tower of London and appeared as Shelburne's personal agent, rather than as an official envoy. Shelburne wanted a settlement in a hurry and had no time for diplomatic subtlety. Under the weak cover of his personal opinion, Oswald told Franklin that Great Britain wanted a separate peace. In response, Franklin took Oswald to a meeting with Vergennes on April 17, where Vergennes and Franklin agreed there could be no separate peace. Two days later Franklin gave Oswald a proposal without Vergennes's knowledge. The cession of Canada, Franklin argued, would be a strong step toward a treaty. The lands could be sold to compensate both Americans who had lost property at British hands and loyalists whose estates had been seized. Oswald returned to London. On April 23 the British cabinet decided to send Oswald back to Paris to set up a negotiation timetable with Franklin, but Oswald would have no other powers.

At a May 23 meeting, the cabinet authorized independence as a precondition rather than as a result of a peace treaty. On June 17 Oswald was named chief negotiator. After Rockingham died on July 1, Shelburne succeeded him, and Fox resigned rather than serve under Shelburne. Jay arrived in Paris from Spain on June 23. He contracted influenza soon after, leaving negotiations to Franklin. Franklin met with Oswald on July 10 and continued the practice of meeting with Oswald informally and only occasionally inviting Vergennes. Franklin presented Oswald with his list of "necessary" and "advisable" articles of peace. The necessary articles included independence, settlement of the boundaries, reduction of Canada at least to its 1774 boundaries, and freedom to fish off of Newfoundland. The "advisable" articles included an indemnity for those whose property was destroyed by British troops, an acknowledgment of error, most-favored-nation status for American ships in Great Britain and Ireland with a corresponding British privilege in American ports, and the cession of Canada. He told Oswald there could be no provision for the loyalists and backed away from his earlier proposal that Canada be used to compensate them. Franklin did not give Oswald a written copy of his proposal. He was already close to violating the June 15, 1781 instructions, and if there was no paper, nothing really happened. The next day Franklin told Oswald he would suspend negotiations until Shelburne's intentions were clearer.

Shelburne sent a dispatch to Oswald on July 27 that embraced Franklin's necessary articles. With the American war virtually over, Great Britain turned to

Gibraltar and its Caribbean interests. Shelburne accepted independence and proposed to cede the lands north of the Ohio River. With an abundance of land, Americans would never develop manufacturing and would instead import British goods. Shelburne would also grant access to the fisheries as a means of splitting the alliance. The cabinet also prepared a new commission for Oswald, which arrived in Paris on August 8 and was not as generous as the July 27 dispatch would indicate. Oswald was to recognize American independence as part of the final settlement and only at the price of ending the French alliance. Franklin objected to such an arrangement but left the matter to Jay. Jay demanded the commissioner's instructions recognize independence and sent Oswald back to London.

While Franklin and Jay had no problem talking to Oswald without involving Vergennes, they did not yet contemplate a separate peace. That would require either an overwhelming offer from Great Britain or some indication that France would not defend American interests. Oswald had not provided the former. Vergennes provided the latter. On August 3, Jay met with Pedro Pablo de Abarca de Bolea, Conde de Aranda, the Spanish ambassador to France, to discuss the western boundary of the United States. Jay requested a line with the southern boundary at 31° north and the western boundary at the Mississippi. A few days later, Aranda produced a map with a western boundary that went from the middle of modern-day Georgia north to Lake Erie, leaving about half of modern-day Ohio as part of the United States. That was unacceptable to Jay but not unexpected.

On August 10 Franklin and Jay met with Vergennes and Rayneval to discuss Oswald's commission and the Mississippi. Oswald's commission authorized him to negotiate with the representatives of the colonies. Vergennes advised the Americans to begin formal negotiations with Oswald. Franklin was willing to go along, but Jay was not. With that issue unresolved, the diplomats moved on to the western boundary. Rayneval spoke for the French. He argued that the United States had no right to the western country. It was a shocking moment for the Americans. For Jay it made sense of the last two and a half years. Now it was clear why the Spanish mission had failed and why Montmorin was little help. It was Paris, not Madrid, that stood in America's way. Jay now believed that France had directed Spanish policy from the beginning.

Jay was wrong and right at the same time. He was wrong in assuming that France directed Spanish policy; he was right about the broader dynamic of the alliance. France wanted to create a client state only strong enough to maintain independence. Jay had come to the realization that France aided the American Revolution to harm Great Britain and protect its own interests. Perhaps this should have been obvious, but many Americans, Jay included, had romanticized the alliance and made it more than it was. Franklin held out hope that Rayneval was speaking for himself alone and pointed to French generosity as a reason to give Vergennes the benefit of the doubt. For Jay, a skilled lawyer, the evidence was in. He and Franklin would have to make a separate peace with Great Britain to save the United States from French diplomacy. Franklin, with regret, agreed.

Jay's next encounter with Rayneval only confirmed his suspicions. Rayneval proposed a new boundary on September 6 that would put Kentucky on the American side, while granting the rest of the land south of the Ohio to Spain and on the north to Great Britain. Rayneval was careful to add that this proposal was his private view. Three days later Rayneval left on a mission to Great Britain. The mission had nothing to do with the United States, but Jay believed he could not take any chances. Jay broke off contact with Aranda, whom Jay regarded as Rayneval's cat's-paw, and told Oswald that he would accept a commission that did not explicitly recognize American independence, but merely stated that Oswald had the power to treat with the United States of America.

Fortunately for Jay, Shelburne wanted a settlement before anything else went wrong. Shelburne had two main concerns—trade and Gibraltar. On August 23 the cabinet sent Lord Howe to reinforce Gibraltar. Shelburne was therefore ready to give the United States most of what it wanted. On August 29 the cabinet decided to advise the king, if necessary, to accept independence as a precondition. The cabinet gave Oswald a new commission on September 27. While Gibraltar's fate was uncertain, Shelburne favored a generous peace. A combined Franco-Spanish fleet attacked Gibraltar on September 13 but failed to dislodge the British. News arrived in London on September 30. Shelburne never reversed policy on independence, but the victory at Gibraltar allowed him to pursue a harder line on the other issues, such as the boundary, the fisheries, and the loyalists.

With Oswald's new commission in hand, negotiations could officially begin. Franklin was ill the first week of October, and Jay took the lead. He completed a draft treaty on October 5. The British would acknowledge American independence and evacuate American territory. The United States would be bounded on the south at 31° north and by the Mississippi on the west. The northern boundary went from the St. Lawrence River to 45° north to Lake Nipissing and across to Lake Huron, putting lower Ontario in American hands. The St. John's River would form the boundary between Maine and Nova Scotia. The United States retained the right to fish in all places permitted in 1763, and each power could freely navigate the Mississippi. The Mitchell Map of 1755, used by the negotiators, mistakenly placed the source of the Mississippi in Canada. Franklin and Jay were willing to sacrifice the bulk of Canada to secure the Mississippi.

The cabinet rejected the draft on October 17. Gibraltar had stiffened British resolve, and the cabinet demanded a number of border adjustments, particularly regarding Canada and Nova Scotia. The cabinet also put the Ohio territory back on the table. Shelburne wanted to bar Americans from the Newfoundland fisheries and deferred any trade articles to a later commercial treaty. Shelburne also wanted compensation for loyalists and a provision for the collection of prewar debts. He accepted the western and southern boundaries, and the navigation of the Mississippi. The news reached Paris on October 24.

Two days later Adams arrived to assume his duties. Franklin had informed him of the progress of negotiations and repeatedly asked him to come to Paris. Adams declined, as he was busy trying to borrow money and gain recognition from the Netherlands. Adams was skeptical of the idea that Yorktown would end the war, but Yorktown did make his job easier. In April 1782 the Netherlands decided to recognize the United States. Two months later the Netherlands offered a loan. The two nations concluded a commercial treaty on October 8, 1782, which endorsed the maritime policies of the Model Treaty.[18] Adams did not relish the prospect of meeting with Franklin and Vergennes, and the last Adams knew, Jay was as pro-French as Franklin. On October 28 Jay gave Adams the full briefing, including the decision to break with France. "Mr. Jay likes Frenchmen as little as Mr. Lee and Mr. Izard did," Adams observed. "Our Allies don't play fair, he told me."[19]

Negotiations resumed on October 30, with Henry Strachey joining Oswald. The two sides agreed on the collection of prewar debts, which Adams separated from the loyalist issue. Strachey fought unsuccessfully to hold the Ohio territory for the British. Jay redrew the northern boundary by abandoning the Nipissing line, setting the Great Lakes as the boundary, and then drawing a line from the Lake of the Woods at 49° north to the Mississippi. No one at the table knew that the Mississippi did not reach that far north. On the northwest, the commission settled on the St. Croix River as the boundary, although where and what that river was remained a mystery until 1842. The western and southern boundaries were uncontested, at least by Great Britain and the United States. Strachey brought the new articles to London, where they were approved at a cabinet meeting on November 11. On November 14 and 15, the cabinet drafted a plan for compensating the loyalists.

Most of the issues now were resolved, leaving only fish and loyalists. Oswald constantly made the case for compensation. None of the Americans were sympathetic. The last sessions began on November 27. By the next day, Strachey was in retreat on the loyalist issue and asked merely that Americans agree to some face-saving article. That left the fisheries. Adams submitted an article giving Americans the right to catch fish everywhere they were accustomed to but was willing to accept only the liberty to dry fish on the uninhabited shores of Nova Scotia and the other nearby islands and coasts. Laurens joined the negotiations on November 29, completing the American team. Jefferson never sailed to Europe. The fisheries dominated the day, and Adams was born for that moment. Adams bombarded the British with arguments that the Americans had a natural right to the fisheries. Oswald was willing to make a deal on this item, as on all things, but saw no way around his instructions. Laurens, Jay, and Franklin closed ranks behind their colleague. The British offered a "liberty" to take fish on the coasts, as opposed to the right to fish off the Grand Banks. The Americans agreed. The Americans also accepted a formal request to Congress to ask the state legislatures to compensate the loyalists. On November 30, 1782, the two sides signed preliminary articles. That night at a celebration, one French guest told British diplomat Caleb Whitefoord that "the Thirteen United States would form the greatest empire in the world." Whitefoord's response was prophetic: "Yes sir, and they will *all* speak English; every one of 'em."[20]

The American diplomatic triumph, impressive as it was, was in direct violation of the instructions of June 15, 1781, but Adams reveled in his defiance: "It is a Glory to have broken such infamous Orders."[21] Jay shared Adams's sentiments. "Had I not violated the restriction of Congress, their dignity would have been in the dust," he wrote to Gouverneur Morris.[22] The commissioners, unlike Congress, did not panic. They did not fear retribution from Congress, but the agreement did complicate relations with France. On the day of the signature, Franklin sent the treaty to Vergennes. Vergennes was not pleased but a few days later told Franklin that he would have done the same thing. Franklin broached the subject of a new loan. Franklin was the only member of the commission who could make such a request or speak of Franco-American unity with a straight face. When Vergennes delayed the loan, Franklin reminded him of the link. "The English, I now learn, flatter themselves that they have already divided us," Franklin wrote. "I hope this little misunderstanding will therefore be kept a secret, and that they will find themselves totally mistaken."[23]

The Anglo-American settlement paved the way for the end of the war. In January 1783 Charles III authorized his ambassadors to make peace without Gibraltar, giving France a free hand. Shelburne wanted to restore normal relations and trade. Vergennes wanted to tend to France's interests in the east. France and Great Britain signed preliminary articles on January 20, 1783. Shelburne was not around to see the end. The American articles toppled the Shelburne ministry and brought in a coalition of Fox (as foreign secretary) and North (as home and colonial secretary) under William Henry Cavendish Bentinck, Duke of Portland. The new government replaced Oswald with David Hartley, an old friend of Franklin's. Merchants on both sides of the Atlantic hoped for a quick resumption of normal trade patterns. Such a settlement was politically impossible. The Portland ministry now turned to saving maritime supremacy and what was left of the empire.

In March 1783 John Holroyd, Lord Sheffield, published *Observations on the Commerce of the American States*, which restated the case for mercantilism. Sheffield argued that the point of overseas colonies was to increase the wealth and power of the mother country. The colonial trade was the chief source of wealth and therefore of maritime power. To open the trade to American shipping, even if the United States could more cheaply supply the West Indies with food, would defeat the purpose of having an empire. Therefore, Sheffield recommended that American ships be barred from the colonial trade. He believed there would be no diplomatic consequences, as Congress was unable to pass any retaliatory measures. Great Britain could exclude American ships from the colonial trade, dump manufactured goods on the United States, and reap the rewards of American trade without offering anything in return. The cabinet closed the door to a commercial treaty with the Order-in-Council of July 2, 1783, which barred American vessels from the colonial trade. The order, considered temporary at the time, was made permanent in 1788 and remained British policy for more than forty years. The belligerent powers signed a final peace treaty on September 3, 1783, folding the Anglo-American articles into a general settlement with France and Spain.

From the start of the American Revolution, the radicals had set the tone for American foreign relations, if they did not always predominate. In one sense the peace treaty was a vindication. The radicals believed that the dynamic of the European balance of power would promote American independence, and they were right. The rivalry between Great Britain and France provided French aid and then a British offer that led to a separate peace. On the other hand, the radicals overestimated the power of American trade to achieve American diplomatic goals without any political commitments. That was the basic assumption behind the Model Treaty. The French wanted more than trade to enter the war. The new idea of free trade could not overcome the tradition of mercantilism, and the British closed the West Indies. The idea of economic coercion as a substitute for military force died hard—and for some died not at all.

CHAPTER 2

# The Failure of the Confederation

To many Americans, the lessons of revolutionary diplomacy confirmed the wisdom of the plan of 1776. Commercial connections were preferable to political engagements, and the United States should avoid entanglement with Europe. Most still believed that the two could proceed on separate tracks. Most also believed that other nations would bid for American trade on American terms and that Europe's wars and the balance of power would provide markets for American agricultural produce as well as opportunity for American shipping. Despite being a wartime policy, the plan of 1776 looked more toward American neutrality than belligerency. Although under the Articles of Confederation the nation achieved some small success in foreign affairs, overall the plan must be considered a failure for two main reasons. First, as the diplomacy of the 1780s revealed, commerce and politics were not the separate things that American policymakers believed. Second, Congress under the Articles of Confederation had no power to coerce other nations. The offer of free trade alone was not sufficient to open colonial ports to American trade or gain American access to the length of the Mississippi.

One of the more fundamental questions of diplomacy in 1783, as much as 1776, was whether or not to conduct it at all. Followed to its logical conclusion, a diplomacy based on trade did not need diplomats. During the American Revolution, William Lee had been an advocate for blanketing Europe with American ministers, but he thought it a wartime expediency. In peace Lee preferred to let European diplomats come to the United States to treat.[1] Privately John Adams agreed but considered that policy impractical and believed Americans should be sent abroad on two conditions: "The First is, to send men of independent minds who will not be tools; men of virtue and conscience. The second is, to persuade Congress to support them firmly. It is infinitely better to have none in Europe than to have artful, unprincipled impostors or depraved men."[2] In short, more Adamses, no Franklins, and no repeat of the instructions of June 15, 1781.

On October 29, 1783, Congress decided against sending more ministers but instructed the commercial commission of Adams, Jay, and Franklin to negotiate treaties with other nations based on the Model Treaty. Congress specifically mentioned Russia, the Holy Roman Empire, Prussia, Denmark, Saxony, Hamburg, Great Britain, Spain, Portugal, Genoa, Tuscany, Rome, Naples, Venice, Sardinia, and the Ottoman Empire. Jefferson replaced Jay when Jay accepted the post of secretary of foreign affairs in 1784. Any American who feared a surplus of American diplomats need not have bothered. By the mid-1780s, only Adams in London and Jefferson in Paris remained. Several attempts to send a minister to the Netherlands failed when no one would serve for the $4,500 per year salary. Without a sufficient government, however, it did not matter how many diplomats Congress appointed.

The Articles of Confederation barely allowed for any exercise of power. "Our foederal Government is incompetent to its Objects," Jay complained to Adams.[3] Congress could assess taxes to be paid by the states but could not compel payment. It could make treaties with the approval of nine states but could not carry out the terms. Any change to the Articles of Confederation required the concurrence of all thirteen states. Upon this rock, attempts to raise a revenue foundered. Rhode Island blocked an impost in 1781, after which Virginia rescinded its ratification. On April 18, 1783, James Madison proposed a 5 percent duty on various imported goods. The amendment slowly worked its way through the states before being blocked by New York in 1786. A congressional committee proposed on April 22, 1784, that Congress should have the power for fifteen years to prohibit exports or imports on vessels from nations that did not have a commercial treaty with the United States. A year later James Monroe moved to give Congress the exclusive power to regulate foreign and interstate commerce. None of these measures passed. "Congress is only a phantom of sovereignty destitute of powers, of energy and of consideration, and the edifice that it should support is falling into ruin," observed Louis Guillaume Otto, Luzerne's successor.[4]

American diplomacy succeeded when nations did not have to be cajoled into accepting American trade. If a nation had no American colonies, the path was much easier. The first trade treaty was with Sweden, which sought American grain. The Swedish ambassador to France approached Franklin soon after the preliminary peace treaty, the two concluding a commercial agreement on April 3, 1783. Each side enjoyed most-favored-nation status, and the treaty provided for a limited contraband list, specifically excluding ship's stores. Like the United States, Sweden was a leading producer of stores.[5]

The Prussian treaty of 1785 was the best example of a treaty based on the Model Treaty. Frederick II was skeptical (as were most European monarchs) about the success of the American experiment, but he did wish to trade. The provisional peace between the United States and Great Britain removed political obstacles. In May 1783 Frederick instructed his ambassador to France, Baron von der Goltz, to approach Franklin. Nine months later Baron von Thulemeyer, the ambassador to the Netherlands, approached Adams. Soon after they met, Thulemeyer sent a draft treaty stating that Prussia intended to import tobacco, rice, indigo, and whale oil, and wished to export Silesian linens, Prussian hemp, Berlin porcelain, hardware, and textiles. Adams modeled a treaty on the Swedish treaty. In July and August 1785 the American commissioners signed the final treaty, followed by Thulemeyer on September 10. Each side held most-favored-nation status, and each power could carry its goods into the other's ports. The treaty stated that free ships make free goods and provided for a limited contraband list. Like Sweden, Prussia had no American colonies and few points of friction with the United States that might lead to war.[6]

American traders ranged even farther away in search of new markets. On February 22, 1784, the *Empress of China* sailed out of New York with a cargo mainly of ginseng, bound for China. The ship arrived at Canton on August 30, sold its cargo, and purchased nankeens (Nanking cloth), silks, tea, and chinoiserie (the catch-all term for Chinese manufactured goods). The *Empress of China* returned to New York on May 11, 1785, and cleared a profit of $37,000. The supercargo, Samuel Shaw, wrote to Jay the next week describing Canton, the procedure for trade, and the opportunity for American merchants. In 1786 Congress appointed Shaw consul, an office he held until 1797. The single largest export item from China was tea. The China trade had the side effect of launching trade with India. On March 24, 1784, the *United States* sailed out of Philadelphia with a cargo of ginseng, naval stores, copper, hardware, and money originally bound for

China. Instead, the ship landed at Pondicherry, India, on December 26, 1784. Elias Haskett Derby, soon to become the merchant king of Salem, linked the two eastern trades with the voyage of the *Grand Turk*. The goods from India were mostly silks, cotton, and coffee. The eastern trades had more potential than profit in the 1780s. The opium trade with China and the ice trade with India lay in the future. Yet these trades testify to a pioneering spirit and a practical effort to circumvent blocked trade routes.

Trade was easier where there was no resistance. Trades that required some sort of government protection suffered. The most glaring example of military weakness as a bar to trade was the American encounter with the Barbary powers of Morocco, Tunis, Tripoli, and Algiers. The Barbary powers considered themselves at war with all powers with which they did not have peace treaties. American ships, no longer under British protection, were fair game. On October 1, 1784, Moroccan pirates seized an American ship, the *Betsey*. The Americans were released in 1785 after Spain's intervention. The same year, Spain concluded a hundred-year truce with Algiers. Spain withdrew its fleet, leaving Algerine pirates free to roam the Atlantic. By July 14, 1785, Algiers was officially at war with the United States. Algerines seized the *Maria* out of Boston on July 25 and the *Dauphin* (or *Dolphin*) of Philadelphia on August 1. Congress sent New York ship captain John Lamb and Thomas Barclay, the American consul-general in France, to negotiate. Barclay succeeded in his mission to Morocco. He arrived on June 21, 1786, and signed an exceptionally favorable treaty two days later. The treaty established a fifty-year peace and gave each side most-favored-nation status. Unlike most Barbary treaties, the Morocco treaty did not call for tribute, and it is unclear why Morocco made peace as easily as it did.[7] Algiers was a far more difficult case. Lamb arrived in Algiers on March 26, 1786, and left empty-handed on April 20. He tried to threaten Spain into helping. When that failed, Lamb offered $30,000 in ransom. The dey of Algiers wanted $60,000. The Algerine crisis lingered for the next decade.

Many American leaders advocated more vigorous action against the pirate states. Jay preferred war to tribute and in some ways welcomed war with Algiers. "In my Opinion it may lay the Foundation for a Navy, and tend to draw us more closely into a foederal system," he wrote Adams.[8] The Barbary pirates were the only issue that turned Jefferson into a hawk. "We ought to begin a naval power, if we mean to carry our own commerce," he wrote Monroe, with one eye on Morocco and the other on Great Britain. "Can we begin it on a more honourable occasion or with a weaker foe?"[9] Jefferson was never really a navy enthusiast and hoped that if the United States could build a navy to defeat Morocco, Great Britain would treat the United States with more respect, preventing the need for a larger navy. Adams believed that if every European power paid tribute and the United States had no money for a navy, there was no choice but to pay tribute. "I agree in the Opinion of the Wisdom and Necessity of a Navy for other Uses, but am apprehensive that it will make bad worse with the Algerines," he wrote to Jefferson.[10]

## The United States and the Great Powers

Problems with Great Britain flowed from the same difficulties as with the Barbary powers—that is, the lack of any coercive power. Despite the setbacks of the order of July 2, 1783, and the lack of a commercial treaty in the final peace, the hope for a complete reconciliation was not yet dead. British merchants and West Indian planters could not believe the order would be permanent. The Americans believed the immutable laws of supply and demand would break down British trade barriers without hectoring the British. However, the American Revolution drew a political line across natural economic zones. The political logic of mercantilism trumped the economic logic of Adam Smith's invisible hand. A committee for trade issued a report on May 31, 1784, that stated British trade was booming in all sectors, including with the United States. American trade sagged. Sheffield was right, and the order of July 2, 1783, stood as official policy. However, the history of Anglo-American trade can be divided into the rules decreed in London and what really happened in America. Colonial planters, and not a few colonial governors, welcomed American produce on American ships. Horatio Nelson spent the 1780s engaged in the thankless and hopeless task of stopping American smuggling in the West Indies. Nevertheless, smuggling could not make up for the loss of official trade, and British restrictions drove American shipping and related industries into a depression.

Far more serious was the British retention of the forts in the Old Northwest—now Ohio, Indiana, Illinois, Michigan, and Wisconsin. The evacuation began smoothly enough when Sir Guy Carleton withdrew his forces from New York

City on December 3, 1783. The British did not, however, evacuate the forts of Michilimacinac, Niagara, Detroit, Point au Fer, Oswego, Oswegatchie, Sandusky, and Presque Isle. British policy regarding the Old Northwest through the War of 1812 may be easily summarized. After Shelburne's offer to cede the territory, every British government, including Shelburne's, regretted it and sought to reverse it in some fashion. In July 1783 Sir John Johnson, son of Sir William Johnson, the legendary superintendent of Indian affairs in the North, held a conference with the Six Nations at Niagara, telling them the king still considered them allies but advising them not to commit hostile acts against the United States. Five months later, Gen. Sir Frederick Haldimand, governor-general of Canada, warned Lord North that the Indian tribes did not believe Great Britain had the right to cede their territory to the United States.

Great Britain's Indian allies, particularly the Mohawk chief Joseph Brant, were key elements in promoting the lucrative fur trade, which was a leading factor in British policy. When Lt. Col. William Hull arrived in Canada in 1784 to arrange for British evacuation of the forts, Haldimand replied that he had no such order and told Hull he believed the mistreatment of the loyalists was the reason. Back in London, Thomas Townshend, Lord Sydney (North's replacement as home secretary), wrote Haldimand on April 8, 1784, instructing him that no fixed term had been set for withdrawal. Sydney hoped to protect the fur trade, as Haldimand did, but portrayed the order as a response to American failure to adhere to the treaty.

The British offered a number of official reasons to keep the forts. In all likelihood, they were mere pretexts, and Great Britain would have held on to the forts for as long as they could get away with it. The loyalists were the first justification. The peace treaty stated that Congress would urge the states to compensate some loyalists whose estates had been seized and prohibited further confiscation of property. Some loyalists remained in the United States but had taken no part in the war. The national mood did not permit any sort of compensation. Henry Laurens believed that the loyalists should be grateful for anything they received short of a hanging. Most states did not go that far but did pass laws barring loyalists from returning, disenfranchising them, seizing their property, or all three. By 1785 the antiloyalist tide crested and became a smaller issue in Anglo-American relations. Soon after, the issue of prewar debts replaced the loyalists as the main reason for the British to hold on to the forts. If treatment of the loyalists was a questionable violation of the treaty, the debt issue was more blatant. Officially the British had no reason to withdraw from the forts, and economically the government felt it had no reason to allow American vessels into the West Indian trade.

Thus John Adams inherited an untenable situation when he took office as the first American minister to Great Britain in June 1785. Before assuming his post, Adams grasped the economic problem. "The Britons boast that All the Prophecies of the Loss of the american Trade, from the independence of the United States have proved false: that the Experiment had been tryed and the Contest decided," he wrote Jay. The British believed they had won. Their products were superior, their prices better, and their credit easier. All other competitors had been driven from the field. Adams believed that while this assertion contained "much exaggeration," there was also "too much Truth."[11] Americans were already used to buying British goods, and Great Britain produced a wide variety of consumer goods aimed at a general market. There was no language barrier to establishing trade between American and British houses. An extensive Anglo-American trade was the default position, and Congress had no power to change it.

Adams hoped his mission could resolve the outstanding Anglo-American issues. After a polite if somewhat awkward reception with George III, Adams began to negotiate with the foreign secretary, the Marquis of Carmarthen. The two met on June 16, 1785. Adams threatened economic retaliation, or at least the prospect of American manufacturing, if Great Britain did not open the colonial trade. Carmarthen did not believe him. Adams insisted that the British withdraw from the forts. Carmarthen insisted on the collection of prewar debts. There relations stood throughout Adams's mission. A meeting with William Pitt in August produced no different results. By then Adams had given up on the power of economic coercion and feared that commercial war might produce a real war. He no longer believed politics and trade could be completely separated.[12]

In October Carmarthen asked for the payment of prewar debts. Adams objected on the grounds that the treaty stipulated only that the creditors be allowed to pursue debts in court. He realized it was a distinction without a difference, and on December 8 he prepared a memorial on the forts. In January 1786 Adams told Jay he expected nothing. He was correct. On February 28 Carmarthen responded that Great Britain would evacuate the forts as soon as provisions were made for British creditors. Adams did not even bother with lesser issues, such as the return of slaves. The problem on the American side, Adams and Jay agreed, was that American violations of the treaty provided an excuse for British violations. On October 13, 1786, Jay submitted a report to Congress detailing state laws in violation of the treaty. The root problem was that Congress had no power to compel the states to obey. That was a common theme in Adams and Jay's correspondence. Privately Adams had a solution: if Great Britain did not abandon the forts, "I would not go and Attack them, but declare War directly and march one Army to Quebec and another to Nova Scotia."[13] It was mere talk and Adams knew it. Even worse, Carmarthen knew it.

Adams attributed British policy to a burning hatred for the United States. "The popular pulse seems to beat high against America," he wrote in July 1785. He believed that, "if this nation had another hundred millions to spend, they would soon force this ministry into a war against us."[14] France and Great Britain concluded the Eden Treaty on September 26, 1786, establishing mutual most-favored-nation status. Adams could see no economic benefit to Great Britain. The United States, not France, was the more valuable trade partner. Adams was wrong about the economics of the Eden Treaty. Such an agreement had been a goal of British policy since Shelburne. But he was right, broadly speaking, about the politics. Political anti-Americanism was popular and, when fused with mercantilism, defeated any free-trade argument. Adams believed that if the United States could not reach a settlement with Great Britain, it would have to do for itself. The United States must encourage its own manufacturing and its own shipping. For Adams free trade was more of a tactic than an ideological principle. By the 1780s it was clear that free trade had not worked as a diplomatic lever and must be abandoned. A commitment to free trade, Adams believed, "would cause the sudden annihilation of all their manufactures and navigation," Adams warned Jay. "We should have the most luxurious set of farmers that ever existed, and should not be able to defend ourselves against the insults of a pirate."[15]

American relations with Great Britain were, in the American view, a case of postwar bitterness overriding economic benefit. Seemingly trade with France should be more open. The two nations were still officially allies, but each side picked up and dropped the alliance when it suited them. In May 1786 Jefferson asked Vergennes if France would help expel Great Britain from the northwestern forts. Vergennes responded that the exact boundary was unclear. Jefferson was going to press the point but feared Vergennes would ask about the American guarantee of the French West Indies.

Franco-American trade was the main problem. Statesmen on both sides of the Atlantic assumed that French trade, both metropolitan and colonial, would replace whatever was lost in British trade. The logic that Americans applied to the British islands applied equally to the French. French diplomats in the United States favored allowing the United States into the colonial trade to secure closer relations. Vergennes agreed but was unsure how much to grant, as "we have to measure the advantages of our national Commerce against that of our navigation, and we shall sacrifice neither the one nor the other to please the Americans."[16] That proved a difficult, if not impossible, balancing act. Even an absolute monarchy had lobbying groups that had to be placated. France opened the ports at Dunkirk, L'Orient, Bayonne, and Marseilles in May 1784. An *arrêt* of August 30, 1784, opened colonial ports to American shipping but prohibited the importation of American flour to the islands and prohibited American ships from taking away sugar, cotton, coffee, and cocoa. In 1785 the French government added a bounty on French dried cod and a duty on foreign dried cod. Notwithstanding, American exports of tobacco and foodstuffs tripled in the 1780s. In 1786 the French West Indies imported £21 million worth of goods from the United States and exported £14 million. French exports to the United States plummeted in the same period, with most of the decline owing to the evacuation of the French army.

French trade never did match up to the hopes projected onto it. French trade was difficult for the same reasons that British trade was easy. First was the language barrier. French trade also had more government controls than British trade. One could not simply strike up a correspondence with a French mercantile house. The credit structure, which made large-scale trade possible, was more difficult to create. French manufactures were not as numerous or as inexpensive as British productions. French goods were aimed at the luxury market, and France could not match British goods in bulk or popularity.

On May 17, 1785, Jefferson was presented to Louis XVI as the new American minister. He took office with the expectation that friendship and free trade would dismantle the system of French mercantilism. "It was an incredibly ambitious undertaking," as Merrill Peterson described, "nothing less than a diplomatic mission to convert all Europe to the commercial principles of the American Revolution."[17] Jefferson embraced the task, the fulfillment of radical diplomacy, that Adams had abandoned. Luzerne described Jefferson for Vergennes in 1784, when Jefferson left for Europe as commercial commissioner. Jefferson was "an enlightened man of integrity and of an excellent Citizen, but one incapable of holding the tiller in stormy weather," Luzerne wrote. He believed that Jefferson would one day replace Franklin as minister. "In that case, My Lord, you would soon perceive that Mr. Jefferson does not join to his theoretical knowledge with much experience and practice of affairs."[18]

Jefferson wasted little time in his quest for free trade, presenting a memorial to Vergennes on August 15, 1785. Jefferson called for an end to the French monopolies, particularly on tobacco, which constituted the vast majority of American exports to France. "In truth no two countries are better calculated for the exchanges of commerce," Jefferson wrote. "France wants rice, tobacco, potash, furs, ship timber. We want wines, brandies, oils and manufactures."[19] What he did not know, and would not until October, is that the tobacco monopoly had already been extended. A group of merchants, known as the Farmers-General, had the responsibility for collecting a number of taxes for the French government, including the duty on tobacco. After a lengthy search for American suppliers, the Farmers-General selected Robert Morris in March 1785. Morris was to purchase three-fourths of his tobacco from Virginia and the rest from Maryland. Two-thirds of the tobacco must be suitable for smoking, and the rest would be used for snuff.

The story of the tobacco monopoly was emblematic of the difficulties of Franco-American trade. Jefferson met with Vergennes to resolve the matter in December. Vergennes was a longtime critic of the Farmers-General and sympathized with Jefferson but explained that the monopoly could not be easily abolished. The Marquis de Lafayette tried to intercede on Jefferson's behalf. On May 10, 1786, an "American committee" met to discuss the future of the contract. It favored either breaking the contract or letting it lapse when it expired in December 1787. Charles-Alexandre de Calonne, the comptroller-general of finances, proposed to let the contract stand and buy an additional 15,000 hogsheads—more than what France would consume. The committee met at Calonne's country seat at Berni on May 24 and accepted the proposal. Calonne informed Jefferson on October 22.[20]

If the point of the contract was to sell tobacco to France, it was successful. What France did not consume, it reexported. The contract drove up the price of all grades of tobacco, giving an economic boost to the Chesapeake region's tobacco farmers. For Jefferson, however, the goal was to reshape the commercial policies of the Atlantic world. Jefferson sought to abolish the monopoly entirely. By October 1786 he temporarily gave up on the effort. Calonne's successor, Charles-Guillaume Lambert, was friendly toward the United States, and Jefferson did not want to cost Lambert his job by pushing the matter. Jefferson raised the issue again in July 1787, calling the monopoly system the "radical evil" that blocked Franco-American commerce.[21]

One consequence of the Berni agreement was a backlash against the American fish and whale oil trade. In an *arrêt* of December 29, 1787, France granted the right of entrepôt, the right to reexport American products, including fish and whale products, from French ports without paying a duty. France then revoked that *arrêt* in February 1788. The duty on cod was intentional, but Lambert blamed the whale oil duty on a bureaucratic error. It was only the latest of many evils suffered by the American fishing industry, the British having imposed heavy duties after the war. Jefferson lobbied against the new restrictions on the American fishing industry. Another *arrêt*, issued on September 28, 1788, barred foreign whale oil from French ports. Jefferson began an extensive study of whaling, relying on numerous American merchants in France for information. Jefferson's completed report, *Observations on the Whale-Fishery*, placed the industry in the context of the overall goal of securing American commerce. Jefferson noted that France had removed the United States "from the *force* of Great Britain" but not from British commerce. The fisheries constituted the only extensive American industry. "The United-States not possessing mines of the precious metals, they can purchase necessaries from other nations so far only as their produce is received in exchange," he wrote. Tobacco was under a monopoly, whale oil was prohibited, and rice was not yet an important article. Jefferson concluded that whether considered "in a political or a commercial light," the September 28 *arrêt* must be repealed.[22] Jefferson had better luck than with tobacco. The king issued an *arrêt* on December 7, 1788, exempting American whale oil from the general ban as of April 1, 1789.

Jefferson was not by his nature an expert in or an advocate of the seafaring industries. His ideal nation, best suited to a republican government, was a nation of yeoman farmers. "Those who labour in the earth are the chosen people of God, if ever he had a chosen people," he famously declared in *Notes on the State of Virginia.* The foreign policy of a farmers' republic would be "to throw open the doors of commerce, and to knock off all its shackles, giving perfect freedom to all persons for the vent of whatever they may choose to bring to our ports, and asking the same in theirs." Such a policy made American produce its own defense. It required neither ships nor troops. Ideally Jefferson would like to "abandon the ocean altogether," letting other nations bid for American commerce.[23] As Jefferson grew older, the more theoretical part of his diplomacy became predominant. Unlike Adams, nothing in Jefferson's experience told him economic coercion, the heart of radical diplomacy, would not work.

If France would not serve as an economic and political counterweight to Great Britain, that left Spain. One could find many Americans who favored Great Britain over France, or France over Great Britain. The only pro-Spanish Americans were on Spain's payroll. However, friendship with Spain seemed to many the only hope against a hostile Great Britain and a doubtful France. The two main issues between the United States and Spain were the boundaries and the navigation of the Mississippi. Most Americans, particularly in the South, viewed Spain and its rich but declining empire with contempt. Spain did not recognize the boundary provisions of the Treaty of Paris and claimed territory as far north as the Ohio River, based on Bernardo de Gálvez's conquest of Pensacola. The Spanish encouraged the southern tribes to seek Spanish protection. The Mississippi question was related to the boundary. The Spanish did not recognize the boundaries established in the Treaty of Paris or the British and American claim to the navigation of the Mississippi. Some local Spanish officials favored opening the lower Mississippi to ease tensions and draw settlers, but officials in Madrid, from Floridablanca on down, were adamant about closing the Mississippi. On June 26, 1784, Minister of the Indies José de Gálvez asserted an exclusive right to the Mississippi where it flowed between Spanish banks. At the same time, the United States made the opposite claim. On June 3 Congress voted not to cede the right of navigation south of 31° north, the boundary with the Floridas established in the Treaty of Paris.

As Floridablanca ordered the closure of the lower Mississippi, he began the process of drawing up instructions for Don Diego de Gardoqui as chargé d'affaires in the United States. Part of a merchant family in Bilbao, Gardoqui had acted as an intermediary for American diplomats during the American Revolution and was the closest thing Spain had to an America expert. He could not grant the navigation of the Mississippi where Spain owned both banks. Gardoqui was to use the Mississippi articles of Jay's draft treaty of September 22, 1781, as a template, conveniently ignoring the fact that that offer was good only during the war. He could offer to put pressure on Great Britain regarding the forts and protect the Mediterranean trade. Gardoqui could also threaten to cut off American trade with Spain. On July 29, Floridablanca issued an "Instruction" to Spanish colonial officials that would serve as Spain's position on the boundaries. Spain accepted 31° north as the boundary of East Florida but demanded a western boundary that would place western Georgia, most of Alabama and Mississippi, part of Tennessee, and the western end of Kentucky in Spanish hands. The United States could not navigate below the junction of the Ohio and the Mississippi. Gardoqui's final instructions of October 2, 1784, had that of July 29 as its basis. Charles III would accept some modification of the boundary, ceding as far south as St. Augustine. Gardoqui could offer most-favored-nation status in Spain and the Canary Islands, but the 1713 Treaty of Utrecht prohibited allowing the United States into the colonial trade. He could offer a military guarantee of American territory if necessary to gain a treaty.

Gardoqui arrived in New York in July 1785 believing he already had the secret to dealing with Jay. Jay was the only American diplomat to bring his wife with him during the American Revolution. Gardoqui observed that Jay was "a very self-centered man, which passion his wife augments, because in addition to thinking highly of herself and being rather vain, she likes to be catered to and even more to receive presents."[24] Properly managed, Jay could deliver six or seven states. To that end, Garqoqui had a large expense account (to be washed through the Gardoqui mercantile house) and no restrictions on how to spend it. He lavished Sarah Jay with attention and arranged for Jay to purchase a prize stallion, a transaction Jay had Congress approve. Gardoqui also gave Washington a donkey.

As might be expected, the negotiation stalled over the navigation of the Mississippi. Jay could not cede it, and Gardoqui could not grant it. On August 25, 1785, Congress reaffirmed a right to the Mississippi. Floridablanca was willing to concede the southwestern boundary and by 1787 offered a line close to the one ultimately agreed to in 1795. However, there could be no Spanish movement on the Mississippi, and Jay believed that the United States would have to give way in order to reach a desperately needed commercial treaty with Spain. In February 1786 Jay told Congress that "the United States will not have that Navigation open to their Citizens unless by *Arms* or by *Treaty* That in the Opinion of your Secretary the Time for the *former* is not yet come." Jay did not believe it prudent to push Spain on the matter. It would have to wait until the Mississippi Valley filled up with more people and "the Affairs of the Confederacy become regulated and arranged."[25] Under this formula, Jay sought a commercial treaty with Spain. On May 23 Gardoqui warned Jay that the United States would give up a great deal of commerce if it insisted on the Mississippi. The next day Gardoqui offered a formal alliance. Jay sought to make an agreement without giving up the Mississippi. As a lawyer, he was careful in his use of language in a contract. On May 29 Jay was willing to forbear the use of the lower Mississippi for twenty-five or thirty years. Ideally that would be acceptable to Spain without giving up the right to the Mississippi. Jay then requested a secret committee to oversee negotiations. Southern members had feared for months that Jay would give up the Mississippi and sacrifice the southern interest for the benefit of northern merchants.

On August 3 Jay presented his treaty to Congress. He began with a primer on the harsh realities of international politics. "France will invariably think it her interest to prefer the good Will of Spain to the good Will of America," he advised. As for Great Britain, "she remembers that we were once her Subjects, and loves us not." Jay concluded that "on good Principles of Policy and Commerce, it is in the Interest of the United States to be on the best terms with Spain." Jay went on to list the economic benefits of the proposed treaty. Each side would enjoy reciprocal trade rights in the others ports. The king of Spain would pay badly needed specie for American ship's masts and timbers. Although American shipping would still be barred from the colonial trade, Jay expected that Spain would need to buy American flour to feed South America. As for the Mississippi, the United States had no choice but to forbear—not cede—its use. Jay believed that the Mississippi was not yet as important as it would be. "It is much to be wished that all these Matters had lain dormant for Years yet to come—but such wishes are vain—these disputes are agitating—they press themselves upon us, and must terminate in Accommodation, or War, or Disgrace," Jay argued. "The last is the worst that can happen, the second we are unprepared for, and therefore our Attention and Endeavours should be bent to the first." The real problem, as always, was the lack of a real central government. "For unblessed with an efficient government, destitute of Funds and without public Credit either at home or abroad, we should be obliged to wait in Patience for better Days, or plunge into an unpopular and dangerous War, with very little Prospect of terminating it by a peace advantageous or glorious."[26]

A week later Charles Pinckney of South Carolina delivered a blistering attack on the treaty, but to no avail. On August 29 Congress voted seven states to six to remove the navigation of the Mississippi as a requirement for a treaty. However, the Articles of Confederation required nine states to ratify a treaty. Gardoqui loaned Henry Lee $5,000 to secure his vote, but when the Virginia legislature found out, it dumped Lee from the delegation. On November 29 Congress approved a motion affirming a natural right to the Mississippi. In April 1787 James Madison presented a motion in Congress, which failed, to move negotiations to Madrid under Jefferson's supervision. Jay's negotiations with Gardoqui lasted another year but went no further. In September 1788 both sides decided to hold off further negotiations until the formation of the new government. Events on the frontier proceeded without input from New York or Madrid. In 1787 Col. James Wilkinson, a recent migrant to Kentucky, wrote to Spanish officials in New Orleans to create a pro-Spanish party in the West by closing the Mississippi to American commerce and inviting the West to join Spain. This plot is generally known as the Spanish Conspiracy, a name unfair to Spain. Wilkinson landed on the Spanish payroll as an informer, but the Spanish council of state declined to create a separatist movement.

In the absence of an effective national government, the states took over some of the functions of foreign policy. Most states passed some sort of tariff on British imports and often on the other states. In June 1784 Madison drafted the Virginia Port Bill, which set aside four ports of entry to Virginia. Without a strong union, Madison wanted to ensure that the profits from the tobacco trade remained in Virginia. Massachusetts passed a navigation act in June 1785 that prohibited the exportation of goods in British ships or other foreign ships without a treaty with the United States as of August 1. Foreign vessels could unload goods only at Boston, Dartmouth, and Falmouth (now Portland), Maine. The act placed tonnage duties on all foreign shipping and high tariffs on imports. Massachusetts abandoned the act in 1786 when the other states failed to follow suit.

## The Constitution

The movement toward the Constitution began with the states seeking to protect their own interests. Under its charter, Maryland owned both banks of the Potomac. In June 1784 Virginia approved a conference with Maryland to resolve the issue. The Mount Vernon Conference convened at Washington's home in March 1785 and agreed that the navigation of the Potomac should be free. Both states sought to bring in the Potomac's near neighbors, and in January 1786 Madison proposed a general commercial conference of all the states. The result was the Annapolis Conference of September 1786. The ill-attended conference produced nothing except a call for a more general convention to be held in Philadelphia in May 1787.

Madison was the leading intellectual force behind the movement to draft the Constitution. The main problem was to reconcile two seemingly irreconcilable truths. First was the conventional wisdom, confirmed by the fate of Rome and recently restated by Montesquieu, that republics had to be small and homogeneous to survive. Second was the fact that the United States had to have free access to the Mississippi to remain an agrarian nation and therefore a republic. Not only was it necessary for the United States to remain a single republic; it needed a much stronger central government. Madison drafted two memorandums in his effort to resolve this paradox. The first, "Notes on Ancient and Modern Confederacies," drafted sometime between April and June 1786, surveyed the history of confederacies—that is, unions of sovereign states under a weak central government. Madison concluded that they all failed. Either inequality among the members invited foreign influence, or a weak government failed to defend against invaders.[27] The second memorandum, "Vices of the Political System of the United States," was drafted in April 1787. Madison argued that in the absence of a central government, state governments that were incompetent to the task were making foreign policy. States passed laws prohibiting the shipping of other states. Madison included his own Virginia Port Bill as the sort of law states should not have the authority to pass. States violated the peace treaty and issued paper money, which complicated the payment of foreign debts. To counter Montesquieu, Madison adapted David Hume's recent argument that in a large commonwealth, purely local interests would be filtered out and national sentiments would prevail.[28]

The Constitutional Convention was the product of a failed American foreign policy. David Hendrickson has described the convention as a peace congress along the lines of Westphalia. Max M. Edling emphasizes the idea of the creation of a fiscal-military state.[29] The nature of the union and powers of the government were the two main questions and were interrelated. The debates, particularly those over the power of government, revived something of the radical-versus-moderate split of the beginning of the American Revolution. As H. James Henderson argued, the radicals relied on a "national ideology" for authority, and when that failed it was necessary to create a "national organization."[30]

Prior to the great compromise on representation of July 16, the dominant question was whether or not there would be a central government. The supporters of the Virginia Plan cited defense against foreign danger as one of the main reasons for a stronger central government. On June 29 Nathaniel Gorham outlined to the small states the dire consequences of disunion. Delaware would "lie at the mercy of Pennsylvania," and both Pennsylvania and New York would fall upon New Jersey. Madison argued that all those who feared a powerful central government should embrace the union. If each state looked to its own defense, all would soon institute powerful governments with large armies: "The same causes which have rendered the old world the Theatre of incessant wars, & have banished liberty from the face of it, would soon produce the same effect here."[31]

Some delegates from the small states feared their larger neighbors more than foreign powers. Gunning Bedford of Delaware warned on June 30 that if the large states destroyed the union by denying equal representation, "the small ones will find some foreign ally of more honor and good faith who will take them by the hand and do them justice."[32] The specter of foreign influence was now out in the open. Bedford's remarks were the main topic of conversation for the next few days. Madison could not believe "that Delaware would brave the consequences of seeking her fortune apart from the other States." Gouverneur Morris painted a lurid picture of civil war. "Our country must be united," he argued. "If persuasion does not unite it the sword will." That would spark a civil war with a worse peace to follow. Morris could not say to what extent foreign powers might intervene but the history of failed confederations did not bode well. Bedford backed off his earlier comments, explaining that he "did not mean that the small states would court the aid & interposition of foreign powers," but rather that the union would be dissolved by the actions of the large states.[33]

The Great Compromise ended talk of disunion. It was good enough to keep the small states in and not bad enough to drive out the large states. The emphasis shifted to the specific powers to be granted. Most of the delegates agreed on forming a national state but differed on how much state was both necessary to conduct foreign relations and compatible with liberty. Charles Pinckney and Alexander Hamilton staked out opposite positions. On June 25 Pinckney painted an idyllic portrait of a free people separated from Europe. Pinckney considered making the people "happy at home" the true goal of republican government. "We mistake the object of our government if we hope or wish that it is to make us respectable abroad."[34] Hamilton responded four days later that the Europeans were neighbors. "Foreign nations having American dominions are & must be jealous of us." He argued that Pinckney made "an ideal distinction" between happiness at home and respectability abroad. "No Government could give us tranquility & happiness at home, which did not possess sufficient stability and strength to make us respectable abroad."[35]

The main foreign policy issues at the convention were the war power, the regulation of commerce, and the treaty power. The convention took up the war power as part of the powers granted to Congress on August 17. Pinckney opposed giving a slow-moving Congress the power to make war and preferred giving the war power to the Senate. Pierce Butler of South Carolina moved to give the president the power to make war. This too was unacceptable. Madison and Elbridge Gerry of Massachusetts proposed to give Congress the power to declare war, "leaving to the Executive power to repel sudden attacks." Roger Sherman of Connecticut approved the change, arguing that the executive should not be able to initiate war. The convention followed suit by a 7–2–1 margin.[36]

Regulation of commerce was the least controversial power granted to Congress. The only question was how far it should be extended. Madison favored a power to tax exports. On August 16 Gouverneur Morris agreed, as such a power would punish foreign nations that restricted American trade and provide a stream of revenue other than direct taxes. John Francis Mercer of Maryland objected to the idea, particularly the notion that the power was needed to fund a navy to protect southern exports. "Were it not for promoting the carrying trade of the Northn. States, the Southern States could let their trade go in foreign bottoms, where it would not need our protection." This was the fullest statement of the agrarian argument that American agricultural produce was so valuable as to be its own protection.[37] The convention returned to the question on August 21. Madison argued for as broad a commercial power as possible. "As we ought to be governed by national and permanent views, it is a sufficient argument for giving ye power over exports that a tax, tho' it may not be expedient at present, may be so hereafter." Madison believed the power to tax exports necessary to lay an embargo. Gerry opposed the export tax as an unnecessary and potentially dangerous power. The convention rejected the power to tax exports by a 7–4 vote on August 21.[38]

The convention took up the general regulation of trade on August 29. Charles Pinckney called for a two-thirds majority on any act respecting foreign commerce. Gouverneur Morris opposed the motion, as Congress needed an unfettered power to regulate commerce and create a navy. Southern delegates were divided on the matter. Madison delivered a full assault on Pinckney's motion, fearing that a two-thirds majority would open the way to foreign influence, which would be more difficult with a simple majority. Like Morris, Madison pointed to "the increase of our maritime strength." The convention rejected Pinckney's motion by a 7–4 vote.[39]

For those who anticipated abuse of the foreign policy powers, the treaty power seemed particularly dangerous. George Mason of Virginia expressed concern that "the Senate by means of the treaty might alienate territory &c. without legislative sanction."[40] On September 7 the convention debated the two-thirds requirement for the Senate to approve a treaty. James Wilson of Pennsylvania preferred a simple majority, as a two-thirds vote gave too much power to a minority. Madison proposed to make a distinction between peace treaties, which the Senate could approve alone, and all other treaties, which would require the president's approval as well. Butler supported the measure as a check on the president. The convention rejected Madison's motion but approved a distinction between peace treaties and others.[41] The next day, the convention considered the distinction. Gouverneur Morris supported the idea of approving peace treaties by a simple majority. Wilson again argued for a simple majority. The convention removed the distinction but retained the two-thirds requirement by a vote of 11–3.[42]

The convention approved and signed the Constitution on September 17 and from there sent it to the states to be ratified. As Frederick Marks has written, foreign policy was the Federalists' best argument. No one could successfully argue that foreign affairs were going well. Everyone who suffered at the hands of a powerless Congress favored the Constitution. Arthur Lee was the only diplomat to oppose it. The others, from the very enthusiastic Jay and Adams to the tepid Jefferson, favored it. Continental Army officers generally favored the Constitution. Ship owners, overseas merchants, and those tied to the shipbuilding industries hoped that the Constitution would lift them out of their economic doldrums.[43]

Foreign policy was a key element in *The Federalist*, a series of essays written by Hamilton, Jay, and Madison under the pseudonym "Publius." Jay wrote the fewest essays but concentrated the most on foreign policy, listing the foreign dangers in "Federalist No. 4." He posited a dangerous world in which "nations in general will make war whenever they have a prospect of getting anything by it, nay that absolute monarchs still often make war when their nations are to get nothing by it." He went on to illustrate the friction points between the United States and other nations. The United States competed for access to the fisheries, the colonial trade, and the trade of China and India. "The extension of our own commerce in our own vessels, cannot give pleasure to any nations who possess territories on or near this Continent, because the cheapness and excellence of our productions, added to the circumstance of vicinity, and the enterprise and address of our merchants and navigators, will give us a greater share in the advantage which those territories afford, than consists with the wishes or policy of their respective Sovereigns." Jay took the union of England, Scotland, and Wales as a model and asked his readers to reach a similar conclusion. "Leave America divided into thirteen, or if you please into three or four independent Governments, what armies could they raise and pay, what fleets could they ever hope to have?" By contrast, a firm union would remedy the defects of government under the Articles of Confederation.[44]

Madison's essays generally focused on the argument that the Constitution did not make an extreme grant of power to the central government. His most famous essay, "Federalist No. 10," had foreign policy, particularly the navigation of the Mississippi, as its background. Madison considered the Mississippi vital to maintaining an agricultural republic. That required a continental union with a strong central government. As noted, much of the theory of republican government held that a republic had to be small and homogeneous, but Madison explained why a large republic was more secure than a small one. In a small republic, one faction or other could seize control and oppress the rest. A large republic would filter out particular interests and allow the public good to come forth.

"Extend the sphere, and you take in a greater variety of parties and interests; you make it less probable that a majority of the whole will have a common motive to invade the rights of other citizens," Madison wrote.[45] This was the theory he wrapped around the reality of a large republic. Madison continued this theme in "Federalist No. 14." Only a strong union could "substitute for those military establishments which have subverted the liberty of the old world." Madison denied that the union was too large. The average distance from the Atlantic to the Mississippi was about 750 miles, well within the bounds of many European nations.[46]

Alexander Hamilton wrote the most *Federalist* essays and covered every aspect of the Constitution. He was a forthright defender of a powerful state, blaming an "overscrupulous jealousy" of power for the difficulties of the confederation.[47] Hamilton addressed foreign policy in his earliest essays. In "Federalist No. 6," he attacked two key elements of American thinking on foreign policy: the ideas that commerce could be entirely separated from politics and that republics were inherently peaceful. A collection of independent republics, or a few confederacies, could not escape the fate of Europe. "A man must be far gone in Utopian speculations who can seriously doubt, that if the these States should either be wholly disunited, or only united in partial confederacies, the subdivisions into which they might be thrown would have frequent and violent contests with each other." To Hamilton republics—particularly Rome, Carthage, and Athens—were as prone to war as any other nation. Commerce served only to "change the object of wars."[48] Hamilton catalogued the causes of war in "Federalist No. 7." First came territorial disputes, "which have at all times been found one of the most fertile sources of hostility among nations." Even after Virginia's cession of land north of the Ohio, tensions over Vermont, separatists in Kentucky and "Franklin" (modern Tennessee), and disputes between Georgia and the Creeks and Cherokees threatened to spark armed conflict. Next came commercial competition. Given the welter of state tariffs and navigation acts, this too boded ill for a friendly neighborhood. Only a strong union could keep the United States out of "the destructive labyrinth of European politics and wars."[49]

Even the Anti-Federalists agreed on the necessity of a central regulation of commerce. On foreign policy grounds, the Anti-Federalist argument against the Constitution fell into two categories. First, the Constitution granted too much power, particularly in allowing Congress to create an army. Writing as "Centinel,"

Samuel Bryan of Pennsylvania called a standing army "that great engine of oppression" and objected to the Constitution for permitting it. The "Federal Farmer," now believed to be Melancton Smith of New York, conceded the necessity of commercial regulation but found those powers in the Constitution implied others that would wipe out state governments. Second, the Anti-Federalists argued that the danger from abroad was exaggerated. Robert Yates of New York, writing as "Brutus," argued that the United States had no real enemies nearby. "We have no powerful nation in our neighbourhood; if we are to go to war, it must either be with the Aboriginal natives, or with European nations," he wrote. "The first are so unequal to a contest with this whole continent, that they are rather to be dreaded for the depredations they may make on our frontiers, than for any impression they will ever be able to make on the body of this country." Yates had no particular fear of Europe. "Some of the European nations, it is true, have provinces bordering upon us, but from these, unsupported by their European forces, we have nothing to apprehend."[50]

Madison might have appreciated the irony. The same people that Madison did not trust to conduct foreign policy, the state leaders generated by local politics, were about to pass judgment on the Constitution. To them foreign policy was a local matter, and it played a key role in the ratification debates. The first five states ratified the Constitution rapidly and overwhelmingly. The vote in Delaware, New Jersey, and Georgia was unanimous, and it was more than three to one in Connecticut. The foreign policy issue in those states was simple. In the event of disunion or separate confederacies, they had large neighbors that could not be trusted to restrain themselves. The small states needed a stronger central government to override the large states. The debate in Pennsylvania had more to do with internal state politics than with foreign affairs, but the Federalists did use diplomacy as an issue. James Wilson, the leading Federalist at the ratifying convention, defended the treaty power and listed foreign policy as one of the chief reasons to ratify. "We are still an inviting object to one European power at least, and if we cannot defend ourselves, the temptation may be too alluring to be resisted." The Constitution, Wilson argued, would create a government that would defend the nation and keep the United States out of European politics.[51]

Pennsylvania was unusual among the large states, both for ratifying by a wide margin and for foreign affairs playing a minor role. In a sense the large states had their own foreign policy interests, and the ratification debate turned on whether or not those interests would be protected by the Constitution. Massachusetts was the second large state to ratify and the first to do so by a narrow margin. Throughout the fall of 1787, Massachusetts Federalists pounded on how the Constitution would benefit Massachusetts. Overseas commerce and the fisheries had suffered badly, and a more powerful government might help revive them. Federalists also observed that Great Britain was a near neighbor. "If disunited the time may come when we may be attacked by our natural enemies," Francis Dana argued. "Nova-Scotia, and New-Brunswick, filled with tories and refugees, stand ready to attack and devour these states, *one by one*." Thomas Dawes observed that "our whole commerce is going to ruin," with three-quarters of southern produce exported in British vessels. "Our sister states are willing we should receive these benefits, and that they should be secured to us by *national* laws." James Bowdoin believed that as matters stood, American commerce would fail "owing to a like want of power in Congress." Thomas Thatcher emphasized national defense. "Will not foreign nations attack us in a weak and divided condition, and once more render us provinces to some potentate in Europe?" he asked. Massachusetts ratified on February 6, 1788, by a vote of 187–168.[52]

Virginia is the best example of a ratifying convention dominated by foreign policy questions. When the Virginia convention met, Maryland and South Carolina had already ratified, while the New Hampshire convention was still deliberating. The Virginia delegates were conscious that Virginia could be the ninth state, officially ratifying the Constitution. As in the other states, foreign policy was a local issue. In Virginia's case that meant the navigation of the Mississippi. Patrick Henry argued that foreign affairs were better conducted under the Articles of Confederation. Seven states were ready to cede the navigation of the Mississippi. Under a stronger central government, those states would have more power and finish the job. Virginia's Anti-Federalists dismissed the prospect of foreign danger and affirmed Virginia's commercial advantages. Henry argued that there was "no real danger from Europe." John Tyler repeated the theory of 1776, that other nations needed American commerce, particularly that of Virginia: "It is the interest of every nation in Europe to keep up the balance of power, and therefore they will not suffer any nation to attack us, without immediately interfering."[53]

The Federalists did not share Henry's optimism for American or Virginia's interests under the Articles of Confederation. "We have become contemptible in the eyes of foreign nations," Edmund Randolph argued. Randolph later contended that Virginia could not defend itself. "Can Virginia send her navy and thunder to bid defiance to foreign nations? And can she exist without an Union with her neighbours, when the most potent nations have found such an union necessary, not only to their political felicity, but their national existence?" Contrary to Henry's view of the nation, Francis Corbin described a nation in collapse. The West Indies were closed to American shipping, and the British dominated the fur trade and held the western forts. American finances were a shambles, making it impossible to pay foreign debts. Only a stronger central government could restore power and honor.[54] On June 25, 1788, Virginia ratified 89–79.

After Virginia ratified, the debate in New York shifted from the merits of the Constitution to whether New York should join the union. New York's Federalists, like those in New England, emphasized trade issues. They also called the Constitution the only hope of regaining the fur trade or of expelling the British from the forts, both of which were New York as well as national issues. Many Anti-Federalists put the union above their objections to the Constitution, and New York ratified 30–27 on July 26, 1788. North Carolina ratified in November 1789. Rhode Island, after being threatened with expulsion from the union, followed in May 1790.

In December 1788 the Comte de Moustier, the French minister to the United States, described American politics for the foreign minister. "The new Congress will infallibly regard a close alliance with whatever European Nation will offer it the most resources as one of the principle means consolidating its authority," Moustier believed. The only two candidates were France and Great Britain, and he recommended sparing no effort in deepening the American alliance.[55] Moustier was not the shrewd observer that his predecessors were. Most advocates of the Constitution saw it as a vehicle for promoting a political separation from Europe, rather than a closer alliance with any power. However, Moustier was right in a way he could not possibly have known. A conflict was coming that would eliminate the breathing room that eighteenth-century neutral powers enjoyed. The Constitution, drafted to guide a small nation through the wilds of balance of power diplomacy, would have to create a nation that could survive a death struggle between France and Great Britain.

# CHAPTER 3

# AMERICAN FOREIGN RELATIONS IN THE FEDERALIST ERA

ON APRIL 30, 1789, GEORGE WASHINGTON took the oath of office as the first president of the United States. Five days later Louis XVI convened the Estates-General of France for the first time since 1614. Of the experiments of 1789, the United States Constitution proved more durable, but the gathering at Versailles had the greater immediate impact. For the next twenty-six years, the French Revolution and the wars it spawned dominated the Atlantic world. The French Revolution destroyed the world in which American diplomacy was born. The ideas of neutral rights and the separation of commerce from politics came from a loosely arranged bipolar system. Neither side had the inclination or, more importantly, the ability to destroy the other. The wars of the French Revolution placed France and Great Britain in a death struggle. They could end only with the destruction of one of the two regimes. Were the tenets of American diplomacy, born of the American Revolution, applicable to a new era? Could the United States impose its will on other nations? In a revival of the moderate/radical debate, the Federalists, in general, said no, and the Republicans said yes.

The supporters of the Constitution expected that it would provide the means to solve the foreign policy problems of the United States. They differed, however, on the nature of and solutions to those problems. Madison was the leading proponent of the postwar version of radical diplomacy. For him the purpose of the Constitution was to create commercial legislation that would force Great Britain to open its empire to American shipping and produce. On April 8, 1789, Madison reintroduced the impost of 1783, which placed a 5 percent duty on various imported goods, mainly from the West Indies. The proposal also included a scale of tonnage duties, with American ships paying the lowest rates, those in a treaty with the United States paying a higher level, and those with no commercial treaty with the United States paying the highest. In September the House passed a bill that distinguished only between American and foreign ships. A year later Madison tried unsuccessfully to reinstate discriminatory duties on British shipping. British trade dominated the American economy. Between August 1789 and September 1790, the United States exported more than $20 million worth of goods. Of these, over $9 million worth went to Great Britain. At the same time, the United States imported about $15.4 million worth of goods, almost $13.8 million from Great Britain.[1]

Hamilton counted on that British trade to fund his financial plans. The story of Hamilton's reports usually belongs to domestic history, but they did have foreign policy aspects as well. As Max M. Edling has observed, Hamilton intended to create a modern, European-style fiscal-military state that could wage war when needed.[2] The funding system recommended in the *Report on Public Credit* would reassure those nations and individuals who had granted loans and encourage new investment. The excise tax would provide an internal source of revenue that could not be reduced or cut off in the event of war. The Bank of the United States would serve the same function as its model, the Bank of England—as a bank of deposit and a source of loans to the government. Finally, the *Report on Manufactures* recommended the development of American industry through bounties granted for useful manufactures. Unlike Jefferson, Hamilton did not believe American trade was its own sword and shield, and did not believe that other nations would automatically line up to sell goods to the United States. Hamilton did not believe that Great Britain would crumble before American economic pressure and did not believe that the threat of economic war could be separated from military war. Forcing a change in British trade policy was a low priority for Hamilton. More open trade would come with time and the logic of economic gain.

The Nootka Sound affair, which dominated European diplomatic life in the first half of 1790, provided the first contest of the two visions of Hamilton and Madison. Nootka Sound was not an ideological battle, but an old-fashioned conflict over colonial empires. In the summer of 1789 the Spanish seized three British merchant vessels that had attempted to establish a trading post at Nootka Sound (now Vancouver). William Pitt ordered naval preparations and demanded restitution and access to the uninhabited parts of North America. Without French support, Spain eventually agreed to both.

In May, Sir Guy Carleton, now Lord Dorchester, the governor-general of Canada, sent Maj. George Beckwith to the United States to lay the groundwork for a possible Anglo-American alliance against Spain. Washington believed that any British actions would involve an expedition that would have to pass through American territory. On August 27, 1790, Washington asked the cabinet, Vice President John Adams, and Chief Justice John Jay what the American response should be if Great Britain asked for permission to cross. Adams recommended a refusal but was under no illusion that the United States could support that decision by force of arms. Jefferson advised delaying giving a direct answer, hoping to induce Great Britain and Spain to bid for American neutrality. Hamilton, after a lengthy discourse, concluded that the United States should probably allow British passage. Both Hamilton and Jefferson wanted to use the crisis for the same end, securing American access to the Mississippi. Hamilton went as far as to tell Beckwith that the United States had no interest in Canada and would accept an alliance with Great Britain to strike at Spain. Spain gave in to British demands and ceded Nootka Sound, and the British never asked for a right of passage.

The Nootka Sound affair ultimately offered no opportunity to wring concessions out of Great Britain or Spain, and the diplomatic problems with those nations that dominated the 1780s continued. George Hammond, the first official British minister to the United States, arrived in October 1791. He had no power to make a commercial treaty but was charged chiefly with investigating American violations of the peace treaty and settling frontier issues. Great Britain still held the northwestern forts. Some British officials, such as John Graves Simcoe, the lieutenant governor of Upper Canada, advocated an aggressive policy of more troops, the creation of an Indian army, and a preventive war against the United States. Most were more cautious. On August 15, 1791, Dorchester told tribal leaders that he would mediate between the Indians and the United States but would not join any hostilities. A month later, Colonial Secretary Henry Dundas instructed Dorchester that the Indian allies were expendable. Dorchester could protect hunting grounds and the fur trade, and defend the Indians in case of attack by the United States but take no further action. Even without substantial British aid, the Shawnees led by Blue Jacket and the Miamis led by Little Turtle defeated an American army under Arthur St. Clair on November 4, 1791.

Relations with Spain had not prospered any more than relations with Great Britain. Spain still recognized neither the American boundary claim nor the right to navigate the lower Mississippi. Jefferson made the navigation of the full length of the Mississippi a top priority as secretary of state. As well as most American statesmen, he considered the Spanish Empire a rotted-out hulk and believed that Spain would eventually have to accede to American demands. Jefferson submitted a report to the president on March 18, 1792, outlining the main points for negotiation and claimed a natural right to navigate the entire length of the Mississippi backed up by Vattel, Grotius, and the other authors on the law of nations.

## The French Revolution

The forts, trade, and the Mississippi were all, for lack of a better word, normal diplomatic issues. Had the French Revolution not intervened, American relations with France would have been dominated by the normal issues of colonial trade and the wartime debt. The French Revolution subordinated all other issues to what became the struggle for the soul of the Atlantic world. The roots of the French Revolution may be traced back to, among other factors, France's long-term debt problem, exacerbated by the expense, with no financial return, of French participation in the American Revolution and the exposure to American republicanism. In 1787 the Assembly of Notables failed to resolve the debt problem, prompting a call for a meeting of the Estates-General, which occurred on May 5, 1789. The Third Estate proposed that all three estates meet in common and declared itself the National Assembly of France. The king at first locked them out but later acquiesced. In Paris revolutionaries feared the king would send the army against them and seized the Bastille in search of weapons on July 14. The National Assembly moved quickly in the direction of a constitutional monarchy. Lafayette and others consulted with Jefferson on a statement of principles. On August 26 the assembly issued the Declaration of the Rights of Man and Citizen.

Old and new revolutionaries cheered the prospect of an alliance of Great Britain's enemies becoming an alliance of free nations. Jefferson emphasized the connection between the French and the American Revolutions. "Our proceedings have been viewed as a model for them on every occasion," he wrote to

Madison, "and tho' on the heat of debate men are generally disposed to contradict every authority urged by their opponents, ours has been treated like that of the bible, open to explanation but not to question."[3] Even those who later became critics approved the French Revolution in its early stages. In October 1789 Hamilton declared his approval: "As a friend to mankind and to liberty I rejoice in the efforts which you are making to establish it while I fear much for the final success of the attempts, for the fate of those engaged in it, and for the danger in case of success of innovations greater than will consist with the real felicity of your Nation."[4]

Some doubted the success of the French Revolution from the beginning. "This unhappy country, bewildered in the pursuit of metaphysical whimsies, presents to one's moral view a mighty ruin," Gouverneur Morris wrote toward the end of 1790.[5] John Adams believed the project of constituting a free government with a unicameral legislature was doomed to failure and so argued in *Discourses on Davila*, published serially in the New York newspapers in 1790 and 1791. Like Hamilton, Adams feared that the French would attempt changes that their history and culture could not sustain. Jefferson considered these views "political heresies" and welcomed the publication of Thomas Paine's *The Rights of Man* in March 1791 as an antidote.[6]

Louis XVI attempted to hold a middle ground between absolute and constitutional monarchy. The Civil Constitution of the Clergy drove the king back toward absolutism, and in June 1791 he attempted to flee the country. He was captured near the border and dragged back to Paris in chains. The Austrian and Prussian monarchs met at Pillnitz on August 27, 1791, to ask the other powers of Europe to join in an effort to restore Louis XVI's full powers. After months of exchanging of threatening notes, France declared war on Austria on April 20, 1792. Initially the wars of the French Revolution had little effect on the United States. The first tangible impact of the French Revolution on the United States came on August 22, 1791, when some ten thousand slaves revolted in Saint-Domingue, present-day Haiti. By the end of the year, Toussaint Louverture had emerged as the leader. The French minister, Jean Baptiste Ternant, asked Washington for $40,000 of war debt to be paid to buy supplies to suppress the revolt. Washington agreed. By 1795 the United States had paid off the war debt in this fashion.

The French war with Austria strengthened the more radical elements of the revolution. The National Assembly suspended the king's authority in August. Prussian and Austrian armies continued to close in on Paris but were stopped by a French revolutionary army at Valmy on September 20. Two days later the renamed National Convention, dominated by the Girondins, abolished the monarchy and created the French Republic. The war to defend the revolution became a war to spread the revolution across Europe. On November 19 the National Convention promised to free the "oppressed peoples" of Europe from monarchy. Next the convention put the king on trial for treason. It voted to convict by an overwhelming margin and then by a narrow margin to execute him, a sentence that was carried out on January 21, 1793. On February 1 the French Republic declared war on Great Britain and the Netherlands.

The radicalization of the French Revolution had a polarizing effect on the United States. Those who opposed the revolution considered themselves vindicated. Some early supporters dropped away. Others fully endorsed the French Republic. Jefferson made support of the French Revolution a litmus test of republicanism. He was convinced that France was a republic on the American model and brooked no dissent.

The French declaration of war against Great Britain turned a continental war into a naval war. American policy since the American Revolution had sought trade in a wide array of goods with belligerent powers. The Republicans, heirs to the radical plan of 1776, continued to believe that American trade was so valuable that no nation would risk being left out of it. The Federalists either abandoned this belief, as with Adams, or never had it, as with Jay. Both France and Great Britain pursued policies intended either to monopolize or destroy American commerce. France made two moves intended to secure American commerce to its benefit. On February 19, 1793, the National Convention opened the French West Indies to American shipping. The profits from the sugar reexportation trade were vital to the French war effort, and France did not have the merchant ships to get sugar from the Caribbean to France. The next day Edmond-Charles Genet set sail on the *Embuscade* as the new minister to the United States.

Genet's public career lasted less than six months, but his impact on American foreign policy, both in the short and long term, is difficult to overestimate. Genet and his fellow Girondins expected that maintaining the close friendship of the

United States would be easier than spreading republicanism throughout Europe. Jefferson believed that the Jacobins, the Girondins' rivals, were the true revolutionaries, but the Girondins bore a greater resemblance to Jefferson's Republicans. Girondin policy tended to lean more heavily on theory than practice and was based on the twin pillars of republican brotherhood and free trade. Genet himself was born to foreign policy. His father had been the head of the translation bureau under the old regime, and the younger Genet was a genius with languages. By the time he was fifteen, he could speak French, English, Italian, German, Swedish, Latin, and Greek but could not keep quiet in any language and had trouble with "no" in all of them. Genet was a spoiled child, craving attention and usually getting it. The nature of the regime exacerbated Genet's less-than-diplomatic personality. The Girondins hoped to remake the world in their own image and had little patience with or respect for the diplomatic rules of monarchy. Prior to the American mission, Genet had been expelled from Russia for his revolutionary exuberance.

In December 1792 the Girondin government prepared Genet's instructions. The Girondins were willing to form a closer alliance that would grant American access to the whole length of the Mississippi and possibly possession of Canada. France also sought a declaration of principles on the spread of republicanism. To that end, Genet was authorized to stir up revolts in Florida, Canada, and Louisiana. Genet was also to warn the United States that if Great Britain defeated France, the United States was next. The Girondins wanted two concessions from the United States: advance payment of the war debt and the enforcement of articles 17, 21, and 22 of the commercial treaty, which permitted each nation to outfit privateers in the other's ports.

The alliance was the main difficulty in American diplomacy. Since 1776 American foreign policy had been based on the idea that the United States should avoid participation in Europe's wars. The French alliance compromised that principle out of necessity. No American of any prominence advocated joining the war on the French side. Washington planned to keep France at arm's length without alienating it. He found the wave of pro-French sentiment the greater obstacle to neutrality. American support for the French Revolution was narrower than it was in 1789 but more intense.

On April 8, 1793, Genet landed in Charleston, where he was the guest of honor at a huge reception hosted by Gen. William Moultrie. Genet prepared privateering commissions and gathered recruits for an assault on Louisiana and the Floridas before departing for Philadelphia on April 18. Genet's delay allowed Washington to have policy in place before the new minister arrived. Washington decided on neutrality, and Hamilton asked Jay to draft a statement to that end. On April 18 Washington submitted a list of questions to the cabinet. The most important were question two—Should the United States receive a minister from the French Republic?—and question four—Were the United States and France bound by the 1778 treaties? The cabinet met the next day. It decided unanimously that the United States should remain neutral and prevent Americans from taking part in the war. The cabinet also agreed to receive Genet, although Hamilton and Secretary of War Henry Knox wanted to receive him conditionally. On April 22 Washington issued the Proclamation of Neutrality, announcing that "the duty and interest of the United States require that they should with sincerity and good faith adopt and pursue a conduct friendly and impartial toward the belligerent powers." Washington warned Americans not to take part in the conflict, stating that the United States government would not protect any American charged with actions violating American neutrality.[7]

The controversy over the Genet mission, as with many other issues of the Washington years, is often portrayed as a conflict between Hamilton and Jefferson. This is an oversimplification, but the framework does illustrate the terms of debate. It also demonstrates the flexible nature of the law of nations. Both Jefferson and Hamilton conducted debate in the language of Vattel, Grotius, and Samuel von Pufendorf. "A clever diplomatist could extract from somewhere among the stately periods of these writers a quotation to re-inforce nearly any legal argument he cared to make," Samuel Flagg Bemis wrote.[8] Statesmen of this era worked backwards. They started with the policies they advocated and then sought justification and explanation in the common language of the law of nations.

Jefferson submitted his answer to Washington's queries on April 28. The central question was the validity of the 1778 treaties. He reviewed the law of nations, including a comparative table of Grotius, Vattel, Pufendorf, and Wolff on when treaties may be ignored. Jefferson concluded that a nation could ignore its treaty obligations if those obligations would place it in imminent danger. He saw none. The biggest potential danger was the mutual guarantee of American territory. Jefferson believed that France could defend its own islands, that the United

States was in no position to aid a French defense of the West Indies, and that it was not in France's interest to invoke that guarantee.[9]

Hamilton's answer, as usual, was much longer. He and Henry Knox replied to Washington on May 2 and, in a letter no less filled with authorities, came to the opposite conclusion. Hamilton believed that Genet should be received conditionally, given the unsettled situation of the French government. Hamilton argued that the United States had signed treaties that bound them to Louis XVI and his successors. With king and monarchy gone, the treaties must be void. Hamilton did not share Jefferson's confidence that France would not invoke the guarantee. If Great Britain attacked the French West Indies, and the alliance was still valid, the United States would have two choices. First, to declare that, as the war was offensive on France's part, the treaties did not apply. Second, to argue that the United States did not have the ability to carry out the guarantee. France would accept neither explanation, and the United States would not be protected by either belligerent. The only way to avoid a charge of ducking a treaty obligation was to declare that the 1778 treaties were dead.[10]

Washington agreed more with Jefferson than with Hamilton and received Genet without restrictions or conditions. Washington considered the 1778 treaties valid but considered the war was offensive on France's part. Therefore, the guarantee of American territory did not apply. With policy set, the administration waited for Genet, who arrived in Philadelphia on May 16. The next day he was the guest of honor at a reception in the City Hotel. Genet presented himself to the president on May 18, a meeting that Jefferson described to Madison. Genet made a point of telling Washington that France would not invoke the guarantee, although it had a right to do so. France only wanted to see the United States peaceful and prosperous, and to that end offered to negotiate a more liberal commercial treaty. "In short he offers everything and asks nothing," Jefferson wrote.[11]

A man of Jefferson's age and experience should have known that there is no such thing as a free lunch. Jefferson expected French friendship and a confirmation that French and American interests were compatible and, at first, he got it. It could not last. On May 22 Genet began to reveal what he wanted in exchange for French friendship. He asked for advance payment of the American war debt, which he intended to use to purchase supplies in the United States. Genet continued to promise that he would not demand the territorial guarantee but always portrayed it as an act of French generosity. On May 27 Genet insisted on the French right to outfit privateers under the commercial treaty. The same day, a French vessel captured a British ship, the *Grange*. On June 5 Jefferson sent Genet a note explicitly barring him from outfitting privateers in American ports. The cabinet also agreed that the United States could not pay off the debt all at once and informed Genet on June 11.

Genet reacted badly to the refusal. He had made the mistake of assuming that enthusiastic crowds translated into an unqualified support for France. On June 19 Genet informed the foreign minister his main obstacles were "the aristocracy" and "old Washington." His plan was to work secretly to have Congress called into session early, where "the majority, conducted by the first heads of the union will be decidedly in our favor."[12] On June 22 in a note to Jefferson, Genet castigated Washington and reasserted his right to outfit privateers in American ports under the 1778 commercial treaty. He implored Jefferson not to hide behind Vattel and to let old rules interfere with republican friendship.

Privateering proved Genet's undoing when the *Embuscade* captured the British vessel *Little Sarah*. Genet renamed it the *Petite Démocrate* and outfitted it as a privateer in Philadelphia. On July 6 Gov. Thomas Mifflin of Pennsylvania reported that the *Petite Démocrate* was set to sail with 120 Americans as part of her crew. Jefferson asked Genet to hold the ship, and on July 8 Genet replied that the ship was not ready to sail. Hamilton and Knox wanted to mount a battery at Mud Island, which Jefferson opposed. In any case, the ship slipped down to Chester and out of range on July 9. On July 12 Washington conducted a cabinet meeting and agreed to ask the Supreme Court for an advisory opinion on the legality of American neutrality. Sometime in the next few days, the *Petite Démocrate* sailed unnoticed to sea, sparing the cabinet the decision Jefferson dreaded.

The larger question of what to do with Genet could not be avoided. The cabinet agreed to put off the question on July 23, pending the advice of the Supreme Court, which refused to give an opinion. On August 3 the cabinet affirmed the ban on privateering, ordering that prizes taken since June 5 be restored. The cabinet also agreed to ask for Genet's recall. Washington agreed with Jefferson that the request should be as mildly worded as possible. Jefferson wanted to make a statement affirming the republican friendship of France and the United States, but Hamilton objected, and Washington sided with Hamilton. The cabinet completed the recall request on August 20.

While the cabinet debated Genet's fate, the French minister left for New York to refit French warships. There he was the toast of New York Republican society led by Gov. George Clinton, whose daughter Cornelia was Genet's biggest admirer. New York Federalists arranged for resolutions supporting Washington and neutrality. Jay and Sen. Rufus King publicly accused Genet of threatening to appeal to the public, a charge Genet angrily denied. He sent the refitted fleet out in October and then disappeared from public view. In December Washington announced Genet's recall in the annual message.

Genet was disgraced in the United States but faced a worse fate in France. The Jacobins, led by Maximilien Robespierre, had taken control of the National Convention on June 2, 1793. They began to execute Girondin leaders at the end of October. Robespierre denounced Genet in the convention on November 27. Genet learned of his peril after Joseph Fauchet arrived as his replacement on February 21, 1794. Two weeks later Fauchet revoked all of the commissions Genet had issued. Fauchet asked Washington's permission to arrest Genet and bring him back to France for trial, but Genet asked for asylum, which the president granted. In November 1794 Genet married Cornelia Clinton and remained in the United States until his death nearly forty years later.

The Genet affair sparked the first serious discussion of the Constitution and foreign affairs since the ratification debate. The Constitution was unclear on which branch had the initiative in foreign policy. The summer of 1793 saw an epic newspaper debate over the Proclamation of Neutrality between Hamilton, writing as "Pacificus," and Madison, writing as "Helvidius." Hamilton published his first essay on June 29. Of his seven essays, the first is the most important on the constitutional question. Hamilton argued that the power to declare neutrality was inherent in the president's authority to negotiate treaties. The power to negotiate a treaty included the power to interpret when and how it should be implemented. The president was "the *organ* of intercourse between this Nation and foreign Nations," Hamilton argued. Moreover, a treaty was a law, and the president had the duty to enforce laws. While Congress had the war power, the president had the power "to preserve Peace till war is declared." The power of the president to receive ambassadors included the right to decide whether those ambassadors should be received. Hamilton noted that Washington received Genet with no constitutional objections, although the Senate might have claimed a share of the decision. "But he is censured for having declared the UStates to be in a state of peace & neutrality, with regard to the Powers at War; because the right of *changing* that state & *declaring war* belongs to the Legislature."[13]

Jefferson was aghast at Hamilton's arguments. He begged Madison to respond, as Jefferson was loath to confront Hamilton directly. Reluctantly Madison agreed. Madison argued that the legislature should control foreign policy. The arguments of "Pacificus," Madison charged, were cheered "by the foreigners and degenerate citizens among us, who hate our republican government, and the French Revolution." For Madison the key power was the war power, not the treaty power. To Madison the war power included all of the decisions that preceded a declaration of war. To declare war was to pass a law, not to execute one. "From this view of the subject it must be evident, that although the executive may be a convenient organ of preliminary communications with foreign governments, on the subjects of treaty or war; and the proper agent for carrying into execution the final determination of the competent authority; yet it can have no pretensions from the nature of the powers in question compared with the nature of the executive trust, to that essential agency which gives validity to such determinations."[14] The idea of executive primacy under the treaty power was itself flawed, in that treaty making was partially a legislative power. Madison also dismissed the president's power as commander-in-chief as a factor in foreign policy.

The aftermath of the Genet affair led to two major personnel changes in the American foreign policy establishment. The first was the departure of Jefferson, who resigned as secretary of state effective December 31, 1793. Washington replaced Jefferson with Attorney General Edmund Randolph. The second was the recall of Morris as minister to France. Morris had always been a controversial choice; the Republicans considered him too aristocratic and had opposed his nomination. Morris was friendly toward France as a nation but was always skeptical of the French Revolution. He considered the Girondins deluded and the Jacobins tyrannical. "The present Government is evidently a Despotism both in Principle and Practice," Morris informed Washington on October 18, 1793.[15] Morris was right, but his honesty won him no friends in the French government. The Genet recall gave the Jacobins the opening to ask for Morris's recall. Washington reluctantly agreed and appointed James Monroe on May 27, 1794. Monroe was an ardent supporter of the French Revolution, and was expected to be more acceptable to France.

The Jacobins replaced Genet's ham-fisted friendship with an iron-fisted approach. They had little interest in the spread of republicanism and concentrated on defeating Great Britain and extending French power. The Jacobins rejected free trade as an ideal and advocated a mercantilism that any ancien régime statesman would approve. The Jacobins threatened destruction to all those who opposed France. Everything was a potential weapon against Great Britain, particularly trade. On May 9, 1793, the convention decreed that all foodstuffs bound for enemy ports on neutral ships were lawful prize, a direct violation of the 1778 treaties. American commerce was at first exempted but finally included on July 27. The convention passed a new navigation act on September 9, proclaiming freedom of the seas. To the Jacobins, freedom of the seas was less an ideological principle than a club to use against Great Britain.

The British government never pretended to be a friend either of free trade or of the United States. The Pitt ministry and its successors fused the protection of British trade with the annihilation of French commerce as a means to destroy the regime. On June 8, 1793, the ministry issued the strictest Order-in-Council of the war. All neutral ships carrying flour, corn, or meal toward France were to be seized and their owners compensated. The British hoped to starve the French armies and achieve a quick victory. The order arrived in Philadelphia on August 24. Jefferson protested on the grounds that food was never contraband of war. His protest was rejected in December, by which time the British had slightly modified their policy. On November 6 the ministry issued a new order, made public in late December, designed to choke off the French colonies and prevent the French recovery of Saint-Domingue. Neutral vessels carrying French colonial products to France or carrying supplies to French colonies were subject to capture. By March 1, 1794, the British seized some 250 American vessels, both denying wealth to France and putting prize money in the British treasury. Lord Hawkesbury of the Committee on Trade framed a new order, issued on January 8, 1794. Neutral vessels carrying French colonial products to France were subject to capture. The extreme measures of June and November were replaced by a more normal application of the Rule of 1756: trade illegal in peacetime cannot be made legal in war. The British posed a western as well as an Atlantic threat. Lord Dorchester spoke to delegates of the Six Nations on February 10, 1794, telling them he expected a war with the United States. Naturally the Six Nations would be allies. News of the November 1793 and January 1794 orders, as well as of Dorchester's speech, arrived in Philadelphia in March.

## The Jay Treaty and the Farewell Address

The debate over British policy revolved around the question of whether or not the United States had the power to coerce Great Britain. The Republicans believed so. On January 3, 1794, Madison proposed a revived commercial discrimination against Great Britain in response to the June 8, 1793, orders. On March 25 Republicans in the House pushed through a one-month embargo. The Senate concurred. The Republicans then sought a sequestration of British debts in the United States, which passed both houses. News of the January 8, 1794, order reached Philadelphia on March 28. On April 15 a committee of the whole in the House approved a non-intercourse bill by an eleven-vote margin. The Republicans' argument rested on the presumption of British economic weakness, exacerbated by the war with France. The United States was Great Britain's largest market for exported goods. It also supplied 90 percent of the flour and meal, two-thirds of the grain, and half of the meat to the British West Indies. The Republicans assumed that the British merchants and the West Indian planters dominated Parliament. This had been close enough to being true during the Stamp Act crisis to give the idea validity. The Republicans saw no need to prepare for war, as they believed that American commerce was so valuable that Great Britain would not risk its interruption by war.

Federalist policy was to prepare for war and negotiate. On March 12, 1794, a delegation of Federalist senators met with Washington and urged him to send Hamilton on a special mission to Great Britain. Hamilton agreed with the idea but recommended Jay. Hamilton did not believe American commerce was a magic wand, nor did he believe that commercial war could be separated from actual war. Hamilton read the economic data in the opposite manner of the Republicans and considered the United States as dependent on British trade as Great Britain was on the United States. He mocked those who "weakly hope that they may hector and vapour with success—that the pride of Great Britain must yield to her interests—and that they may accomplish the object of perpetual animosity between the two countries without involving War."[16] Washington agreed with Hamilton, and the Senate approved Jay 18–8.

Jay had two sets of instructions. Randolph drafted the official instructions, dated May 6, 1794. Jay was to resolve the outstanding issues of the peace treaty, particularly debts, confiscated slaves, and the forts. Jay was also to pursue the full neutral rights agenda. Any treaty should affirm the principle that free ships make free goods and admit American shipping into the West Indies. Randolph also sought to define contraband and legal blockades for the benefit of neutral powers. To those ends, Randolph instructed Jay to negotiate with the nations of the revived Armed Neutrality to form a general agreement or even an alliance. The new version formed as the First Coalition against France was crumbling. It consisted of Denmark and Sweden, and more to the point did not include the Netherlands, Prussia, or Russia, making it unlikely to carry much weight. The Swedish ambassador to Great Britain exchanged notes with American minister Thomas Pinckney on the subject. When Pinckney responded favorably, the Swedish ambassador gushed over the possibility of American entry. The Danish chancellor believed that as the United States had no navy, it would add nothing to the cause. In July Hamilton told Hammond that the United States would not join the Armed Neutrality. It was an indiscreet admission but hardly a shocking one.

Hamilton provided the unofficial instructions. Soon after his appointment, Jay, Hamilton, and several Federalist senators met to plan the mission. They concluded that the most important thing was to tie up the loose ends from the peace treaty. Hamilton wrote to Jay on May 6 to outline a broader vision. Hamilton's approach to a commercial settlement differed from the Republicans'. He too argued that the West Indies depended on American trade. As the British acquired more islands from the French, they would only grow more dependent. But Hamilton cited a 1787 law allowing small vessels to carry products to and away from the British West Indies, which provided a precedent for allowing the same right to American vessels. As the British would need American food, the British should support the American navigation of the length of the Mississippi. In exchange the United States would have to ban the sequestration of debts and accept the Rule of 1756.[17] Hamilton had figured out how to negotiate with the British. If the United States accepted the British maritime framework, it might gain the concessions that would undermine it.

By the time Jay arrived in Great Britain in early June, the British economic and military position had improved. The grain shortages feared in the West Indies did not materialize. Although the continental war with France faltered, Great Britain was in no immediate danger. On June 1, 1794—"the Glorious First of June" in British naval lore—Lord Howe destroyed the French fleet off Brest. Baron Grenville, the foreign minister, wished to reach a treaty, and by August negotiations proceeded to the point of exchanging draft projects. By September the two had reached agreement on some of the issues that had plagued Anglo-American relations for the last decade. Grenville agreed to evacuate the forts by June 1, 1796, with a mutual right to free trade with the Indian tribes. The two nations would create a commission to determine the location of the St. Croix River. Neither party could sequester debts, while each side could seek compensation for seized property. Great Britain would permit American vessels into the West Indies, but those vessels could not reexport colonial products. Grenville could not move on the Rule of 1756. Furthermore, he demanded a cession of land that would connect Canada to the Mississippi in order to provide the British access to the Mississippi promised in the peace treaty. Jay submitted a neutral rights agreement on September 30 but did not press when Grenville refused it. Jay had a keen sense of what was and was not possible, as shown in the negotiations with Spain in 1786, and had already achieved what he and Hamilton thought was possible. Jay signed the Treaty of Amity and Commerce, more commonly known as the Jay Treaty, on November 19, 1794.

The first ten articles of the treaty were permanent. They either wrapped up or established the procedure for wrapping up the loose ends of the peace treaty, providing for the British evacuation of American territory as of June 1, 1796, and opening the Indian trade to both nations. Articles 4 through 7 set up the commissions to resolve the other outstanding issues: the exact course of the Mississippi, the true location of the St. Croix River (and thus the Maine boundary), debts owed to British creditors by American citizens, and American spoliation claims against Great Britain. Article 12 offered a pinhole opening to the West Indian trade. It allowed American vessels of seventy tons or less to carry American products to the British islands. American vessels could carry West Indian products only to the United States. The article would be in force for the duration of the present war and for two years after any peace treaty. The other articles would be in force for twelve years after ratification. Each nation gained most-favored-nation status. Jay abandoned free ships, free goods in favor of the British doctrine that enemy goods on neutral vessels were subject to capture. The ships themselves could proceed and would not be considered prizes. Article 18 noted that the status of goods not obviously contraband was unclear.[18]

The general scholarly consensus is that Jay could not have secured a better treaty. For both Jay and Hamilton, the central problem was that the United States could not enforce its will on Great Britain and had to make the best deal possible. Great Britain was more concerned with current than past controversies, therefore the sections dealing with old crises were easier to draft. The fate of the West was decided on the battlefield as well as the negotiating table. On August 24, 1794, Gen. Anthony Wayne defeated an army of Ottawas and Potowatamies at Fallen Timbers (modern Toledo, Ohio). Wayne's victory led to the Treaty of Greenville on August 3, 1795, in which the United States received title to most of Ohio and part of Indiana. The articles of the Jay Treaty dealing with problems brought by the Anglo-French War did not solve anything but were intended to patch up Anglo-American relations until the war ended.

The treaty arrived in the United States in March 1795 and went to a special session of the Senate in June. Some Republicans consulted with Fauchet on how best to oppose the treaty. Debate began on June 17. On June 19 the Senate moved to expunge article 12, which was considered so small a concession as to be an insult. The Senate approved the treaty on June 24 by a bare 20–10 majority. Five days later, Sen. Stevens T. Mason of Virginia leaked a copy to the Philadelphia *Aurora*, which printed it on July 1. Next the treaty went to the president for ratification. British action complicated matters. On April 25, 1795, the Pitt ministry issued a secret Order-in-Council authorizing the seizure of American vessels headed for France. The British hoped to cripple France and alleviate food shortages in Great Britain. Commanders were authorized to take grain off American ships and pay for it, a policy considered consistent with article 18 of the Jay Treaty. Washington leaned against ratifying until the British made some explanation of the April 25 order.

The prospect of French interference in American politics led Washington to change his mind. On October 31, 1794, Fauchet addressed dispatch number 10 to the foreign minister. Randolph, Fauchet reported, told him that there were very influential Americans who would be friendly to France but were compromised by debts to British merchants. If they were out of debt, they could act freely.[19] The

British intercepted the dispatch in March and passed it along to Hammond in Philadelphia. In July Hammond showed the dispatch to Oliver Wolcott, Hamilton's replacement, and Timothy Pickering, Knox's replacement. The two showed the dispatch to Washington on August 11 upon his return to the capital. Washington summoned a cabinet meeting on August 12 to discuss the treaty. Randolph opposed ratification, but Washington had already decided in favor. When Randolph failed to give a satisfactory account of his conversation with Fauchet, Washington demanded his resignation and replaced him with Pickering. Washington ratified the treaty on August 14, marking the beginning rather than the end of the debate. On August 22 the *Aurora* launched an attack on the treaty. The newspaper, edited by Franklin's grandson, Benjamin Franklin Bache, was an implacable foe of the Federalists. The Federalists now had a problem they had not anticipated—that of conducting a public debate over foreign policy.[20]

A settlement with Great Britain necessarily impacted relations with France and Spain. Relations with Spain were stalled over the Mississippi. In November 1794 Washington appointed Thomas Pinckney as extraordinary envoy to Spain. He arrived in Madrid on June 28, 1795. Pinckney's timing was nearly perfect. French armies came over the Pyrenees to bully Spain out of its alliance with Great Britain and into one with France. On July 22 France and Spain signed the Peace of Basel. Spain feared Great Britain more than France. The main puzzle of the history of the negotiation is whether or not Spain knew of the terms of the Jay Treaty before negotiating with Pinckney. Arthur Whitaker believed that Manuel de Godoy, the Spanish foreign minister, knew the full terms. Samuel Flagg Bemis argued that Godoy did not.[21] Godoy's approach to Pinckney suggests at least that he did not believe the French treaty would protect Spanish America. On August 14 the Spanish Council of State agreed to accept the consistent American demand for the full navigation of the Mississippi and a boundary at 31° north. Furthermore, Spain dropped its pursuit of an alliance. The United States would still not be permitted to trade with the colonies.

On the face of it, this decision suggests that Spain did not know the Jay Treaty did not constitute an Anglo-American alliance. Pinckney's first draft, submitted August 15, called for free navigation of the Mississippi, the right of deposit at New Orleans, reciprocal trade, and the settlement of American claims against Spain for the seizure of American vessels. Godoy replied on September 18 by dropping trade, the right of deposit, and spoliations, and reworking Pinckney's navigation clause. Pinckney was willing to give up a commercial treaty but not the right of deposit. On October 24 Pinckney asked for his passport, considering the negotiation over. Godoy clearly feared hostilities with Great Britain and did not want to alienate a nation that could destroy the Spanish empire in North America. Pinckney agreed to a mixed commission on spoliations, and Godoy granted a privilege to deposit goods at New Orleans. The two concluded a treaty at San Lorenzo on October 27. It was known in the United States as Pinckney's Treaty.

Short of the actual cession of New Orleans, the treaty secured everything the United States could have wanted from Spain. It set the southern boundary of the United States at 31° north and the middle of the Mississippi as the dividing line between Spanish Louisiana and the United States. Pinckney's Treaty marked a triumph of American ideas of neutral rights, establishing that free ships make free goods and setting a strict definition of contraband. Spain permitted Americans to deposit goods at New Orleans. This article would operate for three years. Except for a commercial treaty, Pinckney's Treaty marked a complete Spanish retreat and the best example, in Bemis's words, of America's advantage from Europe's distress.[22]

The treaty sailed through the Senate in February 1796 with no difficulty. At the same time, the Senate approved a treaty with Algiers, ending a conflict that had sputtered along for a decade. The two popular treaties somewhat blunted the political effect of the more controversial and unpopular Jay Treaty. Since ratification, the Jay Treaty had been the subject of a protracted public debate, with each side trying to shape public opinion. The Republicans, believing that Great Britain was vulnerable to economic pressure, considered the treaty a surrender to Great Britain engineered by aristocrats and merchants dependent on British capital. Congress reconvened on December 7 but held off discussion of the treaty pending British ratification. Ratifications were exchanged in London on October 28, and Washington proclaimed the treaty on February 29, 1796.

The House of Representatives has no formal role in the treaty power. However, the Jay Treaty created three commissions—two to settle the boundaries and one to settle the debt question. Those commissions had to be paid for, and money bills must originate in the House. The House took up the treaty on March 1, 1796. The next day, Edward Livingston, a New York Republican, moved that Washington be asked to deliver all papers related to the treaty. The Livingston motion began the first phase of the House debate, in which the central issue was the constitutionality of the treaty. The debate was similar to that over the Proclamation of Neutrality three years before. The central question was whether the president's power to negotiate treaties or Congress's power to declare war would predominate. Naturally the real subject, the treaty itself, was never far from the surface.

As in 1793, the Republicans' vision of congressional power flowed from the power to declare war. As the Jay Treaty required appropriations, this lent further credence to the idea that Congress must have the papers in order to make an informed decision. James Madison saw a constitutional showdown. "It was to be decided whether the general power of making Treaties supersedes the powers of the House of Representatives," he asked, "particularly specified in the Constitution, so as to take to the Executive all deliberative will, and have the House only an executive and ministerial instrumental agency?"[23] In his last speech on the matter, Albert Gallatin made what the Republicans considered their best constitutional and political argument against the Jay Treaty. They believed the treaty constituted an alliance with Great Britain, a power at war. Such an alliance could bring American entry while bypassing the war power. The president and the Senate, Gallatin argued, "have not the power to declare war; but it is for them a duty, a moral obligation to proclaim it." For that reason, Gallatin considered the Jay Treaty unconstitutional.[24]

Toward the end of the debate, Vermont Federalist Daniel Buck returned to what he considered the real reason for Republican opposition. "While our hearts swell with sympathetic emotions for France, our indignation is carried to a degree of madness against Britain; we cry out for the Spirit of Seventy-six; are for plunging into the war to make a common cause with France to extirpate tyrants from the earth."[25] The treaty power served as the foundation of the Federalist argument against the Livingston motion. It was not for the House to judge "whether the Treaty be good or bad; not whether it was proper to make a Treaty at all, or whether a better one might have been made, all these considerations belonging to the Treaty making power, which is vested in the PRESIDENT and the Senate," Robert Goodloe Harper argued.[26]

At the conclusion of the debate on March 24, the House voted on the Livingston motion. By a 61–38 margin, the committee of the whole approved the call for papers. The House then approved the motion 62–37. Three days later the House received a message from the president rejecting the request. Washington noted, as did many of the Federalists in Congress, that foreign policy required secrecy and that to allow the House a right to demand diplomatic papers "would be to establish a dangerous precedent." Furthermore, Washington asserted that the House had no role in the treaty-making power and the approval of the House was not required to carry a treaty into effect.[27] After another week of desultory debate, the House dropped the constitutional issue on April 7.

On April 14 the House voted to separate the measures to execute the Jay Treaty and Pinckney's Treaty. The House voted the appropriations for Pinckney's Treaty without controversy and resumed the debate on the Jay Treaty, shifting from the constitutional issues around the treaty to the merits of the treaty itself. The change in the debate presented a danger to the Republicans. It was easier to argue it was a bad treaty than that the president and Senate had no right to approve it. Yet the constitutional debate spared the Republicans the prospect of a frontal assault on Washington, which a debate over the merits might require. The Federalists knew that Washington's approval was their best card, and they played it for all it was worth. "Has the PRESIDENT OF THE UNITED STATES after twenty years of patriotism become a traitor?" Massachusetts Federalist Samuel Lyman asked on April 15.[28]

Madison laid out the Republican case against the treaty in a lengthy speech on April 15. He attacked nearly every aspect and hit all of the Republican hot-button issues. By allowing British access to Indian territory, Jay gave up too much to gain the forts. He abandoned "free ships make free goods" and a limited definition of contraband, staples of every other treaty. Jay did not need to make any concessions to gain a commercial treaty, Madison argued, restating a fundamental Republican tenet. "A Treaty was surely not necessary to induce Great Britain to receive our raw materials and to sell us her manufactures." Madison saw no danger in rejecting the treaty: "The idea of war, as a consequence of refusing to give effect to the treaty was too visionary, and incredible to be admitted into the question."[29] The basic theme—that the United States had the economic upper hand and that no nation would risk being cut off from American trade—was unchanged since 1776.

The Federalists could not argue that the Jay Treaty was a triumph on the scale of Pinckney's Treaty, but they did argue it was a decent treaty and the best possible. The Federalists had no faith either in economic coercion or the premise that political and economic relations could be completely separated. "We could not have carved for ourselves, for our strength and greatness were not sufficient," Lyman said in response to Madison.[30] On April 28 Fisher Ames of Massachusetts delivered the most memorable speech of the session. To Ames the main question was whether or not the United States would break faith. On this issue hung the question of peace or war. Peace opened a great field of opportunity, but all would be lost in the event of war. "If, however, the vote should pass to reject, and a spirit should rise, as it will with the public disorders to make confusion worse confounded, even I, slender and almost broken as my hold upon life is, may outlive the Government and Constitution of my country."[31] The Federalist dignitaries in the galleries, including Vice President Adams and Justice James Iredell, dissolved into tears. Adams watched the Republican reaction and believed they knew they were beaten. On April 29 the committee of the whole voted 50–49 to approve the appropriations, with Chairman Frederick A. C. Muhlenburg of Pennsylvania casting the deciding vote. The next day the House voted 51–48 to carry the treaty into effect.

Franco-American relations hung on the progress of the Jay Treaty, as well as the course of the new French government. In October 1795 the Directory took executive power from the Committee for Public Safety. Its members were distinguished in having avoided the guillotine. They had no interest in revolution at home or abroad as a policy but rather hoped to conquer as much of Europe as possible and keep the booty for themselves. The directors were unsentimental survivors and would not allow the United States to sign what they considered an alliance with Great Britain. In March 1796 the foreign minister, Charles Delacroix, instructed Pierre Adet, the new minister to the United States, to stir up anti-British feeling in the United States to cause the abrogation of the Jay Treaty and ideally lead to a war between the United States and Great Britain. Such a war would secure Canada to France. On February 15, 1796, Delacroix informed Monroe that France considered the alliance ended by the Jay Treaty. On July 2 the Directory issued a decree that neutral vessels would be treated as they allowed themselves to be treated by Great Britain, meaning that American vessels carrying British goods would be subject to capture. By the end of the year, France had seized 250 American vessels.

In July 1796 Washington replaced Monroe with Gen. Charles Cotesworth Pinckney, brother of Thomas Pinckney. Monroe learned of his recall in November. He did not want to go, nor did the Directory want him to leave, but he gave a farewell address to the Directory on December 30. The Directory ordered the new minister out of the country on January 23, 1797. During the presidential election of 1796, French officials in the United States tried to secure a friendlier government. Gen. Victor Collot attempted to stir up separatist sentiment in the West as a hedge against American hostility. Although Adet preferred Jefferson, he did not believe that any American government could truly be pro-French. "Jefferson, I say is an American and, on this account, he cannot sincerely be our friend. An American is the born enemy of all European peoples."[32]

The Jay Treaty had a number of casualties. The French considered it the end of the alliance, and Monroe's opposition had cost him his job. The treaty also destroyed whatever chance Jay might have had for higher office. The last casualty was Washington. Washington never really wanted all of the offices that had been heaped upon him for the last twenty years. He especially did not want a second term as president. Washington had gotten used to being beyond the criticism reserved for the normal run of politicians. Through the first six years of his presidency, the Republicans had shied away from a direct attack on him, preferring to go after softer targets such as Adams or Hamilton. That deference ended with the Jay Treaty. Washington himself came under direct attack, and he did not like it. He could have had a third term, but Washington's political success lay in his willingness, if not eagerness, to give up power. He had walked away before and determined to do so in 1796 for the last time.

Washington's unique position in American politics required that he offer some advice to the nation as he departed the public stage. In anticipation of retirement in 1792, Washington asked Madison to draft a farewell message. On May 15, 1796, Washington sent the Madison draft and his own materials to Hamilton so that Hamilton could shape them into a formal address. Hamilton sent back a draft on July 30. For decades the full extent of Hamilton's participation was unknown. When revealed, it cast doubt on how much belonged to Hamilton and how much to Washington.[33] It is helpful to think of Hamilton as the equivalent of a modern-day presidential speechwriter. Hamilton did try to slip in some passages that reflected those unusual instances where his and Washington's philosophy differed. However, much of Hamilton's draft meshed perfectly with Washington's thinking and passed unchanged into the Farewell Address. The pen and the style belonged to Hamilton, but the spirit belonged to Washington.

After announcing his intention to retire, Washington turned to the value of the union. The union was the main support of northern shipping and southern agriculture. The union provided "greater security from extant danger, a less frequent interruption of the peace by foreign nations, and what is of inestimable value, they might derive from union an exemption from those broils and wars between themselves which so frequently affect neighboring countries not tied together by the same governments, which their own rivalship alone would be sufficient to produce, but which opposite foreign alliances, attachments and intrigues, would stimulate and embitter."[34] From the union, Washington moved on to foreign relations. He began with fairly innocuous and obvious advice. "Observe good faith and justice toward all nations. Cultivate peace and harmony with all." Washington warned against permanently favoring or opposing any nation. "The nation which indulges toward another an habitual hatred or an habitual fondness is in some degree a slave."[35]

Throughout, Washington warned against faction, particularly based on section, as an invitation to foreign influence. "The great rule of conduct for us in regard to foreign nations, is, in extending our commercial relations to have with them as little *political* connection as possible," Washington argued, keeping the French alliance in mind. "So far as we have already formed engagements let them be fulfilled with perfect good faith. Here let us stop." Washington went on to say that "Europe has a set of primary interests which to us have none or a very remote relation." Union, distance, commerce, and neutrality would keep the United States out of Europe's wars.[36] None of Washington's ideas were new, nor were they intended to be. To Washington the Farewell Address was a distillation of the wisdom gained in the first twenty years of the American national experience.

## The Quasi-War

Washington's successor, John Adams, shared the beliefs and assumptions of the Farewell Address, although Adams would point out that he had argued for the same policies for more than twenty years. Like most of his successors who departed voluntarily, Washington was eager to leave office. "He seemed to enjoy a Tryumph over me," Adams wrote home, describing inauguration day. "Methought I heard him think Ay! I am fairly out and you are fairly in! See which of Us will be happiest!"[37] Adams inherited a calmer relationship with Great Britain than at any point since the American Revolution. However, diplomacy in the age of the French Revolution was a zero-sum game. If relations with Great Britain improved, relations with France must suffer. On March 2, 1797, the Directory renounced the principle that free ships make free goods and permitted attacks on American shipping.

Adams's chief characteristic as a president was his stubborn independence. He was not a party man and took to heart Bolingbroke's description of a patriot king. This disdain for partisan activity placed him in contrast with his inherited cabinet. Adams retained Timothy Pickering as secretary of state, James McHenry as secretary of war, Oliver Wolcott as secretary of the treasury, and Charles Lee as attorney-general. As Washington and Adams were both Federalists, there was no political reason to change personnel. Replacing them would also be impractical. They were at the bottom of Washington's list but were willing to serve. Only Lee became an Adams loyalist. The others were more connected to the unseen presence of the administration, Alexander Hamilton. Wolcott had been Hamilton's deputy. McHenry was an incompetent who owed his political career to good fellowship. Hamilton was aware of McHenry's shortcomings but for a time found them useful. When Adams submitted questions to the cabinet, McHenry sent his to Hamilton, who was more than happy to answer them. Adams was not fooled. Pickering had an even pricklier sense of independence than Adams and saw Hamilton as a like-minded equal rather than as his leader.

Hamilton was used to having the president's ear, and now he did not. He had to approach the new president indirectly. Before the new administration took office, Hamilton wrote to numerous leading Federalists, including those in the cabinet, outlining a plan for negotiation with France. Hamilton recommended sending a three-member commission to France to settle differences and avoid war if possible. He wanted to send a high-profile Republican, such as Jefferson or Madison, to join Pinckney in Paris. To balance the Republican, Hamilton would send a reliable Federalist such as George Cabot of Massachusetts. Henry Knox passed the idea on to Adams. Adams planned to arm and negotiate, and had already decided to repair Franco-American relations by sending a Republican envoy. The day before the inauguration, Adams approached Jefferson about going to France. It was an awkward conversation. The two had broken when Jefferson implicitly attacked Adams in his dedication to *The Rights of Man*. Jefferson told Adams it would be inappropriate to send the vice president. Adams, perhaps sensing that Jefferson gave him a graceful way out, agreed. Adams then asked Jefferson to ask Madison. Jefferson agreed but held out no hope that Madison would accept. Ironically, the cabinet, which normally went along with Hamilton, opposed the idea. Jefferson rendered the question moot on March 6 when he told the president that Madison would not accept an appointment.

Adams called for a special session of Congress, which convened on May 15, and addressed it the next day. He blamed France for the current difficulties, citing the rejection of Pinckney as minister and seizure of American vessels but expressed hope that those difficulties might be resolved. Adams recommended a permanent navy.[38] The president also finalized the commission. Pinckney had to be part of it. His rejection by the Directory was an insult that could not stand. The commission had to have sectional political balance. Adams chose John Marshall, a Virginia Federalist and prominent Richmond attorney, for one position. Adams wanted to appoint Elbridge Gerry for the New England slot. Gerry's politics were indeterminate, but he was someone Adams trusted. When the cabinet objected, Adams named Francis Dana. Dana was a stalwart Federalist, pleasing the cabinet, and was also someone Adams trusted. Adams suspected Dana would refuse the appointment, and when he did that left the way clear for Adams to appoint Gerry. The cabinet completed the commission's instructions on July 15. The Americans were to avoid any blame to the United States for the current crisis. They were to grant no aid to France during the war, make no treaty inconsistent with the Jay Treaty, admit to no restrictions on lawful commerce, and allow no French privileges inconsistent with American sovereignty. A few days later, Marshall and Gerry separately departed for France.

The French government moved in a generally anti-American direction. On July 18 Charles Maurice de Talleyrand-Périgord replaced Delacroix as foreign minister. Talleyrand, the former bishop of Autun, had lived as an exile for four years in the United States and grown to despise Americans as money-grubbers. The Directory ignored Talleyrand on most issues but considered him an expert on the United States. The coup of 18 Fructidor (September 4, 1797) nullified recent elections and purged two directors. The two new directors, Phillipe Antoine Merlin de Douai and François de Neufchâteau, were particularly anti-American, as was the president, Jean François Reubell. France's chaotic internal politics had no effect on its military efforts, as Napoleon Bonaparte marched through Italy.

The Directory saw no need to make concessions to any nation, let alone a small power like the United States.

Adams doubted the mission would succeed, and he was right, although not in the way he imagined. Marshall and Pinckney arrived in Paris on September 27, joined by Gerry a week later. Talleyrand met them but put off a formal reception under the guise of preparing a memorandum on Franco-American relations. Talleyrand then shifted to the use of intermediaries. The first requested that the Americans explain certain elements of Adams's May 16 speech that cast aspersions on France. The Frenchman avoided the word "apology," but that was implied. On October 17, Nicholas Hubbard, an English-born banker in a Dutch house, approached the Americans about meeting the next day with Jean Hottinguer, a Swiss financier. At dinner, Hottinguer got to the point. The United States must assume claims by the American citizens against the French government. Next Hottinguer asked the envoys to loan France money by buying Dutch money at twice the actual value. Finally, the price of doing business with Talleyrand was a bribe—a "*pot de vin*" as Hottinguer put it—of £50,000 ($250,000). Hottinguer first told Pinckney in French and then all three in English. On October 19 Swiss banker Pierre Bellamy joined Hottinguer and repeated Hottinguer's proposals. When the Americans refused, Talleyrand sent Lucien Hauteval, an exiled Saint-Domingue planter, to meet with Gerry. French victories strengthened Talleyrand's hand. Bonaparte imposed the Treaty of Campo Formio on Austria on October 18. In order to ease Austria out of the war, Bonaparte gave it Venice. Europe's oldest republic was now in the hands of the chief defender of absolute monarchy. Word reached Paris a week later, and the French agents threatened the United States with a similar fate. Hottinguer and Bellamy repeated the demand for explanations and money. Pinckney responded, "No, No, not a sixpence."[39]

That was Pinckney's final answer to a request for a loan. In November the Americans demanded official recognition. Hottinguer and Bellamy receded from the negotiations, replaced by old friend Beaumarchais, New York merchant Joseph Pitcairn, and Pierre S. DuPont de Nemours, who later immigrated to the United States. By this time Pinckney was out of the negotiations. Marshall drafted a memorial to Talleyrand in January 1798, demanding formal reception. By that time Marshall too was against any loan. Instead, the Directory issued a decree authorizing the capture of any American ships carrying British goods. Marshall was certain that France would not declare war if negotiations broke down or if the Americans left. Gerry was not, and was willing to discuss a loan. Talleyrand played on Gerry's fear of war and in February asked Gerry to remain behind as a "reasonable" diplomat.

The first dispatches arrived from Paris on March 4, 1798. They contained a full account of the actions of Talleyrand's agents and included events as recent as January. Adams announced the failure of the mission to Congress on March 19. The Republicans demanded to see the dispatches. The Federalists knew what the dispatches said and were eager to comply. Scared by Federalist support, Republican leaders Albert Gallatin and William Branch Giles attempted to reverse course. The motion passed 65–27 on April 2, and Adams delivered the dispatches the next day. Talleyrand's agents asked that their names be left out, so Adams substituted W, X, Y, and Z for Hubbard, Hottinguer, Bellamy, and Hauteval. As Hubbard's participation ended early, the failed mission became known as the XYZ Affair.

The XYZ Affair put the Republicans in a difficult position, to say the least. Since the outbreak of the French Revolution, the Republicans had been unswerving supporters of France. To doubt French republicanism was to be a monarchist or, as Jefferson often put it, a heretic. This belief required the Republicans to swallow a number of camels, accepting the bloody tyranny of the Reign of Terror and the grubby kleptocracy of the Directory as representative of republican government. The first Republican reaction to the dispatches was to deny their accuracy. Jefferson was convinced Marshall had made up the whole affair or at least that Talleyrand's agents were not really Talleyrand's agents. The second was to blame Adams. Joel Barlow, a Connecticut poet and land speculator living in Paris, was representative of the American community there. He considered the reappointment of Pinckney after he had been refused an insult. When Adams attacked France in his first annual message, Barlow "wondered that the answers of both branches of Congress had not been an order to send him to a mad-house."[40]

The Federalists agreed among themselves that the XYZ Affair was an insult and a provocation. There the agreement ended. Adams was a lifelong navy advocate and believed the French threat was best met on the sea. There were ideological and practical reasons for his position. Adams believed, with the English Opposition, that the navy was the politically safest means of defense. Adams was not as fearful of an army as the Republicans but did share the English Opposition's suspicions. His reluctance to augment the army increased with Hamilton's eagerness to command one. In practical terms, Adams never believed that France would invade the United States. That fear was at the heart of the Federalist call for a larger army. It was not completely unreasonable, as most of the nations of continental Europe felt the French boot. But those boots could not walk across the Atlantic. Congress created the Department of the Navy on April 30, 1798. Adams appointed Georgetown merchant Benjamin Stoddert as the first secretary. Stoddert became the president's staunchest ally in the cabinet. At the end of May, the *Ganges* patrolled the coast, followed by the twin frigates *Constellation* and *Constitution.*

Congressional Federalists feared a French invasion, and their eventual rift with Adams came from this issue. Like the cabinet, congressional Federalists looked more to Hamilton for guidance than to Adams. Hamilton and Congress favored an increased army as well as a navy. Congress authorized a large army on May 28 and on June 22 pushed for appointments to a ten-thousand-man "Additional Army." The obvious choice to command the new army was Washington, whose name Adams sent to the Senate on July 4. Washington accepted reluctantly, as he did all public trusts, but with two conditions. First, he would not be called into service until the actual start of hostilities. Until then, the inspector general would command. Second, Washington would choose his own major generals. Pickering and McHenry practically begged Washington to choose Hamilton. Ultimately Washington decided on youth and energy over age and experience, choosing his former aide-de-camp Hamilton as the inspector general. Pinckney and Knox were the other two major generals, but Knox refused to serve under Hamilton. Congress authorized the president to recruit twelve regiments of foot and six light dragoon troops on July 16. Those troops were to form the core of a fifty-thousand-man "Provisional Army," but that army existed mainly on paper.

On June 21, 1798, Adams sent Congress a message celebrating Marshall's return to the United States and transmitting letters from Gerry explaining his decision to stay behind. "I will never send another minister to France without assurances that he will be received, respected, and honored as the representative of a great, free, powerful and independent nation," the president concluded.[41] Did Adams close off negotiations or give France the opportunity to reopen them? His subsequent actions suggest the latter. Nor did Hamilton, despite agreeing with the High Federalists on the need for a bigger army, yet approve a declaration of war. Congressional Federalists ran ahead of both. On June 30 New Hampshire Federalist Peleg Sprague moved in the House of Representatives to extend the conflict by authorizing attacks on all French ships, including unarmed merchant vessels. If passed, it would open the way to a formal declaration of war. A combination of Republicans and moderate Federalists defeated the motion 41–32. Two days later the same motion went down by a larger margin, 52–31.

Many congressional Federalists believed that the United States was already at war with France. Declaring it would clarify the domestic and foreign political situation. However, a July 4 caucus determined that there was not a majority for a declaration of war. Congress voted to abrogate the 1778 treaties on July 7 and on July 9 authorized attacks on French armed vessels anywhere in the world. The lack of a formal declaration gave the war its nickname, "the Quasi-War." Robert Goodloe Harper of South Carolina, the Federalist floor leader, concluded that the moderate Federalists "thought it best to confine [themselves] to defense and preparation, and leave the French either to discontinue their attacks, or to declare war, as they might think best."[42] That was the president's policy as well.

Those Federalists who favored a declaration of war favored acts to limit the influence of France in the United States. The Federalists considered the Republicans little more than pawns of the Directory. The Republicans, of course, harbored the same suspicions about the Federalists and Great Britain. Soon after the XYZ Affair, Federalists in Congress began work on the domestic agenda, particularly the four acts grouped together as the Alien and Sedition Acts. The Alien Act (or Alien Friends Act), giving the president the power to expel dangerous aliens in peace, passed in June. The Alien Enemies Act, granting the same power in war, passed in July. The Federalists hoped to cut off the foreign pipeline to the Republicans, particularly French and Irish immigrants, and passed the Naturalization Act, which repealed the 1795 act and extended the naturalization period from five to fourteen years. The final law, the Sedition Act, was passed on July 10 and signed by the president on July 14, and made it a crime to write, print, utter, or publish "any false, scandalous and malicious writings against the government of the United States, or either house of the Congress, or the President of the United States, with the intent to defame." To pay for the army and navy, Congress passed the Direct Tax, or Evaluation Tax, for the first time placing a direct tax on houses.

By the time Congress adjourned in July, the rift between Adams and the High Federalists was clear. Adams did not really want an army and certainly did not want Hamilton to command it. Instead, Adams chose Henry Knox as inspector general. Washington neither knew nor cared why Adams opposed Hamilton and threatened to resign if Adams did not abide by their agreement to let him choose his subordinates. In October Adams relented. Before the matter was settled, Hamilton devoted himself to the organization of the new army. By August Hamilton decided that war was inevitable, as he became enamored of Francisco de Miranda's plan to liberate South America. Miranda, a native of what is now Venezuela, was a tireless revolutionary. In January 1798 he approached William Pitt about an alliance with Great Britain and the United States to liberate South America. Miranda pitched the plan to Rufus King, the American minister to Great Britain, the next month. King passed the proposal to the Adams administration and to Hamilton personally. Hamilton instantly formed a plan: a British navy, an American army, the liberation of South America, and the American acquisition of Louisiana and the Floridas. For Hamilton, the combination of his command of the army and Miranda's scheme offered the level of fame Hamilton had always craved. As a boy, he wished for a war to take him from the obscurity of being a clerk in a mercantile firm. A decade later Hamilton had his war but was still a clerk. Now he had the chance to be the man who conquered the Mississippi for the United States. Adams had no enthusiasm for the plan. He did not believe the conflict with France automatically brought a conflict with Spain, and he thought the project of making republics out of Spanish America absurd.

As Hamilton committed to war with France, Adams and Talleyrand determined that the conflict would not escalate, even if peace was not imminent. Neither Adams nor Talleyrand wanted a full-scale war, and each expected the other had the same intention. In May 1798 John Quincy Adams reported from his post in Berlin as minister to Prussia that France was making preparations for an invasion of Great Britain. The preparations were so ostentatious that he concluded, correctly, that it was a bluff. Any chance of invasion sank in Aboukir Bay on August 1, 1798, when Adm. Horatio Nelson destroyed a French fleet in the Battle of the Nile, stranding Bonaparte's army in Egypt. Talleyrand was now prepared to seek an honorable retreat. With certain conditions, Adams would give him one. Talleyrand kept up negotiations with Gerry, alternating between threats and promises. Gerry, convinced he had preserved the peace, left France in August.

When Gerry returned to the United States in October, he immediately reported to the president that Talleyrand wished to make peace. Adams did not approve of Gerry's remaining in France but did not question his friend's motives. Gerry's report was not enough to merit a change in policy. Soon after, Adams received similar reports from William Vans Murray, the American minister to the Netherlands. Other than Adams himself, Murray was the most important American in shaping Franco-American relations. As minister to the Netherlands, Murray sat at the diplomatic crossroads of Western Europe. Talleyrand would not yet conduct a direct negotiation and ordered Louis Pichon, the French minister to the Netherlands, to open a back channel in July. Murray's report led Adams to ask the cabinet to decide between war and a new mission.

Not all of the diplomatic overtures were official or welcomed. In June 1798 George Logan, a leading Philadelphia Quaker and Republican, left on a private peace mission to France. He arrived in August and met with the leaders of the French government. The directors, particularly Merlin de Douai, assured Logan of France's peaceful intentions. Logan arrived back in Philadelphia in November. When Logan met Pickering, the secretary of state practically threw Logan out of his office. Logan had a marginally more friendly meeting with Washington. Logan finally met with the president on November 26 and told Adams that France would receive whomever he sent. The president put little stock in Logan's testimony. Congressional Federalists were appalled by the Logan mission and passed the Logan Act on January 17, 1799, prohibiting such private diplomacy. Even though Adams dismissed Logan, the evidence from across the political spectrum pointed toward a lessening of hostilities. In October 1798, Harrison Gray Otis, a Massachusetts Federalist, told Adams that his friend Richard Codman, a Federalist and merchant in Paris, reported that France would accept a new mission. The president's youngest son, Thomas Boylston Adams, arrived in Philadelphia on January 15, 1799. The younger Adams had served as his brother's secretary in Berlin and likely briefed the president on the progress of the Pichon back channel.

Without more explicit overtures from France, American policy would not change. The American navy concentrated on the Caribbean, the area within easiest reach. Adams planned to strengthen the American position in the Caribbean by exploiting the revolt in Saint-Domingue. Adams and Pickering favored opening trade, and Congress passed a bill on February 9, 1799, allowing the president to open trade with Saint-Domingue. The bill, which Jefferson nicknamed "Toussaint's clause," passed on a party-line vote. Adams appointed Edward Stevens, a friend of Hamilton, as consul general. Stevens and Toussaint Louverture concluded an agreement on April 25, 1799, in which Saint-Domingue agreed to cease privateering and the United States agreed to open trade.

The final pieces of the diplomatic puzzle fell into place in February. Adams received more dispatches from Murray that proved the value of the Pichon back channel. Talleyrand wrote Pichon on August 28, telling the envoy that American prosperity was more harmful to Great Britain than France. Pichon passed the letter to Murray, who sent it to Adams. Talleyrand told Pichon on September 28 that he would receive whomever Adams sent. Pichon gave Murray a copy of the letter on October 7. Adams received these dispatches at the end of January and the beginning of February 1799. At the same time, Washington sent Adams a letter from Joel Barlow that said the Directory wanted peace. Washington believed Barlow wrote with the Directory's approval and added that he would support Adams in a just peace. Adams had no use for Barlow, and the feeling was mutual, but Washington's letter seemed to offer a hedge against Hamiltonian opposition. Without consulting the cabinet, Adams appointed William Vans Murray minister plenipotentiary to France on February 18, 1799.

The Hamiltonian Federalists vehemently opposed sending a new mission to France. Pickering scrambled to assure his circle that the nomination was the president's alone. Five days after the announcement, a group of Federalist senators tried to talk Adams out of the mission. He threatened to resign. They then asked Adams to send a commission rather than a single minister. Adams reluctantly agreed and two days later added two more Federalists, Chief Justice Oliver Ellsworth and Patrick Henry. Henry declined and was replaced by Gov. William R. Davie of North Carolina. On March 10 Adams and the cabinet met to discuss instructions. Any treaty must allow Americans to seek spoliation claims against the French government, compensate American shipowners whose vessels had been seized, and not offer a guarantee of French territory in America. That article had become the most troublesome one in the 1778 alliance, and its removal was the chief object of American diplomacy. Soon after Adams appointed the commission Congress adjourned, and Adams returned to his home in Quincy. Delay was part of a two-fold strategy. First, Adams wanted to further gauge French intentions. The president was well aware that Talleyrand's assurances were not necessarily reliable. Second, he wanted to make sure that the navy was at full strength in case the second mission failed.

Murray received word of his new appointment in May and informed Talleyrand of his powers. Talleyrand's response, with a final assurance that Murray and his colleagues would be received, arrived in Quincy on August 6. In the meantime, the Hamiltonians tried to scuttle the mission. Pickering latched onto a change in the French government as the best reason to cancel the mission. On 30 Prairial (June 18) most of the Directory fell from power. Talleyrand, never one to go down with the ship, resigned as foreign minister and was replaced by his political ally Karl Friedrich Reinhard. Pickering asked Adams to call off the mission and convinced Ellsworth to go along. Until then, Pickering continued to draft the instructions, sending his draft on September 14. The envoys were to negotiate only with the foreign minister. Negotiations were to begin within three weeks of arrival and conclude no later than April 1, 1800, in order to avoid a repeat of the XYZ Affair.

Benjamin Stoddert, Adams's best ally in the cabinet, pleaded with the president to return to Philadelphia and take control of the government. On October 10 Adams arrived in Trenton, New Jersey, where the government had moved to escape a yellow fever outbreak in Philadelphia. There Pickering, Wolcott, McHenry, and especially Hamilton tried one last time to convince Adams to cancel the mission. Hamilton raised the prospect of war with Great Britain in the event of peace with France. Adams rejected the notion out of hand, as neither Great Britain nor France could afford to add to their enemies. Adams ordered Ellsworth and Davie to depart on October 16. They set sail on November 3 and landed in Lisbon on November 27. They then sailed to Spain and traveled overland to Paris in order to gather political information on the way. They met Murray in the French capital on March 2, 1800.

The Americans met with yet another change in French government. On 18 Brumaire (November 9, 1799), Napoleon Bonaparte, hero of the Italian campaign and survivor of Egypt, overthrew the Directory and replaced it with the Consulate. Bonaparte was first consul, with Abbé Emmanuel-Joseph Sieyès and Roger Ducos as the others. For a while Bonaparte was willing to pretend he was not a monarch. Soon after, Talleyrand returned to office as foreign minister.

Murray correctly considered the new government a positive sign. Bonaparte wanted to improve relations with the neutral powers of northern Europe, which a settlement with the United States would accomplish. Bonaparte stopped the seizure of American vessels. There was no repeat of the first mission. Bonaparte received the Americans on March 7 and appointed a commission of Joseph Bonaparte (his older brother), Pierre Louis Roederer, and Charles Pierre Claret Fleurieu to negotiate.

Talks began on April 2. Throughout, the central question was the status of the 1778 treaties. Talleyrand instructed the French commission to insist on the validity of the old treaties, while the Americans claimed the right to abrogate them and wished to revise or supersede them. Talleyrand was willing to drop them for a price, namely, the American abandonment of indemnities. On July 22 the French told Ellsworth that they would not pay indemnities but were willing to accept a new treaty to replace the alliance. Three days later, Louis Pichon, acting as secretary to the French commission, told the Americans that France would be willing to accept commercial privileges as a most-favored nation. The Americans agreed. The envoys spent August drafting and rejecting various proposals. Events on the sea drew France toward a settlement. On August 27, Tsar Paul I of Russia proposed the formation of a new League of Armed Neutrality with Sweden, Denmark, and Prussia. A treaty with the United States on terms favorable to neutral rights would boost France's standing with the neutrals.

Roederer stripped the negotiation to its bare bones on September 11. The Americans, he said, wanted to void the alliance, and France did not want to pay indemnities. There was the trade that could bring an agreement. Two days later the Americans met and agreed that normal relations should be reestablished first and other questions dealt with later. The two teams completed a draft on September 27 and signed the Provisional Treaty of Amity and Commerce on October 1. Bonaparte wished to change the agreement to a convention to give it an air of permanence. The revised agreement was signed at Môrtefontaine, Joseph Bonaparte's home, on October 3. Article 2 of the Convention of Môrtefontaine suspended the 1778 treaties until a new treaty could be formed. The convention granted each side most-favored-nation status and reaffirmed the principle of limited contraband.[43]

By the time the treaty arrived in the United States on December 11, 1800, the rift between Adams and the Hamilton Federalists had broken out into open warfare. In May 1800 the Republicans won the legislative elections in New York, delivering New York's electoral votes to Jefferson and Burr. Adams felt free to act against the Hamiltonians, forcing McHenry to resign and firing Pickering, and replacing them with Samuel Dexter and John Marshall, respectively. The Federalist split helped cost Adams a second term. He finished behind Jefferson and Aaron Burr. On December 16 Adams sent the treaty to the Senate. Adams Federalists generally favored it, as did the Republicans. Hamiltonian Federalists (but not Hamilton himself) opposed it. The Senate rejected the treaty on January 23, 1801, by a 16–14 vote. On February 23 the Senate reconsidered the treaty and approved it 22–9, with article 2 removed. The Federalists wanted to ensure that the convention replaced the 1778 treaties. The revised convention was then sent back to France for approval. President Jefferson proclaimed the convention in effect on December 21, 1801.

The intraparty conflict over the Adams years masks the general continuity of Federalist diplomacy. The Federalists armed and negotiated and shunned hopes of remaking the world, believing such dreams were beyond the present capability of American power. This was consistent Federalist policy. Hamilton, rather than Adams, deviated from it in the late 1790s. In their conceptions of the limitations of American power, the Federalists were the heirs to the moderates of the American Revolution, although the Federalists substituted the navy and distance from Europe for a dependence on France. When possible, Washington and Adams pursued the full neutral rights agenda. When impossible, as with Great Britain, they did not. They had no particular faith in commercial coercion as the main weapon of American diplomacy. The Federalists steered an untried government through a turbulent era, avoided a full-scale conflict with any great power, and left office on reasonably friendly terms with all. That was the chief Federalist legacy.

CHAPTER 4

# The Jeffersonian Revolution in Foreign Affairs

Much of the study of Jefferson's presidency revolves around his assertion that 1800 was a "real revolution, as much as 1776." If by revolution one means a return to first principles, Jefferson was correct, especially in foreign affairs. Jefferson planned to return to the pure version of the radical plan of 1776: the use of American trade to impose American will on the European powers. In Jefferson's perfect world there were no armies and no navies, no diplomats and no treaties, no American vessels or manufactures. There were only European powers carrying their manufactures in their own ships to the United States, bidding against each other to sell at the lowest price and to buy American agricultural produce at the highest price. Since 1776 the radicals believed that commercial power would override and avoid the normal course of diplomacy. As Jefferson remarked in his first inaugural address, the United States wanted "peace, commerce and honest friendship with all nations, entangling alliances with none." Commerce, meaning an American shipping industry, was chiefly valuable as a "handmaid" to agriculture.[1] The main difference between 1776 and 1801 was that the great powers that had jabbed at each other, allowing room for neutrals, now were pounding each other to death. Jefferson did not think the wars of the French Revolution invalidated the plan of 1776. Rather, he thought it would work even better. Jefferson believed the French Revolution exacerbated rather than removed the European weaknesses he planned to exploit.

Jefferson's first major crisis, the Tripolitan War, does not fit the framework of Jeffersonian diplomacy. Jefferson disliked the navy and wanted to sell it off as quickly as possible. The Tripolitan War obliged him to keep it. Jefferson hoped the ocean would provide a barrier against the Old World, but he projected American power across the Atlantic. Jefferson warned against entangling alliances with the Old World yet presided over the first American attempt to overthrow a foreign government. Jefferson was a strict constructionist but presided over a war of dubious constitutionality. The only way to remove the Barbary threat, a longstanding goal of Jefferson's, was by force. Also, as in 1784, Jefferson believed an assault on the Barbary powers, who richly deserved it, would give pause to Great Britain and perhaps send a message that would prevent the need for a large-scale navy.

In 1799 the Adams administration concluded a treaty with Tripoli that provided for tribute. No amount of tribute was ever enough. In October 1800 Yusef Karamanli, the bashaw of Tripoli, threatened to go to war if the United States did not pay more. On May 14, 1801, the bashaw had the American flag in front of the consul's office chopped down, indicating a formal declaration of war. In anticipation of trouble, Jefferson sent a squadron commanded by Cdre. Richard Dale to the Mediterranean on May 15, 1801. Dale arrived in July and blockaded the city. The campaign ended inconclusively. The war against Tripoli received constitutional sanction on February 6, 1802, when Congress authorized the president to purchase and arm vessels in order to protect American commerce from Tripoli. It was not a declaration of war and in that way looked forward to the resolutions authorizing the use of force in the twentieth and twenty-first centuries. Richard V. Morris succeeded Dale and arrived in the Mediterranean on May 25. Morris, too, blockaded Tripoli but with even less effect.

Fearful of the cost, Jefferson proceeded with a smaller force in 1803. Jefferson appointed Capt. Edward Preble of the *Constitution* as commander of the Mediterranean squadron. Arriving on September 12, he soon suffered a key loss. The *Philadelphia*, commanded by Capt. William Bainbridge, ran aground on October 31, and its crew of thirty became prisoners. On February 16, 1804, Capt. Stephen Decatur took the crew of the *Intrepid* to burn the *Philadelphia* in Tripoli harbor. Preble began negotiations on June 12, sending Richard O'Brien, former consul at Algiers and former prisoner, to Tripoli. O'Brien offered $40,000 in ransom and $20,000 in gifts, which Yusef rejected. Preble attacked Tripoli on August 3. Preble and O'Brien raised the offer to $80,000 in ransom and a $10,000 tribute, and then to a total of $120,000. Yusef demanded $400,000. Preble resumed bombardment on September 3, and the next day sent the *Intrepid* to set fire to the ships in Tripoli harbor. The attempt failed, and Preble broke off the attack.

William Eaton, the American consul in Tunis, seethed at the capture and enslavement of Americans by the Barbary powers and advocated a more vigorous policy. Eaton wanted to eliminate the Tripoli threat rather than merely punish the bashaw. Yusef had climbed to the Tripolitan throne by murdering one brother and sending the other, Hamet, into exile as the governor of Derne. Eaton and former consul at Tripoli James Leander Cathcart discussed the possibility of using Hamet to form a friendly government in Tripoli. In November 1803 Hamet wrote to Jefferson directly, requesting aid. Jefferson approved the idea. He left the particulars to Eaton, Tobias Lear, the consul at Algiers, and Samuel Barron, the new commodore. Barron commanded the sea operations, Eaton the land, and Lear the negotiations. Barron was initially cool toward Eaton's activities, and the key part, Hamet, fled for his life to Cairo. Eaton sailed to Alexandria and then marched up the Nile in search of his instrument. Eaton found Hamet and signed a treaty with him on February 23, 1805, securing perpetual peace between Tripoli and the United States.

Eaton assembled an army of four hundred men, mainly from the scrapings of Alexandria, and began his march back across the desert on March 3. The army arrived at Derne on April 25. The next day Eaton demanded the surrender of the governor, Mustapha Bey. When Mustapha refused, the *Argus* fired on the town while Eaton surrounded it. Derne fell in the afternoon of April 27. Derne was only the first stage, and Eaton and Hamet prepared an assault on Tripoli. On June 11 Eaton learned that Lear had made peace with Tripoli. The treaty, signed June 4, was better than most with the Barbary states. The United States agreed to pay $60,000 for the release of the crew of the *Philadelphia*, and there was no further tribute. The United States also agreed to evacuate Derne.[2] Joseph Ellis called the Tripolitan War "the ideal minimalist war for Jefferson's minimalist presidency."[3] Certainly, as with most of Jefferson's diplomatic endeavors, he sought the maximum effect with the absolute minimum of force.

## The Louisiana Purchase

Jefferson tried a similar approach of minimal force and expenditure in his signal diplomatic triumph, the Louisiana Purchase. Jefferson had believed since the 1780s that Americans would come to fill up North and South America. Louisiana would one day fall into American hands, and until then Jefferson was content to let it remain in Spain's weak grasp. Two events worked against Jefferson. First, by the 1790s it was clear that Louisiana cost Spain far more than it was worth. Second, with the French defeat in Egypt, the first consul looked west to find an empire. In July 1800 he ordered Talleyrand to open negotiations. Both powers wanted to move quickly in order to avoid British or American interference. Spain and France concluded the Treaty of San Ildefonso on October 1, 1800. Spain sold Louisiana and six warships to France in exchange for an Italian kingdom for the Duke of Parma. Bonaparte wanted the Floridas as well, but Charles IV refused. France could take possession only when it delivered the Italian kingdom. The French offered verbal assurances that France would not sell Louisiana to a third party without offering it back to Spain. As with any event of this magnitude, it could not stay secret for long. Nearly six months later, Rufus King reported from London that France had purchased Louisiana.

Before news of the retrocession reached Washington, the main outstanding issue in Franco-American relations was the American relationship to the revolt in Saint-Domingue. Jefferson and Secretary of State Madison could not countenance a slave revolt, and he feared an "American Algiers," or a pirate state. At the same time, Jefferson wanted to keep a lucrative trade flowing. In March 1801 Jefferson told Louis Pichon, the new French chargé, that the United States would not oppose French policy in Saint-Domingue. The administration leaned toward a French reconquest. In July Pichon again pressed Madison on American policy. By this time, the administration unofficially knew of the Treaty of San Ildefonso. Madison told Pichon that the United States opposed a declaration of independence by Saint-Domingue but nothing more. Pichon had better luck with the president. Jefferson told him that if France and Great Britain made peace, "then nothing will be easier than to furnish your army and fleet with everything and to reduce Toussaint to starvation."[4] Ideally the slave revolt would collapse on its own, without the necessity of a French army in the Caribbean.

For Bonaparte, Saint-Domingue was the key to a revived French empire. Louisiana was to be the breadbasket for the sugar colony, which produced the cash value, and he was willing to co-opt Louverture if possible. In October 1801 Bonaparte planned the expedition under his brother-in-law, Charles Victor Emmanuel Leclerc. Leclerc was to restore the old French empire from its prerevolutionary state. Bonaparte did not specifically call for the restoration of slavery, but the first consul saw no middle ground between anarchy and slavery. Leclerc sailed on December 14 and arrived at Samaná Bay on January 29, 1802. As Jefferson observed, Bonaparte needed peace for his plan to work, and at least temporarily he had it. On October 1, 1801, France concluded a preliminary peace with Great Britain, confirmed in the Treaty of Amiens on March 27, 1802.

To Jefferson, access to New Orleans and the lower Mississippi was vital to the maintenance of an agrarian republic. The task of securing that access fell to Robert R. Livingston, the new minister to France. Livingston, the former secretary for foreign affairs, was appointed to revive the alliance between New York and Virginia Republicans that had become frayed during the contest between Jefferson and Burr in the House of Representatives. At the time of Livingston's appointment, the fate of Louisiana was not officially known. On September 28, 1801, Madison instructed him to inquire if France would continue to allow the right of deposit at New Orleans as under Pinckney's Treaty. If France now owned the Floridas, Livingston should seek the cession of West Florida to the United States for use as a substitute for New Orleans.[5]

The limited policy Madison outlined was applicable only as long as the French army remained outside the Caribbean. Leclerc launched his major offensive in February 1802. Jefferson preferred that the rebellion starve to death rather than go down fighting, since defeated rebels might scatter to the southern states and foment rebellion there. What changed in early 1802 was the means necessary to prevent the Leclerc expedition from succeeding in Saint-Domingue and moving on to New Orleans. Jefferson's tilt toward the French became a tilt toward the rebels, and he refused to impose an arms embargo on them. Jefferson shifted from a policy seeking the mere use of New Orleans to the cession of the city, as well as West Florida. "There is on the globe one single spot, the possessor of which is our natural and habitual enemy," Jefferson wrote to Livingston on April 18, 1802, on the importance of New Orleans. "The day that France takes possession of New Orleans fixes the sentence which is to restrain her forever within her low water mark. From that moment we must marry ourselves to the British fleet and nation."[6] Throughout his career, Jefferson regarded France as the natural ally of the United States and Great Britain as the natural enemy.

Two weeks later Madison sent a formal instruction for Livingston to purchase New Orleans. Jefferson's policy flowed from his perception of American interest rather than any opening offered by France. On May 1 Louverture, perhaps out of design but more likely out of despair, surrendered to Leclerc. Louverture and his deputies, Jean Jacques Desselines and Henri Christophe, were folded into Leclerc's army. This proved to be Leclerc's high point. Yellow fever began to take its toll on the French army. Seeing his opportunity, Louverture plotted his return to rebellion. Leclerc sent him to France, where he died in prison on April 7, 1803. The yellow fever epidemic killed ten thousand French soldiers by July 1802. In October Dessalines and Christophe resumed command of the rebellion. Leclerc himself died on November 2.

In Paris Livingston doggedly tried to carry out his instructions. He drafted a memorandum for Talleyrand in August 1802, intending to talk the French out of Louisiana. Louisiana would be economically useless to France, and French possession of Louisiana would create a permanent rivalry with the United States. On the other hand, if France abandoned its quest for empire and let the United States use New Orleans, the United States would supply lumber and food to France. France would keep its capital and people at home. That would permit France to do what it had dreamed of since the beginning of the American Revolution—replace Great Britain as the chief supplier of manufactures to the United States.[7] While the Saint-Domingue campaign appeared to be going well, Livingston's arguments fell on deaf ears. On October 15 Charles IV signed the transfer agreement. Ten days later Gen. Charles Perrin Victor prepared his expedition to Louisiana. The mission was postponed to December 22 and then to February 1803.

While negotiations in Paris stalled, the dead hand of Spain clutched New Orleans tighter. The right of deposit in Pinckney's Treaty expired three years after ratification. As Spain did not immediately cancel the right, Americans might claim a continued right by various means. Under English common law, failure to restrict a river passage could constitute consent. The king decided to cancel the right of deposit in July 1802 and on July 14 issued a secret order to that effect to the intendant, Juan Ventura Morales. The order was to appear an independent action of the intendant, which would allow Spain to back away if necessary. Morales received the order on October 14, closed the right of deposit on October 16, and published the order on October 18. The effect on American politics was predictable. Westerners assumed the order came by way of Paris, and rumors flew of a French army set to land at any moment. By the end of November the news appeared in

Washington. Jefferson and Madison treated the order as Morales's own and instructed Charles Pinckney, the American minister to Spain, to have the order reversed. Madison told Pinckney and Pichon that there was no telling what angry westerners would do and certainly no way to control them from Washington. The effect on Spain was immediate. On February 28, 1803, Godoy told Pinckney the right of deposit would be restored. The king sent the order on March 1, and the port reopened on May 17.

Jefferson attempted to make ready for whatever emergency presented itself. Throughout the fall of 1802 and winter of 1803, Jefferson stationed militias at various points along the Mississippi in advance of French landing or any aggressive action by Spain. On January 7, 1803, Congress affirmed the American right to navigate the entire length of the Mississippi. Jefferson sent a confidential message to Congress on January 18, 1803, outlining frontier policy. He ordered an exploration of the land west of the Mississippi, the genesis of the Lewis and Clark expedition. Jefferson also proposed a new trade policy toward the Indian tribes of the upper Mississippi Valley. The government would sponsor trading houses that would sell goods below market prices. This trade would plunge the Indians into debt, forcing them to sell their only asset—their land. Most Virginia planters of the eighteenth century were in debt to Scottish merchants, and Jefferson thus knew well the power of debt. Ideally the sale of land would bind the western tribes to the United States, assimilate them into American society, and promote settlement of the West. Jefferson feared that if the French did take Louisiana, their influence would not be contained by the river. Certainly the experience of the 1780s taught the fragility of the American hold on the trans-Appalachian West.

Much of Jefferson's diplomacy was based on the fear of events the administration could not control. As if on cue, the Senate provided another potential danger. On February 16, 1803, James Ross, a Pennsylvania Federalist, offered a series of resolutions calling for $5 million and fifty thousand militiamen raised from the South and West. The president was directed to seize New Orleans or nearby territory if Spain did not restore the right of deposit. Ross, a Pittsburgh resident, was the Federalists' spokesman on western affairs. The Republicans suspected that the Federalists wanted to create an army for its own sake, not for New Orleans, and on February 25 the Senate defeated the Ross resolutions by a 15–11 vote. No western Republican supported them. John Breckinridge of Kentucky offered a less ambitious resolution, calling for the president to raise eighty thousand men from around the country to use as he saw fit. Jefferson did not welcome the Ross resolutions but did not find them useless either. Meeting with Pichon soon after, Jefferson and Madison hinted that the United States would seek an alliance with Great Britain if France did not sell New Orleans. On April 8 the cabinet turned vague threats into policy and agreed that Monroe (the new special envoy) and Livingston should approach Great Britain if talks with France failed. Jefferson was serious about seeking a British alliance but did not believe it would come to fruition. Jefferson believed that the British wanted an American alliance and also that France would do whatever was necessary to prevent it. The mere threat of an alliance was enough to change French policy.

By the beginning of 1803, yellow fever did more for Livingston than months of negotiations. News of Leclerc's death arrived in Paris on January 7, 1803, and the first consul immediately soured on his western empire. "Damn sugar, damn coffee, damn colonies!" Pierre Roederer quoted him as saying.[8] Ice was also Livingston's friend, bottling up General Victor's fleet in Dutch ports until February, further delaying an already delayed mission. Bonaparte's vision again turned east, toward Malta. Bonaparte threatened the British with war over the island on March 12, within earshot of Livingston. The first consul gave up the western project by the beginning of April. Pichon's dispatches, detailing his meetings with Jefferson and Madison, arrived at the end of March. Monroe arrived on April 8, along with news of the Ross resolutions. On April 10 Bonaparte summoned François Barbé de Marbois, the finance minister and an old America hand, to the palace at Saint-Cloud. The next day, the first consul announced that he intended to sell all of Louisiana, rather than just New Orleans, to the United States. Marbois was to make the sale.

Livingston tried to finalize the purchase before Monroe arrived. Livingston unsuccessfully lowballed Marbois, who was content to wait for Monroe's arrival. The eastern boundary of Louisiana was as much of a mystery as the western boundary. Bonaparte could not pry West Florida from Spain, and Marbois was intentionally vague with Livingston on the subject. On April 21 Livingston and Monroe agreed to leave the Floridas out of the treaty, seemingly putting the matter to rest. Only the matter of price remained. War between France and Great Britain loomed over the French presence in the Netherlands in violation of the

Treaty of Amiens. Both France and the United States wanted to conclude an agreement before the war. On April 30 each side agreed to a purchase price of sixty million francs ($11,250,000) for Louisiana. This sum was payable over fifteen years at 6 percent and financed by Baring Brothers of London. The United States would assume twenty million francs ($3,750,000) in American spoliation claims against France. The treaty, concluded on May 2, was dated April 30. In addition to the cession, the key provision was article 3, which promised that the inhabitants of Louisiana would be incorporated into the United States as citizens as soon as possible.[9] Within two weeks Bonaparte cancelled the Victor expedition to Saint-Domingue. Soon after, France and Great Britain were again at war.

Jefferson did not let even his own constitutional qualms stand in the way of a bargain. Jefferson was a strict constructionist, and the Constitution granted no specific power to purchase territory from other nations. Madison had attacked the broad construction of the treaty power during the Jay Treaty debate. Jefferson did not deal with the constitutional problem until January 1803, some nine months after deciding to buy New Orleans and the Floridas. Attorney General Levi Lincoln suggested tacking any new territory onto Georgia and the Mississippi Territory. Gallatin disagreed and saw no alternative but to fall back on the implied powers of treaty making. The limited discussion suggests that Jefferson believed adding a small amount of territory east of the Mississippi posed a minor constitutional problem. Doubling the size of the nation and expanding beyond the Mississippi seemed to require a more explicit sanction. Both Jefferson and Madison drafted constitutional amendments that would allow the government to purchase territory. Philosophical purity gave way to practical political consideration. Facing an October 30 deadline to ratify, as well as the certain opposition of New England, Jefferson accepted Gallatin's original idea. The Senate approved the treaty on October 20, and the president ratified it the next day. Congress passed a government bill in March 1804 dividing the territory into Orleans (now the modern state of Louisiana) and Louisiana. The territories would be ruled as colonial possessions until they filled up with Americans.

The Louisiana Purchase was an anomaly in the history of American expansion in the nineteenth century. Future expansion generally took place when a foreign territory filled up with Americans and either by original design or by circumstance sought independence and annexation to the United States. This was the formula for Texas, California, and Hawaii. Jefferson expected that Americans would settle in Louisiana, which would then be annexed by the United States. This would likely have happened had the Treaty of San Ildefonso not sped up the process. Another pattern in American expansion was for the United States to immediately turn its attention to the piece of territory next to the one most recently acquired. West Florida—the territory south of 31° north, from the Mississippi to the Apalachicola—fit both patterns.

Jefferson's (and later Madison's) dogged pursuit of West Florida has been perplexing to historians. Robert Tucker and David Hendrickson argued that "no compelling interest required wagering the fortunes of [Jefferson's] administration on the possession of West Florida."[10] Such an argument forgets that the original goal was the purchase of New Orleans and West Florida, not all of Louisiana. Jefferson wished to control the entire length of the Mississippi and could not allow West Florida to be held by a European power. Jefferson never got a straight answer out of France about where the boundary was. Monroe later recalled that all parties involved understood the Perdido River to be the eastern limit. Jefferson soon made that assumption the basis for policy. In 1762 France ceded Louisiana east of the Mississippi, except New Orleans, to Great Britain, and the rest to Spain. When Great Britain ceded the Floridas back to Spain in 1783, old Louisiana was restored. Spain and France both bought and sold West Florida without knowing it. Jefferson believed that whoever owned West Florida would eventually cede it to the United States—France out of friendship or Spain out of weakness.

Jefferson moved to assert authority over the disputed territory before Spain could act. On October 4, 1803, the cabinet decided on war if Spain should try to block the transfer of Louisiana. Soon after, John Randolph of Roanoke, a leading Virginia Republican, introduced a bill to extend American jurisdiction to Mobile. The bill passed in February 1804, adding the territory from the Mississippi to the Perdido to the customs district of the Mississippi Territory. The act did not state that Mobile Bay was within the bounds of the United States. On February 18 the cabinet voted to make Fort Stoddert, clearly north of the Spanish-American boundary, the port of entry for the Mobile district. The cabinet also decided to trade the American claim to Texas (which lay within the natural boundaries of the Louisiana Purchase) for the territory to the Perdido. The United States would offer a neutral zone in the west for an eastern boundary at the Apalachicola River and money for the cession of all of East Florida. The Mobile Act appeared in the newspapers in early March and brought a vigorous Spanish protest. For more than a decade, Spain refused to recognize the validity of the Louisiana Purchase. At the Congress of Vienna, Spanish diplomats asked the British to help them recover the territory. Spain only reluctantly conceded the purchase in the Adams-Onís Treaty of 1819.

The French government was usually willing to discuss West Florida but only with a lot more money changing hands. In the fall of 1804, Marbois recommended that the United States offer sixty million francs ($11,250,000) to Spain, which would come back to France as subsidies under the terms of the Franco-Spanish alliance. The administration found France's attitude perplexing. Jefferson and Madison expected a reflexive French friendship and found only opposition. Jefferson needed France to bully Spain for him. In August 1805 Jefferson returned to the plan of 1803, to scare France by seeking a British alliance. Jefferson characteristically overvalued American friendship. He was willing to gamble that the mere prospect of an Anglo-American alliance would spur France to force Spain to give up West Florida. Madison generally shared Jefferson's assumptions but did not think the plan would work. It was one thing to seek an alliance in early 1803, when war was only a possibility. Now that the war resumed, Great Britain wanted one thing from the United States—American acceptance of the British interpretation of maritime law. If Napoleon refused to budge, the United States would be stuck. Jefferson assumed that European war would work in America's favor and that every belligerent would act to ensure that the United States did not join one side or the other.

In 1805 John Armstrong replaced Livingston as minister to France. Like Livingston, Armstrong was hampered by his lack of French. He suspected, not without justification, that Talleyrand hoped to use the West Florida controversy as a money-making scheme. On September 14, 1805, an unnamed Frenchman gave Armstrong a draft proposal in Talleyrand's hand. The United States should offer $10 million and a boundary at the Colorado River of Texas in exchange for the cession of East and West Florida. Armstrong knocked the price down to $7 million and passed the offer on to Washington. Armstrong's dispatches arrived just as the administration was finalizing policy toward West Florida. The cabinet met on November 12 and agreed to offer Spain $5 million ($4 million of which would come back in spoliation claims) and give up the claim to the Rio Grande in exchange for the Floridas. The cabinet met again a week later, having received Armstrong's letter. The cabinet agreed to the Colorado River of Texas as the boundary, with a neutral zone of thirty leagues on either side. Jefferson's reaction to Talleyrand's thinly veiled bribe request was not outrage but parsimony. The president held the line at $5 million. Congress had to approve any sum, and Jefferson guided his lieutenants in the House of Representatives as to the bill he wanted. Not to be outdone in thrift, Congress passed the Two Million Dollar Act in March 1806, appropriating that amount for unspecified diplomatic purposes. John Randolph of Roanoke turned on the president and opposed any appropriation, joined by a dwindling band of Federalists. The money, Randolph believed, was for one of two purposes. Either it was to pay Spain for land the United States already owned or to bribe France to force Spain to give up the Floridas. The first was bad business. The second was poor morality in a republic.

By the time of the Two Million Dollar Act, the maritime crisis caused by the Anglo-French war overtook the Floridas as the main diplomatic problem. The return of war in May 1803 naturally brought the war to the Atlantic and put American commerce between the British hammer and the French anvil. Jefferson always assumed that periodic European warfare would benefit the United States. Each nation would need American supplies and would make any concessions to maintain the flow of American trade. But Jefferson, along with most other American statesmen, had formed this opinion in the classical balance of power age. The wars of the French Revolution were not about jockeying for position; they were about the destruction of one regime or the other. By the time of the Napoleonic wars, they were less about ideology and more about Napoleon conquering everything in his path and Great Britain trying to stop him. Such a war left no room for neutral trade. Henry Adams argued that the British attitude toward the United States was a combination of contempt and dread for the future, "that America was biding her time, that she expected to become a giant."[11] To Jefferson, the United States was already an economic giant that could impose its will on the Old World.

## Jefferson and The War in Europe

Madison's instructions to James Monroe as minister to Great Britain, dated January 5, 1804, laid out the issues that would bedevil Anglo-American relations for the next decade. Monroe was to seek a comprehensive settlement, on American terms, on the issues of impressment, neutral trade (including colonial trade), and blockades. None of these issues was new. Impressment went back to the colonial era. The wooden wall was always Great Britain's primary means of defense, and that wall required sailors to man it. The captain of a shorthanded vessel might send a press gang ashore to round up able-bodied men to serve, willingly or not. Desertion was the main reason for the loss of sailors, pay and conditions for common sailors on warships being poor. Often a shore leave party would come back with fewer sailors than when it began. Those deserters would wait for an American merchantman, whose selling points were higher pay and fewer floggings. The British also considered British subjects who immigrated to the United States deserters. They did not believe that American naturalization removed an obligation to a citizen's nation of birth. A substantial amount of opinion on both sides of the Atlantic held that naturalization added to, rather than subtracted from, one's obligations. The simple solution seemed to be to surrender deserters in exchange for the protection of naturalized Americans. That was impossible as a practical matter. In 1807 Gallatin submitted a report on the American merchant marine concluding that of the eighteen thousand sailors engaged in the foreign trade, nine thousand were deserters according to the more relaxed American rules. To surrender those sailors would cripple American commerce.

The sharp increase in the American carrying trade produced the need for more sailors. As France and Great Britain conquered neutral nations or destroyed their shipping, the United States assumed a greater share. The value of American freight was $6 million in 1790 but spiked to $40 million in 1807. The American share of the colonial reexport trade increased between four and ten times. Jefferson always believed that European war would increase American shipping but was always ambivalent about the prospect, fearing war and damage to American agriculture. To Jefferson, one comforting thought was that any such increase would be temporary. "On the restoration of peace in Europe that portion of the general carrying trade which had fallen to our share during the war was abridged by the returning competition of the belligerent powers," Jefferson remarked in his second annual message. "This was to be expected, and was just."[12]

The return of war in 1803 brought both colonial trade and neutral trade to the forefront. According to the Rule of 1756, the British decreed that trade illegal in peace could not be made legal in war. In 1800 the High Court of Admiralty opened a loophole in the *Polly* decision. The *Polly* was an American vessel out of Marblehead carrying fish to Bilbao. It was seized in October 1799 and found to be carrying sugar from Havana. The admiralty court in Halifax ruled that the cargo did not violate the Rule of 1756. The king's counsel argued that the stop in Marblehead was an attempt to evade British restrictions and appealed the case to London. On February 5, 1800, Sir William Scott ruled that the crown had to prove that a shipowner intended to skirt the law and that the evidence in the *Polly* case was inconclusive. The *Polly* decision did not invalidate the Rule of 1756 but did open the possibility of a broken voyage—that is, making a stop in the United States on the way from a colonial port to a European port.

The Lords Commissioners of Appeals closed that loophole with the *Essex* decision in 1805. In 1799 the *Essex*, an American brig, was carrying wine from Barcelona to Salem. From there the *Essex* set sail for Havana but was captured by a British vessel. The admiralty court on New Providence condemned the vessel as a prize. In May 1805 (the exact date is not certain), Sir William Grant ruled that the shipowner, rather than the government, had the burden of proof. Grant resumed a strict interpretation of the Rule of 1756 and of the doctrine of continuous voyage, that a trip from a colonial port to the mother country was one voyage, regardless of any stops along the way. Great Britain's expansive claims to regulate the colonial trade rested on its naval power. On October 21, 1805, the British fleet, led by Adm. Lord Horatio Nelson aboard the HMS *Victory*, destroyed a Franco-Spanish fleet off Trafalgar, on the coast of Spain. Although not the final naval engagement of the war, it ensured British naval supremacy for the next century.

The same day as Trafalgar, James Stephen published his pamphlet *War in Disguise; or the Frauds of the Neutral Flags*. Stephen was a friend of the Pitt ministry and wrote with Pitt's approval. Stephen's argument was simple: there was no such thing as neutral trade. The American flag was merely a cover for the French and Spanish colonial trades. Therefore, all American vessels engaged in the colonial trade should be seized and the Rule of 1756 strictly enforced. When Stephen's work reached the United States, Madison was ready with a pamphlet of his own. In January 1806 Madison published *An Examination of the British Doctrine, Which Subjects to Capture Neutral Trade, Not Open in Time of Peace*. In the language of Grotius and Vattel, Madison defended the idea that free ships make free goods and condemned the Rule of 1756 as having no validity in the law of nations. Even the British themselves, he pointed out, did not universally apply the rule. Madison believed that Great Britain's real object was a complete monopoly of the West Indian trade and that its appeal to the law was merely a cover for the forcible removal of the United States, the last obstacle to near absolute British maritime supremacy. He was right but chose the wrong target. Madison answered Stephen but in the end had no answer for Nelson.

Jefferson, Madison, and a majority of the Republicans believed that commercial coercion was a sufficient answer to Nelson and pursued it almost to the exclusion of other means of defense. On March 5, 1806, Pennsylvania Republican Andrew Gregg introduced a bill in the House of Representatives to cut off all British imports to the United States in retaliation for the *Essex* decision. Gregg spoke of nonimportation as a strategy without risk. Great Britain needed the American market too much to risk losing it. Federalists considered the bill useless. Gregg's fellow northern Republicans, who wanted to protect the carrying trade, joined him. Southern Republicans did not. For twenty years the southerners regarded the carrying trade as the particular interest of New England and were not willing to risk their profits from exports to Great Britain to protect it. John Randolph of Roanoke, who broke with Jefferson over the Two Million Dollar Act, led the charge against both the nonimportation bill and the carrying trade itself. Randolph considered the colonial trade dishonest and would not risk war to defend "this mushroom, this fungus of war."[13] Jefferson could not have welcomed Randolph's remarks, as they reflected his own private convictions, upon which the president did not have the luxury to act. Randolph precisely identified the ideological box in which the president found himself. Jefferson asserted a theoretical right to the carrying and colonial trades but preferred that Americans not exercise those rights too much, for fear that commerce may overtake agriculture. In April Congress passed a limited nonimportation that would take effect on November 15, 1806. The watered-down act was designed primarily to spur the diplomatic process.

The third problem in Anglo-American relations—the legality of blockades—was also of long standing. Despite having the largest navy in the world, Great Britain never had enough ships to seal off every enemy port. The British regarded a reasonable possibility of capture as sufficient to make a blockade effective. The

Jefferson administration considered only a reasonable certainty of capture as meeting the legal standard. Anything else was a mere "paper blockade." For Americans, the most egregious case of a paper blockade came in the Order-in-Council of May 16, 1806. The order, nicknamed the Fox blockade after foreign minister Charles James Fox, placed Europe from Brest in the west to the Elbe River in the east under blockade. However, it would only be enforced from the Seine River to Ostend. Vessels not carrying contraband or enemy goods, and not bound for another enemy port, could call upon the ports of the northern coast. Fox intended the act to clarify the position of neutrals and allow some leeway for neutral trade, but Monroe saw it as another assault on American trade.

The prospect of conflict between the United States and Great Britain gave new life to the West Florida question. Armstrong continued to negotiate with the unnamed Frenchman who approached him in the fall. However, Florida was a low priority for Napoleon, who preferred to let Spain and the United States bid for French friendship while he dealt with the eastern front. While Florida was the main issue between Washington and Madrid, the West was a more immediate flashpoint. The natural boundaries of Louisiana—that is, the headwaters of each tributary of the Mississippi—placed Texas within the American claim. This was an issue in American diplomacy for the next forty years. Spain did not recognize the validity of the Louisiana Purchase, let alone the American claim to Texas. Jefferson pushed for the extreme claim at the Rio Grande, a stance likely to embroil local commanders. In February 1806 an army of fifteen hundred Americans chased a Spanish garrison off the Sabine River. Lt. Col. Simón de Herrera, the governor of Nueva León, built up Spanish defenses in east Texas in June 1806 in preparation for war with the United States. Gen. James Wilkinson commanded an army about as large, but according to some it was ten times larger. On November 4, 1806, Herrera and Wilkinson made an agreement sanctioned by neither nation's government. Herrera moved his troops west of the Sabine, while Wilkinson pulled back east of the Red and Calcasieu Rivers. That left a lawless no-man's-land between the United States and Spanish territory.

Jefferson expected war with Spain by the middle of 1806. Spanish intransigence had turned him into an aggressive saber-rattler. Jefferson's Spanish policy was based on two assumptions: that the Spanish empire was on the verge of collapse and that France would act as the friend of the United States. The first was true;

the second was not. In May 1807 Madison wrote Armstrong that only the Spanish cession of the Floridas would prevent a war. Armstrong presented a draft agreement to the French government in June. Armstrong proposed to make the Mississippi the eastern boundary of Louisiana and the Rio Grande the western boundary. The United States would trade the territory between the Colorado River of Texas and the Rio Grande for West Florida between the Mississippi and St. Mark's River. If Spain ceded East and West Florida, the United States would pay Spain $5 million and accept the Sabine River as the western boundary of Louisiana. The United States would offer an additional $2 million for the Colorado River of Texas as the western boundary. This proposal, like the others, went nowhere.

It was Jefferson's misfortune to see the triumph of British naval power and the expiration of the Jay Treaty coincide. The Pitt ministry hoped to renew the treaty, and the Jefferson administration wanted to replace it with something better. On April 12, 1804, Lord Hawkesbury proposed to make the Jay Treaty the basis for negotiations. Monroe rejected the offer. In large measure the United States depended on French military pressure on Great Britain to produce a settlement. France crushed an Austro-Russian army at Austerlitz on December 2, 1805, once again knocking Austria out of the war. The defeat only added to the strain on Pitt, and on January 23, 1806, the prime minister died. He was replaced by a coalition nicknamed "The Ministry of All the Talents," led by Baron Grenville. Grenville's partner was Charles James Fox, now the foreign secretary, and a statesman with a thirty-year record as a friend to America. Fox was eager to reach a settlement with the United States. He had the Whigs and the manufacturing interests on his side. However, there was always a limit to pro-American sentiment, and that limit was the military necessity of defeating Napoleon.

Jefferson expected a settlement on American terms. He wrote Monroe in May outlining policy. It was equal parts friendship and bluster. "No two countries upon earth have so many points of common interest and friendship; and their rulers must be great bunglers indeed if with such dispositions they break them asunder," Jefferson wrote. He quickly changed his tone to threats. Coming off the Tripolitan War, Jefferson believed he could credibly threaten the British at sea. "We have the seamen and materials for fifty ships of the line and half that number of frigates; and if France were to give us the money and England the disposition to equip them, they would give to England serious proofs of the stock from which we are sprung, and the school in which they have been taught, and added to the efforts of the immensity of seacoast lately united under one Power would leave the state of the ocean no longer problematical."[14]

Before sending the final instructions, Jefferson appointed William Pinkney to assist Monroe. Pinkney was a Baltimore lawyer and particularly well versed in maritime issues. Secretary of State Madison issued formal instructions on May 17 and had a long list of demands. Madison argued that the British should take no offense at the nonimportation bill, claiming it was a measure to promote American manufacturing. That was a common Madison ploy. The most important issue was impressment, which should precede all other matters. The administration was willing to accept a specific prohibition of seizure on the high seas alone. Next, the administration wanted a limited contraband list that excluded ships' stores. In a related issue, the administration sought a treaty that recognized the doctrine that free ships made free goods, which should be easier if France and Russia pushed for it as well. Furthermore, Monroe and Pinkney should seek a renunciation of the Rule of 1756. Finally, the Americans were charged with ending the practice of paper blockades. The United States would offer most-favored-nation status in return for greater access for American ships to the British West Indian trade.[15]

Jefferson thus offered nothing and asked for everything. The instructions mark the consistency of Jefferson's diplomacy throughout his career. Twenty years before, Jefferson expected that friendship and the logic of free trade would lead to the dissolution of the French tobacco monopoly. In 1806 he assumed the same economic forces would lead the British to dismantle their maritime system. Most historians correctly observe that Jefferson overvalued American trade. He always assumed that the West India planters and manufacturing interest would trump the shipping interest. There is, however, a deeper reason for Jefferson's overreliance on economic coercion. If Jefferson was right, the United States could avoid resorting to a military establishment that might threaten republican government. If Jefferson was wrong, his system of republican diplomacy was impossible, and the United States could not avoid the fate of all republics. Jefferson believed in economic coercion because he had to.

Pinkney joined Monroe in London at the end of June. Their hopes for a quick agreement were soon dashed. Fox's illness delayed the start of negotiations, which began on August 23. Fox died on September 13 and was replaced by Charles Grey, Viscount Howick. Jefferson despaired of success when he heard the news. The British were represented by Henry Richard Vassal, Lord Holland, and William Eden, now Lord Auckland. Holland was Fox's favorite nephew and represented his views. For thirty years Eden had stood guard over the empire and the maritime system. The Grenville ministry wanted a treaty that left Great Britain's maritime claims intact and eliminated the drawback—the American practice of refunding import duties on colonial goods if those goods were reexported soon after. On September 11, 1806, Monroe and Pinkney reported that negotiations had hit a wall over impressment.[16]

Monroe and Pinkney decided to continue with a commercial agreement even without one on impressment. They were nearly rewarded for their faith. Lord Holland was prepared to trade impressment on the high seas for an American promise to give up deserters. Before Gallatin's report on the merchant marine, it seemed feasible. After an exchange of draft proposals, Great Britain asserted the right to pursue deserters on the high seas but agreed to be careful not to impress Americans. The November 5 British project seemed to argue that was impossible. Holland and Auckland advised dropping impressment and moving on to the commercial treaty. On November 11 Monroe and Pinkney notified Madison of their decision to go forward without a settlement on impressment. The two believed that "a satisfactory agreement may be obtained of many of the great points," despite a failure to resolve impressment. Were impressment the only issue, the Americans would have broken off negotiations, but although it was the most important issue, commercial issues required attention. Monroe and Pinkney expressed optimism that they might reach a settlement on blockades and the colonial trade, both in India and the West Indies.[17]

Negotiations resumed their fitful course. On December 6 the commissioners agreed to colonial trade under the *Polly* formula with a limited drawback (a refund on import duties if goods were reexported soon after importation). Soon after, the British learned of the monkey wrench Napoleon had thrown into the works. A French army destroyed a Prussian army at Jena on October 14, ending the Fourth Coalition and removing Prussia from the war. Napoleon marched triumphantly into Berlin nearly two weeks later. French power had no rival west of Russia, and the Hanseatic towns of the north of Germany, as well as the North Sea coast, lay at Napoleon's command. The emperor then closed the ring on Great Britain by issuing the Berlin Decree on November 21, 1806. It was the first building block of Napoleon's Continental System—an attempt to turn Europe into a self-contained economic system, to the exclusion of Great Britain. Napoleon placed the British Isles in a state of blockade. With little naval power, it was a blockade more paper than anything Pitt or Fox could have imagined. All British subjects in French-controlled territory were considered prisoners and their property liable to seizure. All British goods were to be lawful prize, and all vessels carrying goods from the British colonies would be banned from continental ports.

The Berlin Decree had an immediate effect on Anglo-American negotiations. The British proposed to wait for American reaction to the Berlin Decree. Monroe and Pinkney protested that the United States would oppose it. The Americans agreed to a separate statement in which Great Britain reserved the right to retaliate against France. On December 31, 1806, the two sides concluded the Monroe-Pinkney Treaty. Like the Jay Treaty, it would run for ten years after ratification and granted most-favored-nation status. It renewed American trade in the East Indies, with the proviso that American vessels not engage in the coasting trade. Great Britain allowed colonial trade under the *Polly* decision as long as it did not involve trade with a blockaded port. Most of the treaty marked a retreat from Monroe and Pinkney's instructions and certainly a retreat from Jefferson's ideal, adding ships' stores to the contraband list. The treaty made no mention of impressment.[18] Monroe and Pinkney knew the treaty would be a hard sell in Washington and explained their reasons for signing it in a dispatch to Madison on January 3, 1807. Although the British would not officially give up impressment and the right of search, Monroe and Pinkney expressed the hope that "its practice would, nevertheless, be essentially if not completely abandoned." The American commissioners also explained that the Berlin Decree had eliminated any chances of a more comprehensive or favorable settlement.[19] Essentially, Monroe and Pinkney did what Jay did. They accepted the framework of British maritime policy as fixed and sought moderation within it. The British read the treaty as a tacit acceptance of the Rule of 1756. On January 7, 1807, the cabinet issued an Order-in-Council that barred neutral vessels engaging in trade between French or allied ports. This was the original application of the Rule of 1756.

The final treaty arrived in Washington in March. Jefferson would not sign a repeat of the Jay Treaty. The cabinet met on March 17 and agreed not to send the treaty to the Senate. The news reached London in April. Madison sent a detailed critique of the treaty to Monroe and Pinkney on May 20, 1807. First, the British should explicitly reject impressment. The East India article was a step down from the Jay Treaty. The colonial trade article was unacceptable. Madison and Jefferson believed that Great Britain, rather than the United States, should make concessions. Madison argued that Great Britain's colonies depended on American supplies; its navy might soon be in the same position. Great Britain would not dare resort to war. It might have temporarily gained by seizing American commerce, but it would lose the value of the United States as a neutral shipper, for which "she could find no substitute in distributing her manufactures, and ever her fish to their necessary markets, and in obtaining the returns which she wants."[20]

Like the Jay Treaty, the Monroe-Pinkney Treaty was not a triumph, but Monroe did not believe a better treaty obtainable. He later defended the treaty as a temporary expedient. He sought to "get out of the general scrape on the best terms we could" and seek better terms later if possible.[21] Monroe remained at his post until the end of the year, when he was replaced by Pinkney. Monroe was the scapegoat. He was a loyal Jeffersonian whose great crime was seeing reality more clearly than his superiors. The British knew that Jefferson's threat to build fifty ships of the line was hollow. Without a fleet in the way, the British could ignore economic threats. Jefferson might have used the Monroe-Pinkney Treaty the way Washington used the Jay Treaty—as a means of restoring normal relations and buying time. Jefferson instead believed that the United States had the advantage.

## The *Chesapeake* and the Embargo

By April the opportunity for agreement had passed. The Grenville ministry fell in March 1807, having resigned over the king's refusal to accept a limited Catholic emancipation bill for Ireland. The new ministry, under the Duke of Portland, had a more anti-American cast. George Canning, the foreign minister, was probably the most anti-American foreign minister of the period. Canning did not want a war but almost got one as a result of the *Chesapeake* incident. The *Chesapeake* was a forty-gun American frigate that was to form a squadron with the *Wasp*, commanded by Cdre. James Barron, and relieve the *Constitution* and the *Enterprise* on the Mediterranean station. Secretary of the Navy Robert Smith ordered Barron to make ready in January 1807, and the *Chesapeake* went to be refit in Norfolk.

In March the British ships *Halifax* and *Melampus* were anchored in Lynnhaven Bay, off Norfolk. Despite the endemic tension between the United States and Great Britain, British ships frequently put in to American ports for supplies and shore leave. A nearby American port was a great temptation for British subjects to look for a better offer and for American prisoners to escape. Five escaped from the *Melampus*, followed by five more from the *Halifax*. The sailors—some deserters and some impressed Americans—signed on with the *Chesapeake*.

The sight of British sailors deserting and walking through Norfolk to seek other employment was too much for Vice Adm. Sir George Cranfield Berkeley, commander of the North American squadron. He issued a circular to his commanders on June 1, directing any vessel that sighted the *Chesapeake* to board her and search for deserters. At nine in the morning of June 22, the *Chesapeake* set sail for its Mediterranean assignment. She passed the *Bellona* and *Melampus*. Nothing seemed amiss. Around 3:30, the fifty-gun *Leopard*, commanded by Capt. Salusbury Humphreys, hailed the *Chesapeake*. The *Leopard* was ready for battle. The *Chesapeake* was not. Luggage and supplies were strewn on the deck, while men on sick call lay in hammocks. There was nothing unusual about the *Leopard*'s hail, so Barron did not call his men to quarters. Humphreys sent an officer with Berkeley's circular to search the *Chesapeake*. Barron refused the British permission to board. Around 4:30 the *Leopard* fired a warning shot at the *Chesapeake*, and within fifteen minutes it was over. The *Leopard* had crippled the unprepared *Chesapeake*, killing three and wounding eighteen others, and Barron struck his colors. Barron considered his ship the *Leopard*'s prize, but Humphreys was interested only in recovering deserters. He took four sailors. One, Jenkin Ratford, was British-born and had deserted from the *Halifax*. He was later hanged for desertion. Two were black sailors who had enlisted on British ships. The last was an American who had been impressed on the *Melampus*.

The British had crossed a bright red line by attacking an American warship. Jefferson ordered British warships out of American ports on July 2. The same day, a mass meeting in New York City condemned the attack and promised Jefferson its support. There is something of a parallel between the approach of the War of 1812 and the approach of American entry into World War I a century later. Both were primarily naval crises, and in both cases the president did not choose the obvious moment to go to war. The nation was in an uproar over the *Chesapeake* as it would be over the *Lusitania* in 1915. If Jefferson wanted a war, Congress would have granted it. Yet, as Bradford Perkins put it, "Jefferson chose to play the part of a damper rather than a bellows."[22]

First, Jefferson sought an immediate redress for the attack on the *Chesapeake*. Madison issued new instructions to Monroe on July 6. The British must disavow the attack, apologize, and return the sailors taken prior to any other agreement. Next, the United States demanded an end to impressment from American vessels. This demand had already been refused by a ministry that wanted a settlement, and now Monroe faced a more hostile one. Monroe wrote to Canning on September 7. Settlement required four actions: the return of the sailors from the *Chesapeake*, punishment of Captain Humphreys, renunciation of impressment from American private vessels, and a new mission to the United States. Monroe considered the *Chesapeake* incident as merely the logical extension of the British claim to the right of search. Canning did not want war with the United States and was willing to meet Monroe part way. He disavowed the attack on the *Chesapeake* and any claim to take deserters off neutral warships but was willing to send a special envoy, George H. Rose. That was as far as the foreign minister would go. He instructed Rose to keep the *Chesapeake* and impressment from merchant vessels separate issues and to seek the removal of Jefferson's proclamation of July 2.

By the summer of 1807, the defense of neutral rights seemed a losing battle, with both belligerents working to put neutrality out of legal existence. France began to enforce the Continental System more vigorously against American ships, as Napoleon moved to close its last loophole. On June 25 the emperor and Tsar Alexander I of Russia met at Tilsit. Alexander agreed to a formal alliance and to join the Continental System in a secret treaty of July 7. The two powers would also encourage the neutral nations of the north to close the Baltic to British vessels. But the British struck first. In August, the Portland ministry sent Francis Jackson to accompany the British fleet and deliver an ultimatum to the Danish government to give up its fleet. When the Danes refused, the British fleet bombarded Copenhagen. Denmark capitulated on September 6, trading its fleet for a British withdrawal and a return of prisoners. Lord Hawkesbury suggested a similar diplomatic mission be sent to the United States.

How could the United States avoid the fate of Copenhagen? By 1806 and 1807, many began to advocate an embargo of American ships. Armstrong would evacuate the sea until peace returned to Europe. Elbridge Gerry recommended an embargo as a defensive measure, to protect American ships, sailors, and goods from capture. By the late summer and early fall of 1807, Jefferson appeared to lean toward war with Great Britain. The practical problem was that Jefferson's ideological approach to diplomacy prohibited the normal military preparations. Jefferson believed that Great Britain's mounting troubles would do the work of a costly and politically dangerous military establishment. The president recognized, with some discomfort, that he was in the position of cheering Napoleon's conquests.

Napoleon did provide a service in tying up the British military, which Jefferson believed would prevent a full British invasion of the United States. Jefferson would not try to match the British on the high seas. Rather, he would cut off British trade and arm merchant vessels. If that did not work, Jefferson would invade Canada, Great Britain's weak point. Jefferson expected an easy conquest, and such a policy would avoid the "ruinous folly of a navy."[23] Secretary of the Treasury Albert Gallatin feared that war was inevitable and that there was no way to pay for it. He tended to moderate Jefferson's newfound enthusiasm for war. In October the cabinet opposed Jefferson's draft of the annual message as too belligerent. In the message issued to Congress on October 27, Jefferson noted the failure of the Monroe and Pinkney negotiations and the attack on the *Chesapeake*. He did not suggest a course of action but said he believed the British would soon reply to American demands for reparation.

As Jefferson and Congress groped toward a new British policy, the noose around neutral trade drew tighter. The British government issued three Orders-in-Council on November 11, 1807. The most important for the United States was the order allowing neutral trade with enemy ports if the neutral vessel secured a license from London. What appeared to be a loophole in the continental blockade was in fact an effort to turn all neutral trade into reflagged British trade. In response Napoleon issued the Milan Decree on December 17. Any neutral nation that put into a British port, paid a duty in Great Britain, or submitted to examination would be considered British and subject to seizure and sale as a prize. "The Orders in Council of Great Britain necessitated my Milan Decree; thenceforth there were no more neutrals," the emperor explained.[24]

While the belligerents moved against neutral trade, Jefferson backed away from war. By December Jefferson decided on an embargo but went back and forth over whether it was offensive or defensive. The long-delayed nonimportation act of 1806, postponed from November 15, 1806, went into effect on December 14, 1807. At the same time, Washington learned that both France and Great Britain were planning measures against American shipping. The cabinet framed an embargo policy on December 16 and sent it to Congress on December 18. Congress approved the Embargo Act on December 21, and the president signed it into law the next day. It passed the House by a two-to-one margin. The act stated that no American vessels could depart for foreign ports. There was no time limit, but Jefferson did not expect it would take long to have an effect.

However, there was no specific punishment for violation or any means established to enforce it. Even its purpose was unclear. Jefferson often spoke of it as a defensive measure. Madison always saw the Embargo as offensive and defensive, and so defended it in the *National Intelligencer*, the most important Washington newspaper. He argued that the Embargo would deny Great Britain and France a carrier of colonial goods. "The ocean presents a field where no harvest is to be reaped but that of danger, of spoliation and of disgrace," Madison wrote in one essay.[25] That essay provides a clue to both Jefferson's and Madison's thinking. Like most, both tended to see the world through localist eyes, and they thought of the United States as a big Virginia. Jefferson and Madison considered agriculture almost indestructible. Everyone needed food. The carrying trade was a luxury; it was not vital to get American produce from one point to the next. For more than twenty years, Jefferson feared the American pursuit of the carrying trade would lead exactly where it did, to the brink of war with Great Britain. The Embargo would reorient the American economy back toward agriculture where it belonged.[26]

The Embargo was a complete disaster at home. Congress passed four subsequent acts, on January 9, March 12, and April 25, 1808, and on January 9, 1809, to establish penalties and seal the gaps through which trade escaped. The January 9, 1808, act established duties to ensure that coasting and fishing vessels did not engage in the overseas trade. The March 12 act banned exportation to Canada and established duties on foreign vessels. The April 25 act required presidential approval of voyages to the borderlands and allowed the president to suspend the Embargo under certain circumstances. The January 9, 1809, act was the most onerous. Unloading goods required presidential permission. Authorities had the right to arrest those traveling border roads with merchandise. Those arrested had to prove their innocence, rather than the government prove their guilt. Jefferson would have preferred to go further. He wanted to use the army to enforce the Embargo on the borders and explored charging violators with treason. It was all part of the contradiction that was Jefferson—that the author of the Kentucky Resolutions would pursue a policy that would give the Federalists of 1798 pause. But Jefferson could not plug all of the leaks. New Englanders led the way in evading the Embargo, often sending wagonloads of goods into Quebec for shipment across the Atlantic. In such places as Maine, where the boundary had little meaning, the Embargo had none.

France was a secondary target of the Embargo. Jefferson might have expected Napoleon to react to the loss of the chief middleman in the colonial trade or at least take the opportunity to stir up trouble between the United States and Great Britain. He did neither. Napoleon issued the Bayonne Decree on April 17, 1808, which stated that all American vessels in France were presumed to be British, as the Embargo outlawed American shipping. Armstrong tried in vain to change France's policy. In September 1808 the French government considered a broad policy of seizing all American vessels in French ports and arresting all Americans in Europe. By the fall, the emperor relented on a harsh policy toward the United States, accepting the Embargo as part of the Continental System.

The Embargo so consumed the Jefferson administration that he was unable to take advantage of an opportunity Napoleon handed him. In March 1808 Prince Ferdinand forced his father, Charles IV, off the Spanish throne. Napoleon took advantage of Spain's chaos by forcing both to renounce their claims. A month later, Napoleon planted his brother Joseph on the Spanish throne. Partisans of Charles IV and Ferdinand joined forces. In the long run, Spain helped lead to Napoleon's downfall by allowing the British a place to land on the continent. Local juntas in Spanish America refused to follow Joseph Bonaparte. On October 22, 1808, Jefferson's cabinet agreed to seek out "influential persons" in Cuba and Mexico to be told that the United States was willing to see them remain in the Spanish Empire but was unwilling to see them conquered by France. Jefferson would not promise aid in the event of independence but intimated that the United States would prevent another power from conquering them. Jefferson was more explicit to Gov. William C. C. Claiborne of the Orleans Territory, telling him that the administration considered Cuban and Mexican interests the same as American. The continuing Anglo-American crisis prevented Jefferson from taking any other action.[27]

Great Britain was the main target of the embargo, but the action failed to force progress either in Washington or London. By the time Rose arrived in Washington, Jefferson was prepared to separate impressment from reparations for the *Chesapeake*, but not to revoke the July 2, 1807, decree. On February 7, 1808, Rose told Madison the United States should give up deserters. Madison replied that the British should give up impressment. The Rose negotiations were effectively over by March, and the focus of diplomatic action shifted to London. Like Monroe, Pinkney believed Great Britain's real target was American commerce, not France. If France repealed every decree, it would not necessarily change British policy. Madison's instructions to Pinkney of April 30, 1808, authorized him to promise that the United States would repeal the embargo against Great Britain if the government repealed its orders against American shipping. In several meetings with Canning in June and July, Pinkney hinted that if Great Britain repealed its orders and France did not, the United States would go to war with France. For Canning, as with most British statesmen, the embargo was proof the United States would not fight. An American war with France was as much a phantom as an American war with Great Britain. Canning did not even bother to deliver Pinkney's message to the king. Still, Pinkney held out hope for the embargo. In September he reported that British trade felt its effects and urged a vigorous enforcement. Madison agreed and reported to Pinkney the increase of American manufacturing in the absence of some British goods. Madison expected Pinkney would inform Canning of that development. Madison's threat of American manufacturing was no more real than Jefferson's threat to build ships of the line. Jefferson and Madison always assumed that Great Britain would wake up to its economic interests before American manufacturing was too far advanced.

Jefferson admitted defeat in his final annual message. "This candid and liberal experiment having thus failed, and no other event having occurred on which a suspension of the Embargo by the Executive was authorized, it necessarily remains in the extent originally given it," Jefferson told Congress. He defended the measure as having "frustrated those usurpations and spoliations which, if resisted, involved war; if submitted to, sacrificed a vital principle of our national independence."[28] Madison still favored a version of the embargo. Gallatin favored repeal and sent a letter to that effect to George Washington Campbell, a Tennessee Republican and chairman of the House Committee on Foreign Affairs. The formal movement for repeal began on January 24, 1809. Wilson Cary Nicholas of Virginia moved to replace the embargo with war at a future date. Dissident Republicans from the North led the charge for repeal. On February 4, Congress approved March 4 as the date the embargo expired. To replace it, Congress passed a non-intercourse act on February 27, which barred French and British vessels from American ports for one year as of May 20, 1809.

Jefferson's presidency divides neatly in half. The first term was a story of success; the second a dismal failure. Jefferson doubled the size of the nation and secured a vital port with the Louisiana Purchase. He signed a treaty with Tripoli better than any previous treaty with a Barbary power. In his second term he concocted unworkable plans to gain West Florida and sacrificed commerce—and nearly the union and the rule of law—in pursuit of his ideal diplomacy toward Great Britain. Jefferson was successful when he abandoned his ideological preferences. The Louisiana Purchase required a broad construction of the treaty power of the sort the Republicans rejected in the Jay Treaty debate. Jefferson admitted that the Barbary powers were outside his normal framework of diplomacy. The treaty with Tripoli required a navy, an undeclared war, and a somewhat covert operation. The second term was a full test of Jeffersonian diplomacy. He believed France would act as a friend of the United States and bully Spain out of West Florida. Jefferson also believed that the struggle between France and Great Britain would improve, rather than worsen, the chances for using European conflict for the benefit of the United States and for carrying out the plan of 1776. The plan never really worked as intended, and the Napoleonic Wars made it less likely to succeed. For Jefferson the plan of 1776 was vital to a diplomacy compatible with republican government, and the embargo was the logical conclusion. It backfired at home and was useless abroad. Jefferson never acknowledged that his broader vision had failed. Failure was always due to some external factor, which Jefferson believed would eventually be overcome. One could argue that Jefferson left his successor, James Madison, a mess. But Madison had always been at Jefferson's side, and the mess was his handiwork as well.

CHAPTER 5

# Mr. Madison's Wars

Few presidential transitions went as smoothly as that from Thomas Jefferson to James Madison. The two had been political partners for thirty-five years and had no significant philosophical differences. Their main difference was one of temperament. Madison was the more systematic political thinker. He had spent most of his political career crafting a theory of republicanism encompassing the nation's government and diplomacy. His vision was largely the same as Jefferson's but with the mechanics more carefully defined. Europe would likely be at war and in need of American trade. Great Britain was economically dependent on the United States. Spain was militarily weak and would have to retreat in the face of American expansion. France would act as the friend of the United States, in strategic if not political terms. Madison was not prone to Jefferson's grand contradictions, but Madison's presidency did have its ironies. As a member of Congress, Madison was the most forceful advocate for the primacy of Congress in foreign policy. Madison warned that the executive might seek war as a means of aggrandizement and doom the republic to the fate of Rome. As president, Madison presided over four wars: the War of 1812, the war against the Shawnees, the Patriot War in East Florida, and the 1815 Algerine war. The War of 1812 (which eventually included the Shawnee war) flowed from Madison's policies, both in its causes and its execution. The Patriot War was the result of Madison's failure to control his agents, who pushed a more ambitious policy than the president favored. The Algerine War, like Jefferson's Tripolitan War, fell outside of the normal bounds of Republican diplomacy.

Madison suffered from two disadvantages as president. He did not enjoy the overwhelming majority in Congress the Republicans held under Jefferson nor

Jefferson's authority over the party. Republican dissidents made Madison the target of the wrath they could not safely direct at Jefferson. The "Invisibles"—a Republican faction led by William Branch Giles of Virginia, Samuel Smith of Maryland, and Michael Leib of Pennsylvania—thwarted Madison's first personnel move. Madison planned to appoint Albert Gallatin secretary of state and, to blunt opposition, appoint Robert Smith, Samuel's brother, secretary of the treasury. The Invisibles blocked Gallatin, prompting Madison to leave him where he was and appoint Robert Smith secretary of state. Madison did most of Smith's work. Madison retained Jefferson's diplomatic corps, including William Pinkney in London and John Armstrong in Paris. The biggest change came with the appointment of John Quincy Adams as minister to Russia in June 1809. He was one of the few Americans with any expertise on Russia, having served as Francis Dana's secretary from 1781 to 1783. Adams was a nationalist at odds with the sectionalism of New England Federalism and supported the Louisiana Purchase and the Embargo Act.

## The Search for a Policy

Relations with Great Britain were where Madison left them as secretary of state: stalled over impressment, the Orders-in-Council, and the *Chesapeake*. Madison was convinced that in another six months Great Britain would have given in to American demands. The embargo was now a political impossibility, as was any British retreat from its maritime system. Canning considered two items nonnegotiable: the recovery of deserters and the Rule of 1756. On January 23, 1809, Canning issued a new set of instructions to David Erskine, minister to Washington. The government was willing to settle the *Chesapeake* matter without reference to Jefferson's July 2, 1807, order and to repeal the orders of January and November 1807 as they applied to American vessels, under three conditions. The United States should remove restrictions on British commerce in American ports while keeping them in place against France, accept the Rule of 1756, and allow the British to seize any American vessels trading in ports governed by the Berlin and Milan Decrees.

Erskine was unique among British ministers to the United States in that he was friendly to the republic and hoped to reach a mutually satisfactory agreement. He knew the United States would not agree to Canning's demands and downplayed them in his negotiations with Smith. The first condition—the mutual lifting of restrictions—was easily accomplished. In lieu of a guarantee against France, which could be given only in a treaty or by act of Congress, Erskine accepted a presidential proclamation under the Non-Intercourse Act. Erskine intimated to Smith that by acceptance of the Rule of 1756, Canning meant the direct trade between France and its colonies. Smith replied that French trade was prohibited under the Non-Intercourse Act, and Erskine did not press the issue. The third condition was plainly inadmissible, and Erskine let it drop. Erskine issued a note on April 19, 1809, declaring that Great Britain would repeal the January and November 1807 orders as of June 10 in exchange for the American resumption of trade with Great Britain. The president accepted Erskine's offer because it fit what he expected to happen. Eventually Great Britain's economic weakness would lead to a settlement on American terms. Madison did not ask if Erskine's offer was official policy or his own initiative. The offer was too good to let pass. It was a pattern Madison would repeat.

American diplomats had a long and generally successful tradition of ignoring instructions. British diplomats were under tighter control. The agreement reached London on May 21. By then British policy had changed. The Order-in-Council of April 26, 1809, established a blockade from the Ems River to Italy. The license trade allowed under the November 1807 order was abolished with regard to blockaded ports. American ships were to be excluded from the French colonies. The Erskine agreement was incompatible with the new order, and on May 24 the cabinet formally rejected it. Erskine had violated his instructions and received little, from Canning's perspective, in return. There was no guarantee of American action against French trade and no American acceptance of the Rule of 1756. Canning was thinking ahead. The French colonial empire was down to Guadeloupe, but the fate of the Spanish empire was still in doubt, and he wanted to keep that wealth out of Napoleon's hands. More than a decade later, Canning would have the same fight with the Monroe administration. At bottom, he represented the shippers and was a staunch defender of the mercantile system. To Canning, an American flag on a merchantman was as a red flag to a bull.

Canning replaced Erskine with Francis Jackson, who had delivered the ultimatum to Copenhagen. The key issue, as always, was the Rule of 1756. Canning demanded an explicit acceptance of what he considered a normal part of the law of nations. Canning wanted a surrender, not a settlement. Rejection of the Erskine agreement reached Washington in July, and Madison reimposed non-intercourse on Great Britain on August 9. As soon as negotiations began, Jackson accused the administration of helping Erskine violate his instructions. Madison asked for Jackson to negotiate in writing and not in person at the State Department. This changed only the medium of Jackson's accusations, and Madison ordered negotiations ended on October 19.

The British had an open contempt for the United States, which made diplomacy simpler if not easier. French policy was more convoluted. French policy, like British, was driven by the necessities of war. Napoleon wanted the United States to declare war on Great Britain, and Napoleon needed to raise money for his army. This led to a dual policy of seeking American friendship and seizing American vessels. Madison's assumption of French friendship made Napoleon's policy seem more contradictory than it was. While the Austrian campaign was in doubt, Napoleon was willing to placate the United States. Napoleon's victory at Wagram knocked Austria out of the war and removed any urgency about cultivating the United States. By the end of 1809, Napoleon was more committed to the Continental System. He ordered the seizure of American vessels in Spanish ports on December 19. The chief difficulty between France and the United States was the disposition of American property seized by the French. Here the need for money outweighed the quest for an ally. Napoleon resolved the question of American property by issuing the Rambouillet Decree on March 23, 1810. All American vessels taken since May 20, 1809 (the date the Non-Importation Act was known in Paris), would be sold and the proceeds placed in an escrow account, pending final adjudication. In typical Napoleon fashion, he ordered the sale to begin long before the decree was published on May 14.

When Congress convened at the end of 1809, it faced the now annual ritual of framing a policy toward France and Great Britain to replace the one that had most recently failed. In January 1810 Nathaniel Macon, a North Carolina Republican, introduced a bill that would allow American vessels to sail anywhere and to import French and British goods. All French and British ships, public and private, were to be barred from American ports. In February the original bill passed the House 73–52. In the Senate, the Invisibles and the Federalists combined to remove the prohibition on French and British merchant ships. The House refused to accept the Senate version, and the original bill died in April. On April 16 John Taylor of

South Carolina introduced a new bill in the House, misnamed Macon's Bill No. 2. The bill removed all restrictions on American ships sailing abroad and on French and British merchant ships in American ports. If one power removed its restrictions on American shipping, the United States would impose non-intercourse on the other. Despite Republican efforts to alter the bill, Macon's Bill No. 2 became law on May 1, 1810. Sen. William Plumer of New Hampshire believed the bill passed merely because no other action was possible, arguing, "We cannot snatch the trident from George, or the thunder bolt from Napoleon." The only solution was to "stand still, wait events, & shape our course accordingly."[1] No one, including the president, held out any hope that the bill would change either French or British policy.

By July 27, 1810, news of Macon's Bill No. 2 arrived in France. On August 5 the foreign minister, Jean Champagny, Duc de Cadore, delivered a note to Armstrong, which became known as the Cadore letter. Cadore wrote that Napoleon promised to repeal the Berlin and Milan Decrees on November 1, with the proviso that Great Britain would repeal its orders or the United States should resume non-intercourse with Great Britain. Napoleon would prefer war to economic coercion.[2] Yet what Napoleon gave with one hand, he took away with the other. Also on August 5, at Trianon, the emperor ordered the proceeds from the seizure and sale of American vessels to be placed directly in the French treasury. Armstrong celebrated the Cadore letter as a great victory but soon began to have his doubts and asked Cadore for more explicit assurances of French actions. Barely a month after the Cadore letter, Armstrong expected that France would soon return to a full implementation of the Continental System.

The Cadore letter arrived in Washington on September 27. Madison accepted it as a true representation of French policy and informed Congress on November 2, 1810, that France had repealed the Berlin and Milan Decrees. The British had three months to repeal their orders. Madison accepted the Cadore letter for the same reason he accepted the Erskine agreement: his political system required it. Madison, like Jefferson before him, assumed France would act as a friend of the United States. France could inflict military damage on Great Britain that the United States could not, which would allow the United States to punish Great Britain economically. Commercial retaliation carried no threat to republican government. If France did not play the role Madison assigned it in his diplomatic and political machinery, a republican diplomacy was impossible.

## West Florida

Madison faced unfinished business in the Floridas as well as with France and Great Britain. He believed as much as Jefferson that West Florida belonged to the United States and that East Florida would be a valuable acquisition. Vicente Folch, the Spanish governor in Pensacola, was in contact with Gov. William C. C. Claiborne of the Orleans Territory, telling Claiborne he would not accept Napoleon's rule and that he was prepared to cede East and West Florida to the United States. Claiborne and his neighbor, Gov. David Holmes of the Mississippi Territory, were both active in forcing the issue in West Florida. Claiborne met the president in June 1810 and won approval for a plan to stir up a revolt among the Americans there. From Mississippi Holmes reported that Spanish authority in West Florida had disappeared. Secretary of State Smith advised Holmes to monitor West Florida and do whatever he could to determine its residents' true sentiment. Smith did not specify how Holmes should proceed. Andrew McMichael has argued that the circumstantial evidence points to both Holmes and Claiborne actively fomenting rebellion in West Florida.[3]

Many of the Americans in the Baton Rouge district needed no prompting. On July 25 sixteen delegates from four districts west of the Pearl River met at St. John's Plains. The convention decried the anarchy into which the province had fallen but proclaimed its loyalty to Ferdinand VII, as the majority was not ready for a formal break. Loyalty to Ferdinand was short-lived. On September 20 Philemon Thomas, commander of the Baton Rouge militia, intercepted a letter to Folch from Carlos de Lassus, the Spanish governor in Baton Rouge, requesting help. Three days later a party of Americans attacked and seized the fort at Baton Rouge. The convention declared independence on September 26 and asked for American assistance. On October 22 the president received a letter from Holmes containing the declaration of independence and plea for help. Fear of Spanish or British intervention forced Madison to act. After consulting with the cabinet, Madison issued a proclamation on October 27 ordering the annexation of territory to the Pearl River. Madison believed the American claim extended to the Perdido and more likely to the Apalachicola, but only the territory west of the Pearl had revolted. The proclamation remained secret until December 5. Claiborne occupied the territory to the Pearl on December 7, 1810.

Folch believed the only way to save Pensacola was to surrender West Florida and made that offer to Holmes on November 20. Folch backed away from his offer after defeating a small American force at Mobile on December 10. Folch's initial offer led Madison to formulate a policy for East Florida. On January 3, 1811, in a secret message to Congress, Madison asked for the authority to take possession of East Florida, warning Congress of the danger of intervention by a third power. Congress agreed, and on January 15, 1811, Madison signed what came to be known as the No Transfer Resolution. Congress permitted the president to annex East Florida (defined as the territory east of the Perdido and south of Georgia and the Mississippi Territory) if local authority should surrender it or to prevent a foreign power from possessing it. Madison appointed Indian agent John McKee and former Georgia governor George Mathews agents.

## Toward War

Progress in West Florida was not matched by similar progress with France or Great Britain. Armstrong left Paris with no remaining confidence in the Cadore letter. Jonathan Russell replaced Armstrong but as chargé rather than minister. In January 1811 Russell inquired after the fate of American vessels taken after November 1. Cadore's letter implied that the decrees had not been repealed on November 1 but had been by his reply on January 18. However, Cadore was waiting for the imposition of non-intercourse on Great Britain, which would take place on February 2 but would not be known in Paris for several weeks. French policy made William Pinkney's job in London more difficult. Pinkney continued the American protest against the Fox blockade as a paper blockade, which Americans considered a violation of the law of nations, and intimated that the French decrees had been repealed. His only evidence was Madison's proclamation, while the continued French seizure of American vessels proved the contrary was true.

In February 1811 Congress debated a new non-intercourse act against Great Britain. Macon's Bill No. 2 did not require additional congressional action; non-intercourse was automatically imposed on one power when the other repealed its ordinances against American shipping. Its passage suggests the majority of Republicans did not care about technicalities and took the opportunity to strike at Great Britain. It passed on February 28, and the Senate and president rapidly assented. The act barred British goods and ships from American ports but allowed American goods and vessels to sail out. The act also sanctioned the Cadore letter, declaring that Madison's proclamation of November 1810 would be proof of French repeal in American courts.

Madison signaled a change in policy toward Great Britain. Madison had dinner with Joseph Gales, the editor of the *National Intelligencer*, on April 13. The dinner discussion appeared in the April 16 issue. Gales reported that the negotiations to be conducted with Augustus John Foster, the new British minister, would fail. Great Britain would have to renounce the Orders-in-Council, the Rule of 1756, and impressment.[4] Madison's policy was clear by April. He intended to paper over differences with France and make demands on Great Britain. Monroe replaced Smith as secretary of state in March. By contrast he was inclined toward a compromise with Great Britain and grilled Louis-Barbé-Charles Sérurier, the French minister to the United States, about the Berlin and Milan Decrees. The British threat was always more direct. The British could seize American vessels anywhere, while France could take only those in French ports. On May 6, 1811, Secretary of the Navy Paul Hamilton ordered the USS *President* to sail out and defend American commerce. Ten days later the *President*, commanded by Cdre. John Rodgers, sighted a vessel believed to be the British frigate *Guerrière*. It was in fact the *Little Belt*, a sloop with half the *President*'s firepower. The *President* quickly defeated the *Little Belt*.

Foster arrived in Washington in July. He asked for reparations for the *Little Belt* and was summarily denied. Prime Minister Spencer Perceval ordered Foster to defend the Orders-in-Council. As long as Napoleon and the Berlin and Milan Decrees remained in place, Great Britain could not lower its wooden wall. If Foster hoped for more out of Monroe than Madison, he was soon disappointed. Foster protested American actions in the Floridas. Monroe defended the American claim. Within a month of his arrival, Foster's mission was effectively over. The only accomplishment was an agreement on compensation for the *Chesapeake*, reached on November 12, 1811.

Many Americans considered the nation to be in a two-front war with Great Britain. Westerners blamed the British for frontier trouble. British Indian policy was more opportunistic than anything else. By the fall of 1811, trouble reached a crisis point, brought by two Shawnee leaders, the warrior Tecumseh and his younger brother Lalawethika, a mystic. In April 1805 Lalawethika reported a revelation from the Master of Life and in August took his disciples to Greenville,

Ohio. In November he met with a delegation of Senecas, Shawnees, Wyandots, and Ottawas, and outlined his religious vision. Lalawethika told the assembled tribes the Master of Life commanded them to return to the old ways. The tribes should reject the tools and culture of the Americans. The Americans were not created by the Master of Life, but by the Great Serpent. Lalawethika took the name Tenskwatawa—translated as the Open Door—and was generally known as the Prophet. William Henry Harrison, the governor of the Indiana Territory, tried to talk the Delawares out of the Prophet's movement. The Prophet won more followers on June 16, 1806, when he told the Delawares he would make the sun stop. That day saw a total eclipse of the sun—information available in a farmer's almanac. In 1808 the Prophet convinced Harrison that his movement was not a threat, and Harrison sent food and other supplies. That April the Prophet left Greenville to establish a new settlement, Prophetstown, where the Wabash and Tippecanoe Rivers meet in what is now Indiana. At the same time, Tecumseh met with Matthew Elliott, the British superintendent for Indian affairs.

By the middle of 1809, Harrison had reversed position and moved against the Shawnees. He signed the Treaty of Fort Wayne with pro-American Miamis, Potowatamies, and Delawares on September 30, gaining three million acres of land. After Fort Wayne, Tecumseh turned his brother's religious movement into a political movement, planning to establish a pan-Indian confederation. After a tense confrontation with Harrison in August 1811, Tecumseh went south to recruit the Upper Creeks. Harrison determined to break up Prophetstown before Tecumseh returned and marched an army north on September 26. On November 6 the army was one mile from Prophetstown. The Shawnees struck first early the next morning, planning to kill Harrison and disrupt the army. The attack failed, and Harrison marched on the now abandoned settlement.

French opacity, open British hostility, and frontier trouble formed the backdrop for the Twelfth Congress, eventually known as the War Congress. Madison's third annual message, delivered November 5, 1811, was far more pessimistic that the one the year before announcing the repeal of the Berlin and Milan Decrees. Madison threw most of the blame on the British, noting that Great Britain had not repealed its orders. Yet he was forced to admit that France had offered no proof of a change in policy. He then turned back to the British, advising Congress to improve the nation's defenses.[5] Madison abandoned the pretense that relations with Great Britain were determined by relations with France. He fell back on the essential truths of Republican diplomacy, that Great Britain was the natural but vulnerable enemy of the United States and that France was the natural friend.

As Speaker of the House, Henry Clay of Kentucky took charge of translating the president's message into policy. Clay led a band of between twenty and thirty Republicans known as the War Hawks. They were mostly young, born around the time of the American Revolution, and came from the South and the West. Clay seeded the major committees with these men, most importantly placing Peter B. Porter of Buffalo, New York, at the head of the Foreign Relations Committee. Porter's committee issued a report on November 29, 1811, that echoed the assumptions and recommendations of Madison's message and ignored French policy for an attack on Great Britain. British depredations demanded enlarging the army, calling the militia into national service, preparing the navy, and arming merchant vessels. The House approved all of the measures by deceptively wide margins. Antiwar Republicans, such as John Randolph's Tertium Quids, and the Federalists made up the bulk of the opposition. Some Federalists went along with the majority, bowing to the inevitable. Among the Republicans, Donald Hickey points to a "scarecrow" faction that opposed war but hoped that stronger measures would be enough to frighten the British into a settlement.[6]

The chief differences between the administration and the War Hawks were over speed and goals. The War Hawks believed that negotiations had come to an end. Madison was prepared to wait until the end of the session, ideally with the United States in a better defensive position. Madison's goal was the abolition of the British maritime system, with a possible invasion of Canada as a means to an end. The War Hawks saw the permanent acquisition of Canada as the goal of any war. To the western War Hawks, the maritime issues were an abstraction. Impressment was an affront to national honor but was not as concrete a problem as Tecumseh and his ties to the British. Like Jefferson before them, the western War Hawks were prepared to abandon the sea, defeating 62–59 in January 1812 a bill (which Clay supported) to build ten frigates. Congress settled on stockpiling naval timber, fortifying harbors, and deploying gunboats. The Republicans were not anxious to face the task of paying for their programs. In January 1812 Gallatin recommended a $10 million loan, as well as internal taxes to replace the trade revenue that would be lost in war. Congress did not approve Gallatin's report until the middle of February.

A new embargo completed the Republican program. Madison sent a secret message to Congress on April 1, 1812, requesting the measure. Porter submitted legislation for a sixty-day embargo to the House. After passing by nearly thirty votes, it went to the Senate. The House, as well as Madison, saw the embargo as a preparation for war. Sen. Michael Leib recognized the opportunity to make the embargo a substitute for war and moved to extend it to ninety days. The House reluctantly agreed, as did the president, who signed it into law on April 4. With preparations complete, Madison waited for the British response.

On several fronts, the question of war or peace was left to events beyond Madison's reach. By the spring of 1812, the mission of Gen. George Mathews seemed out of control. The West Florida portion of the assignment was put off in June 1811, when Folch refused to surrender the territory. Mathews then turned east. He was authorized to take East Florida if given by local authorities or under imminent threat of capture by a third power. In the absence of a revolution, Mathews decided to create one. In August 1811 he informed Monroe that although East Florida had only around thirty-seven hundred Americans, they were ready for revolt and could seize the province. Mathews recruited local planter John Houston McIntosh as the leader of the "Patriots of East Florida." Monroe's exchange of notes with Foster over East Florida became public in November. Monroe defended the American claim to East Florida as part of the Louisiana Purchase, and Mathews took that assertion as carte blanche to do whatever was necessary to complete the transaction. The Patriots seized undefended Fernandina on Amelia Island, at the mouth of the St. Mary's River, on March 17, 1812. The next day Mathews and McIntosh ceded their conquests to the United States. A few days later Mathews proceeded to his next target, St. Augustine. Some two hundred Patriots laid siege to the city. Madison and Monroe had no fear of war with Spain and were willing to play along with Mathews up to a point. The administration expected war with Great Britain but had no wish to see it come prematurely. Foster, acting as Spain's guardian, protested the seizure of Fernandina on April 2, 1812. Two days later, Monroe wrote Mathews repudiating his revolution. Madison replaced Mathews with Gov. David B. Mitchell of Georgia on April 10, instructing the new envoy to return Fernandina and Amelia Island to Spain when he deemed it safe and to protect the Patriots from punishment.

While Washington waited, London debated and Paris plotted. In April 1812 Henry Brougham, a member of Parliament at the beginning of a long reformist career, began an inquiry into the Orders-in-Council. His main concern was the British economy rather than cultivating American good will, as Great Britain had suffered from an economic depression since 1810. The great manufacturing centers of Manchester, Yorkshire, and Sheffield begged for the restoration of trade with the United States. The ministry of Spencer Perceval tried to hold to the mercantilist order but was hard-pressed to maintain it against the economic logic of repeal. Prince Regent George issued a proclamation on April 21 promising a repeal of the Orders-in-Council if the French government provided proof it had repealed the Berlin and Milan Decrees. A week later the House of Commons began to consider the petitions for repeal, and even members from constituencies loyal to Perceval began to give way. The city of Liverpool petitioned for repeal on April 27. The last bulwark of the orders fell on May 11, 1812, when an assassin shot Perceval at the House of Commons. The new government, led by Robert Banks Jenkinson, Earl of Liverpool (formerly Lord Hawkesbury), continued to hear the petitions.

The prince regent's proclamation had an effect in Paris. Joel Barlow, the new American minister, could not get a straight answer on the status of the Berlin and Milan Decrees. On May 10, 1812, Barlow learned of the "Saint-Cloud Decree," dated April 28, 1811, which announced that the Berlin and Milan Decrees no longer applied to American shipping. Hughes-Moret, Duc de Bassano, Cadore's replacement as the French foreign minister, gave Barlow a copy on May 11, explaining that although the decree had never been published, it had been sent to Sérurier for communication to the American government. The decree was a complete fraud, as Barlow suspected. It was created to forestall a clash with the United States and help promote difficulties between the United States and Great Britain. Before Barlow could obtain more information, Bassano left Paris to join Napoleon in preparation for the coming war with Russia.

The machinations of the European courts were only imperfectly known in Washington. The *Hornet* arrived in New York on May 19, carrying news as late as that of May 1. The campaign against the Orders-in-Council had only begun when the *Hornet* departed. The dispatches arrived in Washington on May 22. For the past several weeks the administration had prepared the public mind for war with pieces in the *National Intelligencer*. Madison sent a formal message to Congress on June 1 presenting the case against Great Britain. First came impressment, an indignity that no nation could be expected to accept. Second, Madison denounced the system of blockades, both paper blockades against European ports and effective blockades of British vessels hovering outside of American ports. Although Madison did not specifically mention the Rule of 1756, he attacked the whole system of the Orders-in-Council. Madison denied the British argument that France would have to repeal its decrees before Great Britain repealed the orders. Madison always feared that war would lead to debts, taxes, and a standing army, all fatal to republican government. By 1812 Madison considered submission to the British a greater danger.[7] Madison's vision of republican diplomacy, by demanding that Great Britain dismantle its maritime system, ensured the United States would go to war. Madison's vision also ensured the United States would be unprepared.

## The War of 1812

On June 4 the House of Representatives approved a declaration of war by a 79–49 margin. Dissident Republicans joined the Federalists in opposition. The Senate took up the war bill on June 9, where the Federalists combined with the Invisibles. Some Republicans called for a maritime war alone, rather than an attack on Canada. The Federalists proposed a "triangular war" with France as well as Great Britain, a proposal resting on two assumptions: that Madison was in league with Napoleon and that Napoleon was in league with the Devil. The Federalists did not expect a declaration of war on France to succeed but believed its defeat would prove their case. There was some sentiment among the War Hawks for a war with France, but the triangular war lost by a 17–15 vote. On June 17 the Senate approved a declaration of war on Great Britain, 19–13. The president signed it the next day. Monroe delivered the bad news to Foster at three that afternoon.

For Madison the maritime issues caused the war, and their resolution was the main objective. Beyond the concrete issues were the more abstract motivations. Roger Brown points to three. One was national honor, which resonated particularly with the War Hawks. Madison alluded to national honor in his attack on impressment. A related issue was the prestige of republican government, which concerned southern War Hawks such as John C. Calhoun. Northern Republicans saw a war with Great Britain as the key to their political survival. They believed war would put New England Federalists in the same box the Federalists had tried to put the Republicans in during the Quasi-War with France.[8]

Madison had terrible timing. Brougham moved for a repeal of the orders on June 16. James Stephen, the leading defender of the orders, was absent on that day, signifying that Liverpool was ready for repeal. The House voted to revoke the orders on June 17. Robert Stewart, Viscount Castlereagh, the new foreign minister, instructed Foster to give the United States two weeks to remove restrictions on British trade. On June 23 Liverpool revoked the orders. Two days later Castlereagh sent new instructions to Foster to seek the readmission of British trade. Castlereagh believed the main cause of conflict had been removed. Madison seemed to agree. Foster held his last meeting with Madison on June 23. Madison told him that Great Britain could have peace if it repealed the orders and negotiated on impressment. Madison expected that French military pressure would help persuade the British government. Federalist hyperbole notwithstanding, Madison had no agreement with or allegiance to Napoleon. Nevertheless, Madison expected France to take up the vast majority of the British military effort. Yet even with an unfinished war in Spain, the emperor launched another. On June 24, 1812, Napoleon and his Grande Armée marched toward Russia to punish that nation for flouting the Continental System. Napoleon planned to occupy Moscow and wait for the government in St. Petersburg to surrender. But the Muscovites abandoned their city and burned it, denying Napoleon quarters and supplies. The French emperor began to retreat with his depleted army on October 19.

In Washington Anthony St. John Baker, the British secretary of legation, assumed Foster's duties. In July he received Castlereagh's instructions of June 17, along with cease-fire proposals from British officials in Nova Scotia. Madison met with Baker in early August and demurred on the subject of a cease-fire, arguing that he could not stop a war Congress had begun. In reality Madison considered Castlereagh's instructions and Baker's authority insufficient. On August 14 Baker received the June 25 instructions confirming the repeal of the orders. He again appealed for a cease-fire on August 16. Madison still refused but instructed Russell to tell Castlereagh the United States would accept the repeal of the orders and would make peace if the British renounced impressment as well. At the same time, Castlereagh rejected Madison's offer of June 23. Madison saw the repeal of the orders as a sign of weakness and overplayed his hand. He made his stand on the one issue where no British government would budge.

Madison expected a short war. The conquest of Canada would lead the British to abandon impressment. Most Republicans assumed that an underdefended and underpopulated Canada would soon fall into American hands. Some British officials on the scene shared that concern. For twenty years the government of Upper Canada (now Ontario) had encouraged American settlement across the border with cheap land and lower taxes. Gen. Sir Isaac Brock had no confidence in the fidelity of the so-called Late Loyalists. He need not have worried. First, the Americans in Canada were similar to the French during the American Revolution in aiding neither their government nor the invaders.[9] Second, the American campaign against Canada was a disaster on three fronts. Gen. William Hull crossed into Canada from Detroit on July 12, 1812. He soon became concerned about his supply lines and withdrew. Brock followed Hull across the Detroit River, and Hull surrendered Detroit on August 16. The American armies in New York fared no better. At Niagara Maj. Gen. Stephen Van Renssalaer commanded the New York militia and Gen. Alexander Smyth the federal troops. Smyth refused to take orders from Van Renssalaer. In October the New York militia attacked Queenston but failed to take it. Smyth later attempted to cross the Niagara but broke off the attack on December 1. Gen. Henry Dearborn's northern army undertook the least action. Dearborn commanded an army of some eight thousand men, including militias from New England. His objective was Montreal. When Dearborn crossed into Canada in November, the New Englanders refused to follow. Dearborn retreated from Canada on November 23. By January 1813 the first Canada campaign was over.

Events on the southern frontier were no more decisive. The Patriots continued their war for independence. In June they elected McIntosh "Director of the Territory of East Florida" and in July elected delegates to draft a constitution. The Patriots made no military progress, and the prospect of a full American involvement faded. Mitchell resigned as agent, replaced by Thomas Pinckney. Monroe ordered Pinckney to keep troops in East Florida until the Patriots were safe. In February 1813 Congress passed a bill that allowed Madison to take West Florida between the Pearl and Perdido Rivers. James Wilkinson occupied Mobile on April 15, completing the West Florida saga. The administration decided to conclude its involvement in East Florida. On February 15 Secretary of War John Armstrong ordered Pinckney to quarter his troops until further notice. Don Luis de Onís, the representative of the Spanish government at Cadiz, promised amnesty for the Patriots. Armstrong then ordered Pinckney to withdraw American troops. After Madison repudiated the Republic of East Florida on April 19, 1814, Gov. Sebastián Kindelán sent the Seminoles to ambush the Patriots. The movement collapsed in May 1814.

The main bright spot for the United States in the first six months of the war was the navy. The *Constitution* defeated the *Guerrière* 750 miles east of Boston on August 19 and won the American frigate its nickname, "Old Ironsides." American victories in single-ship engagements sent the *Times* of London into a panic. The U.S. Navy proved that its ships, officers, and men were as good as their British counterparts. Unfortunately, the British always had more of all three. Sheer numbers gave the British the advantage on the high seas. The British government authorized reprisals against American ships in October and imposed a blockade from Charleston to Florida. They extended the blockade to the Delaware and the Chesapeake on December 26. British manning of the wooden wall had been the prime cause of the war. In January 1813 Madison proposed a solution to the impressment issue, excluding foreign sailors from the American merchant marine in exchange for a British renunciation of the right of search. The proposal passed Congress as the Seaman's Bill in February 1813.

Throughout the War of 1812, American diplomacy succeeded better than American arms. On September 21, 1812, Count Nikolai Petrovich Rumientsev, the Russian chancellor, gave Tsar Alexander I's offer of mediation to John Quincy Adams. Adams sent the proposal on to Washington on September 30. American relations with Russia were better than with any other nation. The United States did not yet border Russian colonies, and Russia and the United States held the same principles of neutral rights. The bipolar world of the Napoleonic Wars brought the two great neutrals closer together. Adams frequently met with Rumientsev and Alexander, who both cultivated American friendship. "Our attachment to the United States *is obstinate—more obstinate than you are aware of*," the chancellor told Adams in 1810.[10]

Andrei Daschkov, the Russian minister to the United States, made a formal offer of mediation on March 8, 1813. His timing was fortunate. The financial system was already starting to creak. In the absence of a national bank, which Congress let die in 1811, Gallatin had to ask Congress for direct taxes and seek discounted loans from wealthy merchants. Madison immediately accepted the offer and pursued the chance to use the mediation to force Great Britain into an agreement on maritime rights. In a tradition that went back to the Treaty of Paris, Madison chose a politically balanced commission. Apart from his skills as a diplomat, Adams had the advantage of being from New England without being a Federalist. Next, Madison selected James A. Bayard, a Delaware Federalist who opposed the war but without the taint of pro-British sympathies. Perhaps at the insistence of both Russia and the war's financial backers, Madison chose his closest adviser, Gallatin. Monroe issued instructions on April 15, 1813, which showed no change in the American position. Monroe blamed the war on impressment and blockades, and therefore the envoys should seek an end to those practices in any peace.[11] Gallatin and Bayard sailed in May, arriving in the Russian capital in July.

Monroe's instructions reflected Madison's expectation of a more successful 1813 campaign against Canada. Dearborn's forces attacked York (now Toronto) on April 27 and burned the town three days later. The British attempted an invasion of the United States but were stopped at Sackett's Harbor, New York, on May 29. American fortunes improved in the West. On September 10 Oliver Hazard Perry defeated a British squadron at Put-in-Bay, Ohio, at the west end of Lake Erie. Naval supremacy allowed William Henry Harrison to cross into Upper Canada on September 27, where he defeated an army led by Tecumseh at the Battle of the Thames on October 5. Tecumseh was killed, but American gains were short-lived. James Wilkinson attempted another campaign against Montreal, which was repulsed at Chrysler's Farm on November 11. He broke off the attack the next day. By the end of the year, the British had captured Fort Niagara and burned Buffalo. The British extended their blockade to Long Island Sound in November 1813, pointedly leaving New England outside. Madison asked for and received a new embargo in December.

The Federalists gained seats in the 1812 elections and pressed Madison on the nature and conduct of the war. On June 10, 1813, Daniel Webster, a freshman Federalist from New Hampshire, introduced a series of resolutions demanding an accounting of the Saint-Cloud Decree. The Federalists sought to prove either that Madison was working with Napoleon or was tricked by the emperor. Republicans in both houses went along to put the matter to rest. Webster personally delivered the resolutions to the president on June 21. In the Senate a coalition of Invisibles and Federalists struck at Madison's diplomatic corps. The Senate rejected Jonathan Russell as minister to Sweden on July 9, judging a minister to Sweden unnecessary. Gallatin had not resigned as secretary of the treasury, giving his opponents in the Senate the chance to force Madison to choose what office Gallatin should have. Madison met the Senate on July 16 and refused to remove Gallatin from the cabinet. Three days later the Senate rejected Gallatin as peace envoy, while approving Adams and Bayard.

Like Madison, Castlereagh was not opposed to ending the war. However, he knew that a Russian mediation would involve neutral rights, and Castlereagh wanted to avoid that discussion. The British minister to Russia issued an oral rejection on August 20, followed by a formal note on September 1. Castlereagh kept a back channel open. Under Castlereagh's direction, financier Alexander Baring wrote Gallatin on July 22, telling him the British would reject mediation but would negotiate directly at London or Gothenburg, Sweden. Furthermore, the British would not negotiate on the basis of Monroe's instructions of April 15, 1813. Castlereagh formally offered direct talks in November. News of the offer arrived in Washington on December 30. Madison formally accepted on January 5, 1814, and added Henry Clay and Jonathan Russell to the original commission. The Senate approved Gallatin only after he resigned from the cabinet. Clay and Russell arrived at Gothenburg on April 13, 1814.

The balance sheet of the war at the end of 1813 showed a stalemate. Neither side especially wanted the war or was committed to a long-term conflict, but neither was willing to give in on peace demands. Everything fell apart for the United States in 1814. After the disaster of the Russian campaign, Napoleon returned to Paris, raised another army of 350,000 men, and marched east. A coalition of allies and German nations attacked the emperor at Leipzig on October 16, 1813. Three days later the latest eastern campaign was over. Napoleon retreated back to Paris. The Russians gave chase and entered the French capital on March 31, 1814. Talleyrand, now the Prince of Benevento, begged Alexander to restore Louis XVIII to the French throne. After failing to have his son named as successor, Napoleon abdicated on April 11. The allies packed him off to what was intended to be a genteel exile on Elba.

The Federalists cheered Napoleon's downfall and hoped that the only obstacle to peace had been removed. The Republicans had no use for Napoleon but feared that the only barrier against destruction had fallen.[12] In the long term the Federalists were correct. In the short term the Republicans' fears were well grounded. The British press urged an all-out war on the United States. "As we urged the principle, No peace with Bonaparte! so we must maintain the doctrine of, No peace with James Madison!" the *Times* blared on April 15, 1814. Madison cut a poor figure as a monster, but the *Times* continued its assault over the next several weeks. Great Britain shall "inquire a little into the American title to Louisiana" and punish the United States for invading Florida.[13] Press bombast aside, British policy moved in the same direction. On April 25, 1814, Vice Adm. Sir Alexander Cochrane, commander of the North American Station, extended the blockade to the entire American coast. To this point the British had left New England alone to encourage thoughts of a separate peace. Now the British made no distinctions among Americans.

At the same time, the American financial system collapsed. Recruitment remained fairly consistent, but there was no way to pay the bounties recruits demanded. Boston banks holding the most hard money refused to lend throughout the war, and by 1814 New York and Philadelphia banks were reluctant to throw good money after bad. Madison bowed to the new reality. In April Congress removed the embargo laid the previous fall. The cabinet met on June 23 and 24 to reconsider impressment as a necessary article of peace. Almost the whole cabinet chose to refer maritime issues to a separate treaty and first restore peace. News from Europe led the cabinet to reconsider, and on June 27 the cabinet agreed to seek a treaty silent on impressment. A war for free trade and sailors' rights was now a war for survival.

If there was a time for the British to finish the war, it had come. The American offensive in Canada ended in July. After driving the Americans from Upper Canada in July, the British began a concerted assault on the Chesapeake, along coastal New England, and in upper New York. The capture of the American capital seemed the quickest way to end the war. A British fleet commanded by Adm. Sir George Cockburn sailed up the Patuxent on August 18, landing troops under Maj. Gen. Robert Ross at Benedict, Maryland. After defeating the militia at Bladensburg on August 24, the British marched on Washington that night and burned the White House, the Capitol, and other public buildings. Madison and the rest of the government had planned to go to Frederick, Maryland, but instead fled to the Virginia countryside, where Madison himself rallied the local troops. The British left the capital the next day and took Alexandria on August 28.

The loss of Washington was a psychological trauma that temporarily rallied southern and mid-Atlantic Federalists to Madison. Unfortunately for the British, Washington was no more a centralized capital in 1814 than Philadelphia was in 1777. Furthermore, the capital had no particular strategic value. For strategic advantage, the British turned north to Baltimore. Maj. Gen. Samuel Smith, Madison's longtime nemesis, commanded Baltimore's defenses. His forces held off Ross's assault on September 12, killing Ross in the process. The next day, Adm. Alexander Cochrane began the bombardment of Fort McHenry but broke off the assault early in the morning of September 14. The giant star-spangled banner, immortalized by Francis Scott Key, still flew over the fort.

The northern campaigns were more successful for the British. In July Nantucket leaders wrote to Cochrane suing for peace. On August 23 Nantucket declared its neutrality. As an island, Nantucket was especially vulnerable to British pressure, but other towns on Cape Cod and in Rhode Island made their own deals to avoid destruction. To the north the chief British objective was the occupation of large parts of Maine to improve military communication between New Brunswick and Montreal. The British captured Castine on September 1 and transformed it into a British naval base. In Montreal Gen. Sir George Prevost poised to strike the fatal blow. Over the summer of 1814 he gathered an army of veterans of the war in Spain and amassed an army of thirty thousand by September. Henry, Earl of Bathurst, the secretary of state for war and colonies, directed Prevost to take either Sackett's Harbor on Lake Ontario or Plattsburgh, across the border in upper New York. Prevost chose Plattsburgh to shorten his supply lines. He crossed the border on September 3. Capt. Thomas Macdonough and his squadron, led by the *Saratoga*, defeated the British on Lake Champlain on September 11. The ground offensive crumbled, and the cautious Prevost retreated back to Canada a few days later. The summer campaign had mixed results for the British. However, they now held the advantage. The question was, did the British have the will to continue?

The peace negotiations planned for Gothenburg were moved to Ghent, in modern-day Belgium, at Great Britain's request. The American envoys had the task of preserving a nation in collapse against a victorious foe. They were still bound by the instructions of April 1813 and January 1814, which demanded a settlement of the maritime issues, especially impressment. The British had an equally ambitious agenda but one more closely related to battlefield results. Castlereagh instructed his diplomats to seek the cession of the Ohio Valley in the form of an Indian buffer state, improvement of the Canadian boundary in the northeast, and British access to the Mississippi. The Americans were to lose the fishing rights granted in the Treaty of Paris. The Americans did not know the internal discussions of the British government, but the commissioners they met on August 8 were a clear sign of a difficult negotiation. At the head of the commission stood Lord Gambier, best known as the commander of the Copenhagen expedition. Next came William Adams, an expert in maritime law. The youngest member was Henry Goulburn, at the start of a long career in the colonial office. He was then an undersecretary and appeared to be a young man in a hurry, bucking for a promotion by teaching Brother Jonathan some law. The meeting at Ghent allowed Lord Liverpool to keep his team on a short leash and closely supervise them from London. British decisions at Ghent were made by Liverpool, Castlereagh, and Henry, Lord Bathurst, secretary for war and colonies.

On the first day, the British demanded the Indian buffer state, the revision of the Canadian boundary, and some equivalent concession for the fisheries. Adams replied the next day that the Americans could treat on impressment and the border but not on the Indians or the fisheries. Castlereagh issued more explicit instructions on August 14, calling for an American retreat to the Greenville line of 1795 and a ban on the purchase of Indian lands. The British presented the new demands at a meeting on August 19. It was the last joint conference until December 1. An American note of August 24 rejected the British proposals and offered peace based on status quo ante bellum. News of the burning of Washington reached London on September 27, leading the government to adopt a policy of delay in order to press the advantage of anticipated military victories. The American envoys learned of Washington's fate on October 1. A week later the British issued an instruction putting Indian affairs where they were in 1811, subject to the approval of the tribes themselves. The note attacked the American acquisition of Louisiana and West Florida and demanded part of Maine.

On October 17 London learned of the British defeats at Baltimore and Plattsburgh, and the basis for a hard line against the United States collapsed. The next day Bathurst abandoned the buffer state and proposed to negotiate on what he considered a more conciliatory basis, *uti possidetis*. The Americans flatly rejected this proposal in a note of October 24. Madison considered British demands so shocking (and politically useful) that he sent the buffer state proposal to Congress on October 10 and sent the *uti possidetis* proposal to Congress on December 1, something of a breach of diplomatic procedure. The Americans began drafting their own treaty project at the end of October. The main dispute within the American delegation was over whether to grant British access to the Mississippi. Gallatin, Adams, and Bayard agreed to allow access in exchange for American access to the fisheries. Clay and Russell objected. When Clay refused to sign such a treaty, the Americans agreed to a draft silent on both issues. Clay, the poker player, believed Great Britain would fold on *uti possidetis* as it had on the buffer state. The American project of November 10 proposed a return to status quo ante bellum, a settlement of the northwestern boundary from the Lake of the Woods to 49° north, and a commission to determine the northeastern boundary. On maritime issues there would be a temporary ban on impressment, limitation on blockades, and indemnity to Americans for lost property.

The Americans had good timing, as Liverpool was nearing a decision to end the war. The desire to squash the United States faded before the reality of paying for a longer war. Liverpool estimated the American war would cost another £10 million ($44 million) for any meaningful result. That cost might be acceptable if peace in Europe were certain. The allies, having vanquished Napoleon, quarreled with each other at Vienna. Russia wanted Poland and was ready to fight Great Britain to get it. Prussia and Austria each wanted Saxony. France could still explode. Bathurst wrote to the Duke of Wellington on November 4, proposing to send him to America or Vienna. Wellington replied that he would go to America but could not depart until the spring. Furthermore, he argued that the British military position did not justify a demand of *uti possidetis*. Wellington's reply arrived in London on November 13, followed by the American project. Liverpool informed Castlereagh on November 18 that he saw no reason to continue the American war.

Great Britain would not consent to maritime concessions and still wished to exclude the United States from the fisheries. On November 28 Gallatin again proposed an article on the Mississippi and the fisheries, and Clay exploded in a profanity-filled tirade. The joint meeting on December 1 got off to a promising start but collapsed over the fisheries. The British had no instructions to grant access and argued that silence must mean an American surrender. The last two issues on the table were the fisheries and the islands off the coast of Maine. The British cared about the fisheries and not the Mississippi, except as a vehicle to extract concessions. The opposite sentiment prevailed in the American camp. Clay once again refused any concession on the Mississippi, arguing it was far more valuable than the fisheries. That was a common southern and western argument going back to 1779. John Adams had not had to answer it in Paris in 1782, as the American commission supported him. His son was not so fortunate. Even Gallatin warned Adams that the Americans might have to give up the fisheries to make peace. The Americans agreed in a note on December 14 to accept a treaty silent on the fisheries and the Mississippi. Bathurst accepted the note, and the two sides signed the Treaty of Ghent on December 24, 1814.

The treaty settled nothing but the war itself, restoring peace and providing for the mutual evacuation of territory. Article 4 established a commission to adjudicate the islands off the coast of Maine. In 1817 the commission awarded Moose, Dudley, and Frederick Islands to the United States, with Deer, Campobello, and Grand Manan Islands awarded to Great Britain. Articles 5 and 6 established similar commissions for the northeast and northwest boundaries. Those were settled by the Webster-Ashburton Treaty in 1842 and the Convention of 1818, respectively. Article 9 left the Indian tribes on their own. Article 11 required unconditional ratification, as the British hoped to avoid a repeat of the Treaty of Paris and the Jay Treaty.[14] The treaty was silent on every other contentious issue, including blockades and impressment. On July 3, 1815, Adams signed a commercial convention with Great Britain at London that restored trade on the terms of the Jay Treaty for four years.[15]

The war continued during the negotiations. In September Massachusetts governor Caleb Strong sent a mission to negotiate a separate peace with Lt. Gov. John Cooper Sherbrook of Nova Scotia. Bathurst made no commitments but encouraged the conversation. At the same time, Strong asked for a New England convention. The Hartford Convention convened on December 15, 1814, and adjourned on January 5, 1815. Massachusetts, Connecticut, and Rhode Island attended the convention, joined by two delegates from Vermont and one from New Hampshire. The deliberations do not survive. The final report demanded a repeal of the three-fifths compromise, a single term for presidents, and a ban on consecutive presidents from the same state. On foreign policy matters, the convention called for a limit on embargos and two-thirds vote for a declaration of war. The convention sent a delegation to Washington to deliver the report, expecting to impose terms on a beaten administration.

Madison's timing was now perfect. As Great Britain launched an offensive in the southwest in the fall of 1814, Madison sent Andrew Jackson to command the defenses at New Orleans. Jackson was already a hero on the frontier, having crushed the Creeks at Horseshoe Bend on March 27, 1814. British forces led by Gen. Edward Packenham took up a position opposite Jackson at New Orleans on December 23, 1814. Jackson defeated the last British push on January 8, 1815, securing American control of New Orleans. Had the British won, they would likely have held the city hostage until the United States ratified the treaty rather than relaunch the war.[16] News of the battle arrived in Washington on February 4, followed by the Treaty of Ghent on February 15. The Senate approved the treaty 35–0 the next day. Madison signed on February 17 and proclaimed the treaty on February 18. Coupled with New Orleans, a narrow escape had become a victory.

Madison had one piece of unfinished business. Jefferson's first foreign policy crisis was a Barbary war, as was Madison's last. In July 1812 Hadji Ali, the dey of Algiers, demanded additional tribute from the United States. Consul Tobias Lear borrowed to pay the $27,000 the dey demanded. Still, that was not enough, and the Algerines seized the merchant vessel *Edwin* in August. Nothing could be done until after the War of 1812. Madison had as little patience with the Barbary pirates as Jefferson and asked Congress for a declaration of war on February 23, 1815. The House voted 94–32 for war on March 1, followed by a 27–2 vote in the Senate on March 2. Stephen Decatur, William Bainbridge, and William Shaler—two navy captains and a sometime secret agent—formed the American negotiating team. Napoleon's return to France prompted a delay. When the administration decided that the former emperor could not restart the war, the mission sailed in May. It was a fast negotiation. Decatur arrived at Algiers on June 28 and demanded a new treaty. The new dey, Omar Bashaw, approved a new treaty at gunpoint. Algiers agreed not to ask for tribute and to pay an indemnity of ten thousand Spanish dollars for the *Edwin*. The treaty was signed on June 30, and Shaler picked up the money on July 3.[17] For the United States, the Barbary wars were finally over.

# CONCLUSION

# The Significance of the Founding Era

Three years to the day after the United States went to war with Great Britain, Napoleon lost his last chance to remain on the French throne. Wellington's victory at Waterloo on June 18, 1815, ended the Napoleonic Era and the wars that came with it. The allies at Vienna patched together an approximation of the pre–French Revolution diplomatic system. The world into which American diplomacy had been born and matured died. Napoleon went off to a more secure exile at Saint Helena. A new revolution, the Spanish American wars of liberation, replaced the French Revolution as the main focus of American diplomacy. For a century after the Congress of Vienna, American relations with European nations were determined by American issues, rather than by the spillover of European conflicts.

The United States had come through its final encounter with the Napoleonic Wars in one piece. Political figures as far apart as John Adams and Henry Clay saw the outcome of the War of 1812 as proof the republic could fight and win a war with a European power unbound by the rules that constrained a republic. Madison agreed that the war went a long way toward demonstrating the permanence of republican governments, where the record of ancient and modern history seemed to prove otherwise. Yet Madison and the majority of the Republicans tacitly admitted that Hamilton's style of republic was better prepared for war than Jefferson's. Madison asked Congress to recharter the bank of the United States in 1811, but Congress did not agree until 1816. Congress also provided for a more permanent army and navy. The great issues of Anglo-American relations were left to rest. As secretary of state, John Quincy Adams brought up the Rule of 1756 and blockades in an opportunistic fashion but without threats of economic punishment.

In some ways the year 1789 marks an obvious dividing line in the history of American foreign policy. In the United States a stronger central government replaced a weak, if not nonexistent, government under the Continental Congress. In Europe the French Revolution began, leading to the destruction of the Westphalian balance of power and creating a bipolar system more analogous to the Cold War than to the eighteenth-century system. Yet a case can be made for continuity, at least in the case of the American formulation of foreign policy. The radical and moderate approaches to foreign policy, first apparent in 1775, retained a recognizable shape until 1815. No foreign policy system remains unchanged for forty years, and some people and ideas migrated from one camp to the other.

The most durable principle of American foreign policy was that the United States should remain separate from the political system of Europe while taking advantage of it. Europe represented both a physical threat and a moral contagion. *Common Sense*, the Model Treaty, Washington's Farewell Address, and Jefferson's first inaugural address all echo this theme. The principle was so obvious that it became diplomatic boilerplate, remaining the unchallenged position of American foreign policy until 1914 and then the dominant one until 1949. The only challenges to this idea came out of necessity, as with the 1778 alliance, or out of political affinity for the French Revolution. Few Republicans advocated joining France's war on monarchy; yet pro-French sentiment (and to a certain extent Federalist pro-British sentiment) undercut the idea of the separate spheres of the Old and New Worlds. Ideological affinity returned as an issue in Spanish America. Henry Clay called for an alliance of the Western Hemisphere to counter the Holy Alliance. John Quincy Adams applied the principle of political separation southward as well as eastward. Parallel to a political separation from Europe was the desire to trade with all on a reciprocal basis. The radicals and their heirs believed that politics and economics could be kept separate; the moderates and their heirs did not.

Thus the radicals and moderates differed on how that separation from Europe should be achieved. The radicals conceived of America as an economically mighty nation that could dictate terms to European powers. This belief was overstated but not entirely misplaced. The moderates feared that the nation would need a protector that would demand more political and diplomatic guarantees. Battlefield results led the moderates to win the debate. Some moderates, particularly Jay, lost faith in France as a benefactor. Some radicals, particularly John

Adams, gave up on the power of trade as a substitute for the regular tools of diplomacy. The radical and moderate split was blurred by the debate over the Constitution. Most agreed that only a congressional power to regulate trade could properly harness American economic power. The debates over how much power to give the government—and over respectability abroad—were essentially debates over how to secure separation from Europe.

The Federalists embodied much of the moderate position. The United States could not force its will on Europe. Therefore the United States should see to its own defenses and avoid Europe's wars. Unlike the moderates, the Federalists had no faith in French friendship. That became a pillar of Republican diplomacy. Otherwise, the Republicans were the heirs to the radicals. They believed the European nations that needed American trade in an age of limited war would need it more in an age of total war. Twelve years of Federalist rule followed by sixteen years of Republican rule, under similar European conditions, affords a good chance for comparison. The Federalists did not advance the neutral rights agenda, but they did not believe that would be possible. The Federalists saw to the army and navy and avoided mortal danger. The Quasi-War with France was limited and not existential. The Federalists handed the Republicans a well-defended nation in one piece. The Republicans assumed the United States had the upper hand and could use the Napoleonic Wars as a means to advance their territorial and maritime agendas. On land the results were mixed. Jefferson purchased Louisiana, but a quizzical French policy stymied Jefferson and Madison. The sea was not the natural element of an up-country Virginian. The United States under Jefferson and Madison achieved none of its maritime goals regarding Great Britain and France, ultimately embarking on a war with Great Britain for which the United States had been kept woefully unprepared as a direct result of Jeffersonian ideology.

For the next century the United States faced far different issues from those of the founding era. The wars and near misses were about American issues—the borders with Mexico and Canada, the preservation of the union, and the final fate of the Spanish colonial empire. Europe went to war in 1914, and the old issues returned. Europe split into two camps, each seemingly bent on the other's destruction. War to the death extended to the sea, which meant the revival of the contest over blockades, continuous voyage, and the definition of contraband. In 1914 the

United States was a different nation, and Woodrow Wilson answered the great questions in a much different manner than the statesmen of the founding era.

# Appendix: Excerpts from Related Documents

### 1. Joseph Ward to John Adams, October 23, 1775

*The radicals expected a quick victory over Great Britain. Here, Joseph Ward, a cousin of Gen. Artemus Ward, outlines his expectations to his fellow radical, John Adams.*

Source: Adams, *Papers*, 3:236–37.

I have long been waiting for an opportunity to communicate some intelligence worthy of your notice, but nothing very important has taken place since you left the Camp; and every action with the Enemy has been published in the Newspapers, which has superseded the necessity of communicating those events by Letter. The general face of our public affairs both civil and military appear much as they have done for months past. By all the intelligence we receive from the *Tyrant Country*, it appears that the *Heathen still rage and the people imagine a vain thing*—That they can enslave America; *but none of these things move us*, the Spirit of War and Liberty thrives by persecution, and I trust they will be invincible in this Country. I humbly conceive we have a glorious prospect before us notwithstanding the gathering Storm. We are yet in blossom, but ripen fast, and when we have done playing with petitions and making kites for George, I expect we shall exert our united vigour with a direct line to "Liberty Peace and Safety," and soon reach the summit of human happiness and glory.

That the united efforts of the free the brave and the hardy millions of independent Americans whose minds are enlightened and animated with the divine Spirit of Freedom, should ever be enslaved by the British Tyrants is incredible among men! Nothing but the curse of Heaven (which we devoutly deprecate) can spread the cloud of despotism over the extensive region of America. *Fear* or *folly* only can produce our ruin; I am happy in believing that *these* do not dwell in the Great Council of America—but that Wisdom and Fortitude with a steady hand and persevering firmness will guide our political helm until we arrive at the haven of perfect Freedom.

I expect soon to hear that the Continental Congress have published the Confederacy of the Colonies—compleated the Republic of America—and formed a *commercial* Alliance with France and Spain. Such tidings will be musick in my ears, as I apprehend nothing short of such a plan will secure our Liberties; and if America should be enslaved it is probable freedom will expire thro the World. It is a great and glorious Prize which the Americans contend for, *the happiness of all future ages, and the freedom of the World* as the Liberties of all Nations may in some degree be connected with ours.

## 2. Robert Morris to Charles Lee, February 17, 1776

*In contrast to the radicals, the moderates preferred a reconciliation with Great Britain but only on terms that protected American liberty. Robert Morris describes the moderate position on foreign affairs at a critical juncture.*

Source: Smith, *Letters of Delegates*, 3:269–70.

You will doubtless have heard the various reports of Commissioners coming out to treat with us. I wish it to be true, provided they come with proper Powers; but to come limited to terms inconsistent with Freedom will be doing nothing. France is certainly filling her West India Islands with troops, the ostensible reason for doing so is that upon reconciliation between Great Britain and this Country the Great Force introduced into America during the disputes, may be employed to seize their Islands unless well prepared for defence; but I fancy their real design is to be able to take advantage whenever the event of this war, wherever opportunity offers; and I don't conceive this a proper time for this Country to make Treaty's with any Foreign Power, we don't want their assistance to defend our Country, it is only protection to our Trade that we can want from any Country in Europe, the benefit of that trade will always most readily be admitted as a full compensation for the

Protection of it hereafter, altho' the Ministers of Great Britain were not satisfied with it; If we by resistance obtain proper terms, reconciliation and connection with Great Britain, we want no other protection than hers. If by our own Force of Conduct, we establish an Independent Empire, notwithstanding the utmost exertions of Britain, there is not a Nation in Europe, but will be glad to treat and trade with us on our own terms; therefore I think it best to persevere in our own measures, and depend on our strength, which I believe is quite sufficient; and if so, we shall ever after hold a respectable consequence in the World. But notwithstanding these notions I am of opinion with you that we shou'd know the sentiments and dispositions of Foreign Nations, of and towards us; and you cannot doubt but measures have been taken to obtain such knowledge—*a word to the wise.*

## 3. Chevalier de la Luzerne to Comte de Vergennes, June 14, 1781

*Luzerne exercised a great influence over Congress and used that influence to minimize the diplomatic role of John Adams. Here Luzerne describes the political maneuvering that led to Adams's replacement by a five-member peace commission.*

Source: Giunta et al., eds., *Emerging Nation*, 1:190–91.

Congress has been pondering whether it would be advisable for it to name a plenipotentiary other than Mr. Adams; the recall of that Minister appearing subject to great difficulties, it was proposed to give him two coplenipotentiaries; Mr. Jay was named unanimously, and Mr. Franklin was placed in nomination to be the third. General Sullivan, who named him, found insurmountable difficulties in having this choice adopted; this Delegate and his party were opposed in their turn to the nomination of Mr. Jefferson, Governor of Virginia, and of Mr. Henry Laurens, who was successively chosen despite the disadvantages and the type of disadvantage there is in naming as a negotiator for peace a Minister who is a prisoner of the enemy. The impossibility of managing to name any one of these three Candidates persuaded General Sullivan to represent with new fervor the services of Mr. Franklin and the consideration which he enjoys, the injury done him in appointing a Colleague for him, the necessity of mitigating by a mark of shining confidence the bitterness of this first treatment; he observed that having been unjustly treated upon false reports, he merited some sort of satisfaction, and that a zealous servant who had had such a part in the revolution for its whole duration was the most proper to preside at its consummation; after this preamble, he proposed to add these three Candidates to the two already named; objections were made with regard to the expense and the number; as for the first point, it was replied that American plenipotentiaries would always be approved if they were content with a modest and republican manner, that besides the subject was too important for these expenses to be regarded; as for the number, if one examined the diplomatic collections, one would find that the Republic of Holland had had three, four, and five plenipotentiaries at almost all the peace conferences in which it had taken part. The party opposed to Mr. Franklin then proposed to choose the three Candidates in succession, while leaving this Minister for last. General Sullivan saw the trap, and responded that all three should be elected or rejected together. His firmness brought together all the parties, and the three candidates were named at once unanimously, so that the declared enemies of Mr. Franklin were themselves obliged to give him their votes.

## 4. Richard Oswald to Thomas Townshend, November 30, 1782

*In negotiating with the Americans, Richard Oswald retreated on almost every important point. Here he explains his retreat on the fisheries and defends his actions as necessary to secure a peace treaty.*

Source: Giunta et al., eds., *Emerging Nation*, 1:695–97.

If We had not given way in the Article of the Fishery, We should have had no Treaty at all. Mr. Adams having declared that he would never put his hand to any Treaty, if the restraints regarding the 3 Leagues and 15 Leagues were not dispensed with, as well as that of denying his Countrymen the Privilege of Drying Fish on the unsettled parts of Nova Scotia.

Mr. Fitz-Herbert and Mr. Strachey finding this, and there being a discretionary Power in Mr. Strachey's Instructions, regarding the whole of this Article, as well in extent as manner, they thought it adviseable to avail themselves of it rather than send again to London on this critical occasion, for farther Instructions, which although in the most certain prospect of obtaining assent to such Dispensation might have been of bad consequence, not only in the loss of so much time, but in leaving the Commissioners in such humour, as in the interim, to have suggested some new demands under the head of one or more of the Articles, which might have been of worse consequence, than that of giving up these Restraints of Fishery. One Specimen of which We had yesterday, while sitting with them and under hesitation on this Subject, when one of those Gentlemen, pulling a Paper out of his Pocket, proposed that His Majesty should recommend to His Parliament, to make Provision for the payment of certain Effects which had been seized by order of His Generals and entirely out of the Line of the consequences of Military Irregularitys, and such as they could bring undoubted proofs of. And which he said ought to be paid upon the same principles of Justice, as was urged in favour of the recovery of Debts. On these and other accounts, and being in a manner certain that without an Indulgence in this Article of Fishery, there would have been no Treaty with America. The above mentioned Gentlemen thought it best to close with the Commissioners by admitting this Article in the way they proposed. In which they not only had my concurrence, but I own I used the freedom to encourage and press them to give their consent; being of Opinion that I would be under no difficulty in shewing that the Grant was not of that Importance as to be put in comparison with the consequences of splitting with America at this time. Among other things it occurred to me that if our caution in this particular regarded our Marine, and an apprehension of its being abridged by this Interference of the Americans to a greater extent in this Trade, we might come to suffer much more by what the Commissioners insinuated and indeed threatened in case of a Refusal, which was to pass an Act of Navigation, by which, after a certain time all the Ports of America should be shut against English ships, in so far as the Exportation of their produce should be concerned. – And in the other view of the Profits of the Fishing Trade, and our being deprived of such part of it as the Americans would gain by this admission, I was of Opinion that in leaving the Fishing Sea Ports in the West of England, I would not have far to go Inland, to be satisfied that the Loss by continuing the Dispute some time longer with the Americans, or even laying the foundation of a National Grudge, would, ten times over, counterbalance the amount of the said Loss; even supposing that the Conditions of those Restraints could be enforced; by keeping the Americans to their proper distances, which I am of opinion would be difficult if not doubtfull. Or if attempted by our Men of War on that Station, might be the means of bringing on

Quarrels of States, instead of being useful in preventing Quarrels of Fishermen, as one of the Motives insisted on in justification of this Refusal.

## 5. Robert R. Livingston to the American Peace Commissioners, March 25, 1783

*The Provisional Treaty placed Congress in a difficult position. It secured all major goals but at the cost of violating the instructions of June 15, 1781, and risking a breach with France. Here Livingston praises the treaty but condemns the means taken to achieve it.*

Source: Adams, *Papers*, 14:361–62.

I am now to acknowledge the favor of your joint Letter by the Washington, together with a Copy of the preliminary Articles—Both were laid before Congress—The Articles have met their warmest approbation, and have been generally seen by the People in the most favorable point of view.

The steadiness manifested in not treating without an express acknowledgment of your Independence previous to a Treaty, is approved; and it is not doubted but it accelerated that declaration. The Boundaries are as extensive as we have a right to expect, and we have nothing to complain of with respect to the Fisheries—My Sentiments as to English Debts you have in a former Letter, no honest Man could wish to with hold them. A little forbearance in British Creditors till People have recovered in part the losses sustained by the war will be necessary to render this Article palatable, and indeed to secure more effectually the Debt. The Article relative to the Loyalists is not quite so accurately expressed as I could wish it to have been. What, for instance, is intended by *real British subjects*? It is clear to me that it will operate nothing in their favor in any State in the Union; but as you made no secret of this to the British Commissioners, they will have nothing to charge you with, and indeed the whole Clause seems rather to have been inserted to appease the clamours of these poor Wretches, than to satisfy their wants. Britain would have discovered more candour & magnanimity in paying them three months expence of the war establishment which would have been an ample compensation for all their losses, and left no germ of dissatisfaction to bud and blow, and ripen into discontents here—another Administration may think the noncompliance of the Legislatures with the Recommendations of Congress on this subject a sufficient cause for giving themselves and us new trouble—You however were perfectly right in agreeing to the Article—the folly was theirs, who did not either insist upon more, or give up this.

But, Gentlemen, tho' the issue of your Treaty has been successful, tho' I am satisfied that we are much indebted to your firmness and perseverance, to your accurate knowledge of our situation, and of our wants for this success; yet I feel no little pain at the distrust manifested in the management of it, particularly in signing the Treaty without communicating it to the Court of Versailles 'till after the Signature, and in concealing the separate Article from it ever when signed. I have examined with the most minute attention all the reasons assigned in your several Letters to justify these Suspicions. I confess they do not appear to strike me so forcibly as they have done you, and its gives me pain that the Character of Candour and Fidelity to its Engagements, which should always characterize a great People should have been impeached thereby. The concealment was in my opinion absolutely unnecessary. For had the Court of France disapproved of the terms you had made after they had been agreed upon, they could not have acted so absurdly, as to counteract you at that late day, and thereby have put themselves in the power of an Enemy, who would certainly betray them, and perhaps justify you in making terms for yourselves.

### 6. Thomas Jefferson to John Jay, August 23, 1785

*Jefferson's political career reflects the tension between his ideological preferences and the need of representing the whole nation. Here he outlines his preference for an agrarian political economy, in conflict with the policy of carrying American goods on American ships.*

Source: Jefferson, *Papers*, 8:426–27.

I shall sometimes ask your permission to write you letters, not official but private. The present is of this kind, and is occasioned by the question proposed in yours of June 14 "Whether it would be useful to us to carry all our own productions, or none?" Were we perfectly free to decide this question, I should reason as follows. We have now enough lands to employ an infinite number of people in their cultivation. Cultivators of the earth are the most valuable citizens. They are the most vigorous, the most independant, the most virtuous, and they are tied to their country and wedded to it's liberty and interests by the most lasting bands. As long therefore as they can find emploiment in this line, I would not convert them into mariners, artisans, or any thing else. But our citizens will find emploiment in this line till their numbers, and of course their productions, become too great for the demand both internal and foreign. This is not the case as yet, and probably will not be for a considerable time. As soon as it is, the surplus of hands must be turned to something else. I should then perhaps wish to turn them to the sea in preference to manufactures, because comparing the characters of the two classes I find the former the most valuable citizens. I consider the class of artificers as the panders of vice and the instruments by which the liberties of a country are generally overturned. However we are not free to decide this question on principles of theory only. Our people are decided in the opinion that it is necessary for us to take a share in the occupation of the ocean, and their established habits induce them to require that the sea be kept open to them, and that that line of policy be pursued which will render the use of that element as great as possible to them. I think it a duty in those entrusted with the administration of their affairs to conform themselves to the decided choice of their constituents: and that therefore we should in every instance preserve an equality of right to them in the transportation of commodities, in the right of fishing, and in the other uses of the sea. But what will be the consequence? Frequent wars without a doubt. Their property will be violated on the sea, and in foreign ports, their persons will be insulted, emprisoned &c. for pretended debts, contracts, crimes, contraband, &c. &c. These insults must be resented, even if we had no feelings, yet to prevent their eternal repetition. Or in other words, our commerce on the ocean and in other countries must be paid for by frequent war. The justest dispositions possible in ourselves will not secure us against it. It would be necessary that all other nations were just also. Justice indeed on our part will save us from those wars which would have been produced by a contrary disposition. But how to prevent those produced by the wrongs of other nations? By putting ourselves in a condition to punish them. Weakness provokes insult and injury, while a condition to punish it often prevents it. This reasoning leads to the necessity of some naval force, that being the only weapo[n] with which we can reach an enemy. I think it to our interest to punis[h] the first insult: because an insult unpunished is the parent of many oth[ers]. We are not at this moment in a condition to do it, but we should put ourselv[es] into it as soon as possible. If a war with England should take place it see[ms] to me that the first thing necessary would be a resolution to abandon the carrying trade because we cannot protect it. Foreign nations must in that case be invited to bring us what we want and take our productions in their own bottoms. This alone could prevent the loss of those productions to us and the acquisition of them to our enemy. Our seamen might be emploied in depredations on their trade. But how dreadfully we shall suffer on our coasts, if we have no force on the water, former experience has taught us. Indeed I look forward with horror to the very possible case of war with an European power, and think there is no protection against them but from the possession of some force on the sea. Our vicinity to their West India possessions and to the fisheries is a bridle which a small naval force on our part would hold in the mouths of the most powerful of these countries. I hope our land office will rid us of our debts, and that our first attention then will be to the beginning a naval force of some sort. This alone can countenance our people as carriers on the water, and I suppose them determined to continue as such.

## 7. Francisco Rendón to Don José de Gálvez, February 12, 1785

*American expansion and pressure on the Spanish colonial frontier were the main issues in Spanish-American relations throughout the period of the early republic. Here Francisco Rendón, the Spanish agent in the United States, outlines the sources of American hostility toward Spain.*

Source: Giunta et al., eds., *Emerging Nation*, 2:551–52.

I observe with sorrow, Your Excellency, that the general public who make up this Republic is ignorant of the great part which our Benevolent Sovereign has taken in making it possible for them to shake off the British yoke which was oppressing them, and that without exception, in all societies, the people complain that from beginning to end the Court of Spain had declared itself opposed to the ideas of the Americans. Their angry prejudices have led them to publish in their newspapers different pieces which every day contribute more toward turning the public against the Spanish nation. To give Your Excellency an idea of this I am taking the liberty of copying an article published in today's paper, word for word: "The insulting memorial of the Court of Spain must be considered very seriously. That Court, not content to exclude our citizens from navigation on the Mississippi River (which in truth cannot be important or detrimental to Spain), but as they desire to demonstrate a total contempt of us, they also declare that they do not recognize the United States as a Power. What is this if not an implicit claim to all their former possessions? If they do not recognize the United States as a Power, will they be willing to consent to fixing territorial limits with us? Will they tacitly agree to abandon Georgia and part of South Carolina which they have always considered as belonging to them and which to this day is regularly attested in their wills from father to son just as in the territories of New Spain? The warehouses of naval stores and the men who are now in New Orleans are proof enough of their designs, and make it imperative for us to be on our guard against them."

These circumstances and other similar ones which I have had the honour of reporting to Your Excellency in previous letters, show the need for our Court to negotiate with these states and settle the different points which are now causing enmity between the two nations. Your Excellency can be sure that if negotiation is postponed, the time is not far distant when the Americans who are settled on the Mississippi declare themselves to be enemies of His Majesty's possessions which border on those lands, leading to very disagreeable results. The American population in those parts is multiplying so rapidly that the settlement called Kentucky alone has added thirty thousand souls since peace was declared, an emigration from the eastern states and of many families in Europe is continuing.

It seems to me that the incomparable desire to navigate that river and go out into the Gulf of Mexico which the Americans openly profess makes it imperative that His Majesty be prepared immediately to prevent the violent claims of those colonists from becoming a discord which can be repaired only with great difficulty and much time. The present moment appears to be favourable for the establishment of a treaty that can be mutually profitable to the two nations, so that the restrictions contained in articles of such a treaty can serve as a shield against the attempts of the settlers, and it is probable that by that method the settlers will contain themselves and adjust to the rules agreed upon by the two nations.

## 8. James Wilson's Speech at the Pennsylvania Ratifying Convention, December 11, 1787

*The Federalists skillfully exploited foreign affairs as an issue in support of the Constitution. Here James Wilson argues not only that the Constitution will secure the United States against foreign danger, but will also act as an agent to spread liberty worldwide.*

Source: Jensen et al., eds. *Ratification of the Constitution,* 2:583–84.

The adoption of this system will also secure us from danger and procure us advantages from foreign nations. This, in our situation, is of great consequence. We are still an inviting object to one European power at least, and, if we cannot defend ourselves, the temptation may become too alluring to be resisted. I do not mean, that, with an efficient government, we should mix with the commotions of Europe. No, sir, we are happily removed from them and are not obliged to throw ourselves into the scale with any. This system will not hurry us into war; it is calculated to guard against it. It will not be in the power of a single man, or a single body of men, to involve us in such distress, for the important power of declaring war is vested in the legislature at large; this declaration must be made with the concurrence of the House of Representatives. From this circumstance we may draw a certain conclusion, that nothing but our national interest can draw us into a war. I cannot forbear, on this occasion, the pleasure of mentioning to you the sentiments of the great and benevolent man whose works I have already quoted on another subject. Mr. Neckar had addressed this country in language important and applicable in the strictest degree to its situation and to the present subject. Speaking of war, and the great caution that all nations ought to use in order to avoid its calamities: "And you, rising nation," says he, "whom generous efforts have freed from the yoke of Europe! let the universe be struck with still greater reverence at the sight of the privileges you have acquired, by seeing you continually employed for the public felicity. Do not offer it as a sacrifice at the unsettled shrine of political ideas, and of the deceitful combinations of warlike ambition; avoid, or at least delay participating in the passions of our hemisphere; make your own advantage of the knowledge which experience alone has given to our old age, and preserve for a long time, the simplicity of childhood. In short, honor human nature, by showing that when left to its own feelings, it is still capable of those virtues that maintain public order, and of that prudence which insures public tranquility."

Permit me to offer one consideration more that ought to induce our acceptance of this system. I feel myself lost in the contemplation of its magnitude. By adopting this system, we shall probably lay a foundation for erecting temples of liberty in every part of the earth. It has been thought by many, that on the success of the struggle America has made for freedom will depend on the exertions of the brave and enlightened of other nations. The advantages resulting from this system will not be confined to the United States; it will draw from Europe many worthy characters who pant for the enjoyment of freedom. It will induce princes, in order to preserve their subjects, to restore to them a portion of that liberty of which they have for many ages been deprived. It will be subservient to the great designs of Providence with regard to this globe; the multiplication of mankind, their improvement in knowledge, and their advancement in happiness.

### 9. Samuel Shaw to John Jay, December 21, 1787

*With the closure of traditional American markets in the European colonies, Americans sought opportunities elsewhere. Here Samuel Shaw, the agent for the owners of the* Empress of China *and consul at Canton until 1797, describes trade in China and the political situation there.*

Source: Giunta et al., eds. *Emerging Nation*, 3:683–86.

Having in the letter which I did myself the honor of addressing to you towards the close of the last season, mentioned the several matters which came within my observation, relative to the Commerce which the Europeans carry on with this part of the world, I have only to remark generally on this subject, that a detail of it at present, such is its uniformity, would be to involve merely a repetition of the greater part of what was then written. I shall therefore confine myself rather to the quantity, if I may be allowed the expression, than to the manner, of the commerce for the current year.

Since the Year 1784 the trade here has been constantly tending to the disadvantage of the Europeans. The imports collectively taken, hardly defray the first costs, and the exports have increased in a ratio beyond all possible conjecture. By an average, at the most moderate computation, the price of every sort of Tea, bohea only excepted, is advanced more than forty per cent, nor is it yet at the highest. Such is the demand for this Article, that the Chinese hardly know *how much* to ask for it, and should the rage of purchasing it continue only another year, it is not improbable that it may double its price. I shall for your information annex a list of the shipping at Wampo; and though the number for the English does not exceed that of the last year, yet from the size of the ships, the quantity of tonnage is greatly increased. In the opinion of judicious observers, the English seem to be aiming not only at a monopoly of the tea trade for Europe, but appear to have in view the exclusive Commerce of this division of the Globe. The new plan of Government for Bengal and its dependencies—their late establishments both to the eastward and westward—the prohibition to their subjects in India against selling their ships to foreigners—And in short their whole conduct favour the suspicion. This object, and to be sure it is no trifling one, is now considered as the great idol of the English Nation; and in consequence of it the current of popular opinion carries rapidly along every measure which the Company think fit to adopt. How far our republican friends the Dutch, whom it most nearly concerns, will suffer any attempts of this kind, a few years must determine. The settlement of the English at Pulo Pinang, which enables them to command the whole of the navigation from the Peninsula of India, that of Malaya, and of the Island of Sumatra, has not a little alarmed them; and the settlement at Botany Bay on the south east coast of New Holland, has increased their apprehensions. I say nothing of the opposition the English might expect from the Swedes and Danes, who certainly find their advantage in this Commerce; or from the French invariably their Enemies. Perhaps a commercial confederation of these Nations, for their mutual benefit, not unlike the armed neutrality during the late war, may be adopted, as the best means of checking and defeating such exorbitant pretensions.

With respect to our own Commerce this way yet in its infancy, I shall only observe that inconsiderable as it has hitherto been and is this year especially, it is viewed with no small degree of jealousy by our late mother Country. Gentlemen in all parts of the World, of whatever nation they may be, can esteem and sometimes love one another. But Englishmen and Americans merely as such, in any place, as at Canton, where the former have the ascendancy, can barely treat each other with civility. It is to national prejudices only, not yet done away, that I have reference, for I have found among them men who are an honor to their species.

No national civility on their part have been offered us at Canton, either last year or the present; but at Macao, in the interval, there was a full tender of them made me, with a general invitation to their table. These however I thought proper to decline without assigning a reason, as circumstances rendered any explanation unnecessary. In my own particular I have no cause of complaint. The usual compliment of a visit has been mutually paid and returned, and we frequently meet at other tables, and also at the Danish Concert. They have themselves a public weekly concert, but for the reasons mentioned I never attend it. After saying thus much concerning the English, I should be guilty of the highest ingratitude were I to omit testifying on this occation, my entire satisfaction in the reception and treatment I have met with from the Chiefs and Gentlemen of the other nations, not only at Canton, but during a residence of six months at Macao. It has been and continues to be in all respects proper, and in many instances really friendly.

Though little can ever be known of China by persons restricted to such narrow limits as are the foreigners who trade here, yet we see enough to give us very unfavourable ideas of its government. The laws may be good, but its police is extremely defective. It would shock your humanity were I to give a sketch of the misery which is here daily exhibited; and what excites the indignation of every foreigner, is that the number of these wretched objects not being considerable, it is evidently in the power of the Magistracy amply to provide for them. This is not the only instance which contradicts the generally received idea of the excellence of the Chinese Government. At present there are great disturbances in many parts of the Empire, and the insurrections in the Island of Formosa, and the adjacent Country threaten consequences of a serious nature. The war in that quarter has raged upwards of a twelvemonth—and its issue is yet doubtful. The oppressions exercised by the Government have reduced the inhabitants of those parts to a state of desperation, which had had the most pernicious effects on the agriculture and commerce, not only of that but of the neighbouring Provinces.

From this painful view of the effects of despotism, I turn with pleasure to the contemplation of that happiness which an American enjoys, under the Government of equal laws and a mild administration. Surely, if we avail ourselves of the experience of other nations, and make a proper use of the advantages with which heaven hath blessed us, we cannot fail in due time of becoming a great and a happy people.

In addition to the observations in my former letter respecting the article of Genseng, I shall only observe that the sales of it this Season confirm me in the opinion of the great advantages which our Country may derive from it. The annexed list will shew the quantity brought here, and the price for the best has been from one hundred thirty to two hundred dollars the pecul, (133 1/3 lbs. English) at which it now stands, though probably it will rise twenty or thirty dollars before the departure of the last ships.

It was my intention after dispatching our ship last season to have gone to Bengal, but the vessel in which I had engaged my passage lost so much time at Macao that her destination was changed for Manilla, and I was reduced to the necessity of remaining behind. I am now making a second attempt, have engaged my passage and expect to sail the first week in January. On my return here in August next I hope to meet Mr Randall from America, by whom I flatter myself I shall have the honor of receiving your Commands. The Commercial engagements I have made, in behalf of Mr Randall and my self, will involve the necessity for me if not for us both, to return at the close of the ensuing season to America. I therefore take the liberty of begging you will be pleased to communicate this circumstance to Congress; and I humbly hope that honorable body will not be offended that I take this step without their permission previously obtained. The loss of time which the waiting for such permission must involve would be prejudicial to us in the extreme, and this with the consideration that the office of Consul at Canton is rather honorary to the person vested with it, than essential to the Commerce of our Country, I presume to flatter myself will be admitted as my excuse.

## 10. Proclamation of Neutrality, April 22, 1793

*With the Proclamation of Neutrality, President George Washington announced that the United States would not take sides in the war in Europe, despite having an alliance with France. Notice that Washington never uses the word "neutrality."*

Source: Richardson, ed., *Messages and Papers*, 1:156–57.

Whereas it appears that a state of war exists between Austria, Prussia, Sardinia, Great Britain, and the United Netherlands of the one part and France on the other, and the duty and interest of the United States require that they should with sincerity and good faith adopt and pursue a conduct friendly and impartial toward the belligerent powers.

I have therefore thought fit by these presents to declare the disposition of the United States to observe the conduct aforesaid to those powers respectively, and to exhort and warn the citizens of the United States carefully to avoid all acts and proceedings whatsoever which may in any manner tend to contravene such disposition.

And I do hereby also make known that whosoever of the citizens of the United States shall render himself liable to punishment or forfeiture under the law of nations by committing, aiding, or abetting hostilities against any of the said powers, or by carrying to any of them those articles which are deemed contraband by the modern usage of nations, will not receive the protection of the United States against such punishment or forfeiture; and further, that I have given instructions to those powers to whom it belongs to cause prosecutions to be instituted against all persons who shall, within the cognizance of the courts of the United States, violate the law of nations with respect to the powers at war, or any of them.

## 11. Thomas Jefferson's Description of a Cabinet Meeting on Edmond Genet, August 20, 1793

*Edmond Genet gave the Washington administration no choice but to ask for his recall. Here Jefferson describes the debate within the cabinet. Jefferson tried to separate the conduct of Genet from the policy of France, while Hamilton and Knox drew no such distinction.*

Source: Jefferson, *Papers*, 26:730–32.

Aug. 20. We met at the President's to examine by paragraphs the draught of a letter I had prepared to Gouverneur Morris, on the conduct of Mr. Genet. There was no difference of opinion on any part of it, except on this expression. "An attempt to embroil both, to add still another nation to the enemies of his country, and to draw on both a reproach, which it is hoped will never stain the history of either, that of *liberty warring on herself*." H. moved to strike out these words "that of liberty warring on herself." He urged generally that it would give offence to the combined powers, that it amounted to a declaration that they were warring on liberty, that we were not called on to declare that the cause of France was that of liberty, that he had at first been with them with all his heart, but that he had long since left them, and was not for encouraging the idea here that the cause of France was the cause of liberty in general, or could have either connection or influence in our affairs.—Knox according to the custom jumped plump into all his opinions.—The Pr. with a good deal of positiveness declared in favor of the expression, that he considered the pursuit of France to be that of liberty, however they might sometimes fail of the best means of obtaining it, that he had never at any time entertained a doubt of their ultimate success, if they hung well together, and that as to their dissensions there were such contradictory accounts given that no one could tell what to believe.—I observed that it had been supposed among us all along that the present letter might become public; that we had therefore 3 parties to attend to. 1. France, 2. her enemies, 3. the people of the US. That as to the enemies of France it ought not to offend them, because the passage objected to only spoke of an attempt to make the US., *a free nation*, war on France, *a free nation*, which would be liberty warring on herself and therefore a true fact. That as to France, we were taking so harsh a measure (desiring her to recall her minister) that a precedent for it could scarcely be found, that we knew the minister would represent to his government that our Executive was hostile to liberty, leaning to monarchy, and would endeavor to parry the charges on himself, by rendering suspicious the source from which they flowed: that therefore it was essential to satisfy France not only of our friendship to her, but our attachment to the general cause of liberty, and to hers in particular. That as to the people of the US. we knew there were suspicions abroad that the Executive in some of it's parts were tainted with a hankering after monarchy, an indisposition towards liberty and towards the French cause; and that it was important by an explicit declaration to remove these suspicions and restore the confidence of the people in their government. R. opposed the passage on nearly the same ground with H. He added that he thought it had been agreed that this correspondence should contain no expressions which could give offence to either party.—I replied that it had been my opinion in the beginning of the correspondence that while we were censuring the conduct of the French minister, we should make the most cordial declarations of friendship to them: that in the first letter or two of the correspondence I had inserted expressions of that kind but that himself and the other two gentlemen had struck them out: that I thereupon conformed to their opinions in my subsequent letters, and had carefully avoided the insertion of a single term of friendship to the French nation, and the letters were as dry and husky as if written between the generals of two enemy nations. That on the present occasion however it had been agreed that such expressions ought to be inserted in the letter now under consideration, and I had accordingly charged it pretty well with them. That I had further thought it essential to satisfy the French and our own citizens of the light in which we viewed their cause, and of our fellow feeling for the general cause of liberty, and had ventured only four words on that subject, that there was not from beginning to end of the letter one other expression or word in favor of liberty, and I should think it singular at least if the single passage of that character should be struck out.—The President again spoke. He came into the idea that attention was due to the two parties who had been mentioned France and US. That as to the former, thinking it certain their affairs would issue in a government of some sort, of considerable freedom, it was the only nation with whom our relations could be counted on: that as to the US. there could be no doubt of their universal attachment to the cause of France, and of the solidity of their republicanism. He declared his strong attachment to the expression, but finally left it to us to accommodate. It was struck out of course, and the expressions of affection in the context were a good deal taken down.

## 12. Alexander Hamilton, "Americanus No. 1," January 31, 1794

*Alexander Hamilton was the most prolific defender of Federalist foreign policy. As "Americanus" in the follow-up to his "Pacificus" essays, Hamilton attacks the idea that the French Revolution represented the cause of liberty, and by extension the idea that American foreign policy should rest on the idea of republican brotherhood.*

Source: Hamilton, *Papers*, 15:670–71.

None can deny, that the cause of France has been stained by excesses and extravagances, for which it is not easy, if possible, to find a parallel and at which reason and humanity recoil. Yet many find apologies & extenuations with which they satisfy themselves, they still see in the cause of France the cause of Liberty; they are still sanguine in the hope that it will be crowned with success; that the French Nation will establish for themselves not only a free but a Republican Government, capable of promoting solidly their happiness. Others on the contrary discern no adequate apology for the horrid and disgusting scenes which have been and continue to be acted. They conceive that the excesses which have been committed transcend greatly the measure of those which were reasonably to have been expected with every due allowance for circumstances. They perceive in them proofs of atrocious depravity in the most influential leaders of the Revolution. They observe, that among these, a Marat and a Robespierre, assassins still reeking with the blood of murdered fellow Citizens, monsters who outdo the fabled enormities of a *Busirsis* and a *Procrustes*, are predominant in influence as in iniquity. They find every where marks of an unexampled dissolution of all the social and moral ties. They see no where any thing but principles so wild so extreme passions so turbulent so tempestuous, as almost to forbid the hope of agreement in any rational or well organized system of Government: They conclude, that a state of things like this is calculated to extend disgust and disaffection throughout the Nation, to nourish more and more a spirit of insurrection and mutiny, facilitating the progress of invading armies, and exciting in the bowels of France commotions, of which it is impossible to compute the mischiefs the duration or the end: that if by the energy of the national character and the intrinsic difficulty of the enterprise the enemies of France shall be compelled to leave her to herself, this era may only prove the commencement of greater misfortunes: that after wading through seas of blood, in a furious and sanguinary civil war, France may find herself at length the slave of some victorious Scylla or Marius or Caesar: And they draw this afflicting inference from the whole view of the subject, that there is more reason to fear, that the CAUSE OF TRUE LIBERTY has received a deep wound in the mismanagements of it, by those who, unfortunately for the French Nation, have for a considerable time past, maintained an ascendant in its affairs—than to regard the Revolution of France, in the form it has latterly worn, as intitled to the honors due to that sacred and all important cause—or as a safe bark on which to freight the Fortunes the Liberties and the Reputation of this now respectable and happy land.

## 13. Alexander Hamilton, "The Defence No. II," July 25, 1795

*Even though he left office in January 1795, Hamilton remained a key Federalist opinion maker. Here he lays out the fundamental Federalist defense of the Jay Treaty, that the choice was between the treaty and a destructive war with Great Britain.*

Source: Hamilton, *Papers*, 18:493, 495–96.

Previous to a more particular discussion of the merits of the Treaty, it may be useful to advert to a suggestion which has been thrown out, namely that it was foreseen by many, that the mission to Great Britain would produce no good result, and that the event has corresponded with the anticipation.

The reverse of this position is manifestly true.

All must remember the very critical posture of this Country at the time that mission was resolved upon. A recent violation of our rights too flagrant and too injurious to be submitted to had filled every American breast with indignation and every prudent man with alarm and disquietude. A few hoped, and the great body of the community feared, that War was inevitable.

In this crisis two sets of opinions prevailed; one looked to measures which were to have a compulsory effect on Great Britain, the sequestration of British debts and the cutting off of intercourse wholly or partially between the two Countries—the other to *vigorous preparation* for war and *one more effort* of negotiation by a solemn mission to avert it.

That the latter was the best option no truly sensible man can doubt, and it may be boldly affirmed that the event had entirely justified it. . . .

Few nations can have stronger inducements than the U States to cultivate peace. Their infant state in general—their want of a marine in particular to protect their commerce would render war in an extreme degree a calamity. It would not only arrest our present rapid progress to strength and prosperity, but would probably throw us back into a state of debility and impoverishment from which it would require years to emerge. Our Trade navigation and mercantile capital would be essentially destroyed. Spain being an associate with Great Britain a general Indian war would probably have desolated the whole extent of our frontier. Our Exports obstructed, Agriculture would have seriously languished. All other branches of industry must have proportionally suffered. Our public Debt instead of a gradual diminution must have sustained a great augmentation and drawn with it a large increase of taxes and burthens on the people.

But this perhaps was not the worst to be apprehended. It was to be feared that the war would be conducted in a spirit which would render it more than ordinarily calamitous. There are too many proofs that a considerable party among us is deeply infected with those horrid principles of Jacobinism which proceeding from one excess to another have made France a theatre of blood and which notwithstanding the vigorous efforts of the national representation to suppress it keeps the destinies of France to this moment suspended by a thread. It was too probable that the direction of the war if commenced would have fallen into the hands of men of this description. The consequences of this even in imagination are such as to make any virtuous man shudder.

It was therefore in a particular manner the duty of the Government to take all possible chances for avoiding War. The plan adopted was the only one which could claim this advantage.

To precipitate nothing, to gain time by negotiation, was to leave the country in a situation to profit by any events which might turn up tending to restrain a spirit of hostility in Great Britain & to dispose her to reasonable accommodation.

The successes of France which opportunely occurred allowing them to have had an influence upon the issue so far from disparaging the merit of the plan which was pursued serve to illustrate its wisdom. This was one of the chances which procrastination gave, and one which it was natural to take into the calculation.

Had the reverse been the case, the posture of negotiation was still preferable to that of retaliation and reprisal; for in this case, the triumphs of Great Britain the gauntlet having been thrown by us, would have stimulated her to take it up without hesitation.

By taking the ground of negotiation in the attitude of preparation for war, we at the same time carried the appeal to the prudence of the British Cabinet, without wounding its pride, and to the justice and interest of the British Nation without exciting feelings of resentment.

## 14. James Madison's Petition to the General Assembly of the Commonwealth of Virginia, October 12, 1795

*The Republicans considered the Jay Treaty at best a surrender to Great Britain and at worst an alliance. Here Madison gives the Republican argument, that the treaty was unnecessary for peace with Great Britain.*

Source: Madison, *Papers*, 16: 96–103.

Even "waiving the merits of the respective complaints and pretensions of the two parties," as to the inexecution of the Treaty of Peace, it is reasonable to view the two parties as equally culpable, or equally blameless, and to determine that the execution of the Treaty of Peace equally by both ought to have been provided for. Yet, whilst the United States are to comply, in the most ample manner, with the article unfulfilled by them, and to make compensation for whatever losses may have accrued from their delay; Great-Britain is released altogether, from one of the articles unfulfilled by her, and is not obliged to make the smallest compensation for the damages which have accrued from her delay, in fulfilling the other. . . .

Without remarking the inexplicit provision for redressing past spoliations and vexations, no sufficient precautions are taken against them in future. On the contrary, by omitting to provide for the respect due to sea letters, passports, and certificates, and for other customary safe guards to neutral vessels, "a general search warrant" (in the strong but just language of our fellow-citizens of Charleston) is granted against the American navigation. Examples of such provisions were to be found in our other Treaties, as well as in the Treaties of other nations. And it is matter of just surprize, that they should have no place in a Treaty with Great-Britain, whose conduct on the seas so particularly suggested and enforced every guard to our rights that could be reasonably insisted on.

By omitting to provide against the arbitrary seizure and imprisonment of American seamen, that valuable class of citizens remains exposed to all the outrages, and our commerce to all the interruptions hitherto experienced from that cause.

By expressly admitting that provisions are to be held contraband in cases other than when bound to an invested place, and impliedly admitting that such cases exist at present; not only a retrospective sanction may be given to proceedings against which an indemnification is claimed, but an apparent license is granted to fresh and more rapacious depredations on our lawful commerce; and facts seem to shew that such is to be the fruit of this impolitic concession. It is conceived that the pretext set up by Great-Britain of besieging and starving whole nations, and the doctrine grounded thereon, of a right to intercept the customary trade of neutral nations, in articles not contraband, ought never to have been admitted into a Treaty of the United States. . . .

Whenever the law of nations has been a topic for consideration, the result of the Treaty accommodates Great-Britain in relation to one, or both of the republics at war with her, as well as in the abandonment of the rights and interests of the United States.

Thus American vessels bound to Great-Britain, are protected by sea papers against French and Dutch searches; but when bound to France or Holland, are left exposed to British searches, without regard to such papers.

American provisions in American vessels, bound to the enemies of Great-Britain, are left by Treaty to the seizure and use of Great-Britain; but provisions, whether American or not, in American vessels, cannot be touched by the enemies of Great-Britain.

British property in American vessels is not subject to French or Dutch confiscations—French or Dutch property in American vessels, is subjected to British confiscation. Articles of ship building bound to the enemies of Great-Britain for the equipment of vessels of trade only, are contraband—bound to Great-Britain for the equipment of vessels of war, are not contraband. . . .

The proposed Treaty nevertheless, puts Great-Britain in all respects gratuitously on the footing of the nations most favoured, even as to future privileges, for which the most valuable considerations may be given; so that it is not only out of the power of the United States to grant any peculiar privileges to any other nation, as an equivalent for peculiar advantages in commerce or navigation, granted to the United States; but every nation desiring to treat on this subject with the United States is reduced to the alternative, either of declining the Treaty altogether, or of including Great-Britain gratuitously, in all the privileges it purchases for itself. An article of this import is the greatest obstruction next to an absolute prohibition, that could have been thrown in the way of other Treaties; and that it was insidiously meant by Great-Britain to be such, is rendered the less doubtful, by the kindred features of the Treaty. . . .

A Treaty thus unequal in its conditions, thus derogating from our national rights, thus insidious in some of its objects, and thus alarming in its operation, to the dearest interest of the United States in their commerce and navigation, is, in its present form, unworthy of the voluntary acceptance of an independent people, and is happily not dictated to them, by the circumstances in which a kind providence has placed them. A Treaty thus incompatible with our constitution, thus unequal in its conditions, thus derogating from our national rights, thus insidious in some of its objects, and thus alarming in all its operation; is not only unworthy of the voluntary acceptance of an independent and happy people, but is an abject sacrifice which ought to have been rejected with disdain in the most humiliating and adverse circumstances. It is sincerely believed that such a Treaty would not have been listened to at any former period, even when Great-Britain was most powerful, at her ease, and the United States most feeble, without the respectability they now enjoy. To pretend that however objectionable the instrument may be, it ought to be considered as the only escape from a hostile resentment of Great-Britain, which would evidently be as impolitic, as it would be unjust on her part, is an artifice too contemptible to answer its purpose. It will not easily be supposed, that a refusal to part with our rights without equivalents, will be made the pretext of war on us; much less that such a pretext will be founded on our refusal, to mingle a sacrifice of our commerce and navigation, with an adjustment of political differences. Neither is there any evidence in history, or in human nature, that nations are to be bribed out of the spirit of encroachment and aggression, by humiliations which nourish their pride, or by unreasonable concessions, which extend their resources and their power. To do justice to all nations, to obtain it from them by every peaceable effort, in preference to war; and to confide in this policy, for avoiding that extremity, or for meeting it with the firmness under the blessing of Heaven, when it may be forced upon us, is the only course of which the United States can never have reason to repent.

## 15. John Adams to Elbridge Gerry, July 8, 1797

*Elbridge Gerry was a longtime friend of John Adams. Gerry's role in the mission to France was to serve as the president's eyes and ears. Here Adams tells Gerry what he should expect on his first foreign mission.*

Source: Adams, *Works*, 8:547–48.

I wrote you a line, yesterday, but was so busy I could not enlarge. The Secretary of State will send you your instructions, and as ample a collection of documents as we can prepare. Mr. Marshall will sail next week; but you may reach Amsterdam from Boston as early as he will, though you cannot sail so soon. There is the utmost necessity of harmony, complaisance, and condescension among the three envoys, and unanimity is of great importance. In such a negotiation the attention should be to the great objects, and smaller matters must sometimes be yielded or neglected.

It is my sincere desire that an accommodation may take place; but our national faith, and the honor of our government, cannot be sacrificed. You have known enough of the unpleasant effects of disunion among ministers to convince you of the necessity of avoiding it, like a rock or quicksand.

There have been many instances of three ambassadors at a time. The Dutch at Munster had eight. In modern times they have not been common, and in this case, it ought to be considered by the French, as it will be considered by the world, as a great compliment and a signal mark of respect.

I wish you to get acquainted at Amsterdam with our bankers there, Messrs. Willink and Van Staphorst, and in France, if you are received there, to inquire into the conduct and character of our late and present consuls, and their inferior agents, and to find out what kind of speculations have been carried on there. You will see that Mr. Blount, the senator, has been speculating with the English, but some suspect this to be only a feint, and that the real design was upon France or Spain, or both. Swan, Hichborne, Edwards, &c., in connection with others in this country, have been speculating, and I fear these speculators have done this country no good.

As to our being a divided people, all nations are divided. France is divided; so are Holland, England, Italy, and Germany. There will ever be parties and divisions in all nations; but our people will support their government, and so will the French theirs. Not to expect divisions in a free country, would be an absurdity.

It is probable there will be manœuvers practised to excite jealousies among you, both by Americans, English, Dutch, and French; this should not produce too much irritation, but should press you closer together. You will hear a great deal of affected contempt, as well as a great deal of affected esteem and admiration of America. Neither should affect you much. But I cannot enlarge. I wish Mrs. Gerry health and comfort, and that you may acquire glory enough to compensate for all your cares.

N.B. I must give you a hint about economy. I would be as plain and cheap as possible in dress, equipage, lodgings, livery, and every thing. I would not give many feasts to Americans. Decorum must be observed. You will be surrounded with projectors and swindlers. You will not be deceived by them.

## 16. Alexander Hamilton to James McHenry, June 27, 1799

*As the Adams administration turned toward peace with France, Hamilton's dreams of glory were dashed. Despite the appointment of a second mission, Hamilton expected a war with Spain and planned the conquest of Louisiana and the Floridas.*

Source: Hamilton, *Papers*, 23:227–28.

It is a pity, My Dear Sir, and a reproach, that our administration have no general plan. Certainly there ought to be one formed without delay. If the Chief is too desultory, his Ministers ought to be the more united and steady and well settled in some reasonable system of measures.

Among other things—It should be agreed what precise force should be created *naval* and *land*, and this proportioned to the state of our finances. It will be ridiculous to raise troops and immediately after to disband them. *Six* ships of the line & *twenty* frigates and sloops of war are desireable—more would not now be comparatively expedient. It is desireable to complete and prepare the land force which has been provided for by law. Besides eventual security against invasion, we ought certainly to look to the possession of the Floridas & Louisiana—and we ought to squint at South America.

Is it possible that the accomplishment of these objects can be attended with financial difficulty? I deny the possibility. Our Revenue can be considerably reinforced. The progress of the Country will quickly supply small deficiencies, and these can be temporarily satisfied by loans—provided our loans are made on the principle that we require the aliment of European Capital & that lenders are to gain and their gains to be facilitated not obstructed.

If all this is not true our situation is much worse than I had any idea of. But I have no doubt that it is easy to devise the means of execution.

And if there was every where a disposition without prejudice and nonsense to concert a rational plan I would chearfully come to Philadelphia and assist in it. Nor can I doubt that success may be ensured.

Break this subject seriously to our friend *Pickering*. His views are sound and energetic; and try together to bring the other Gentlemen to a consultation. If there is every where a proper temper & it is wished send for me & I will come.

## 17. James Madison to Charles Pinckney, November 27, 1802

*Both Jefferson and Madison had long sought the navigation of the Mississippi and the use of the port of New Orleans. Here Secretary of State Madison explains the importance of the Mississippi to Charles Pinckney, the minister to Spain. Madison also addresses the problem of having colonial empires as neighbors.*

Source: Madison, *Papers* 4:146–48.

A letter from a confidential citizen at New Orleans, of which a copy is inclosed, had just informed us, that the Intendant at that place, by a proclamation from which an extract is also inclosed, had prohibited the deposit of American effects, stipulated by the Treaty of 1795; and as the letter is interpreted, that the river was also shut against the external commerce of the U States from that port. Whether it be the fact or not that this latter prohibition has also taken place, it is evident that the useful navigation of the Mississippi so essentially depends on a suitable depositary for the articles of commerce that a privation of the latter is equivalent to a privation of both.

This proceeding is so direct and palpable a violation of the Treaty of 1795, that in candor it is to be imputed rather to the Intendant solely, than to instructions of his Government. The Spanish Minister takes pains to impress this belief, and it is favoured by private accounts from New Orleans, mentioning that the Governor did not concur with the Intendant. But from whatever source the measure may have proceeded the President expects that the Spanish Government will neither lose a moment in countermanding it, nor hesitate to repair every damage which may result from it. You are aware of the sensibility of our Western citizens to such an occurrence. This sensibility is justified by the interest they have at stake. The Mississippi is to them every thing. It is the Hudson, the Delaware, the Potomac and all the navigable rivers of the atlantic States formed into one stream. The produce exported thro' that channel last year amounted to $1,622,672 from the districts of Kentucky and Mississippi only, and will probably by fifty per Cent more this year (from the whole Western Country, Kentucky has alone exported for the 1st half of this year $591,432 in value) a great part of which is now or shortly will be afloat for New Orleans and consequently exposed to the effects of this extraordinary exercise of power. Whilst you presume therefore in your representations to the Spanish Government, that the conduct of its officer is no less contrary to its intentions, than it is too good faith, you will take care to express the strongest confidence, that the breach of the Treaty will be repaired in every way which justice and regard for a friendly neighbourhood may require.

I have communicated the information received from New Orleans to the Chevalier D'Yrujo, with a view to obtain his immediate interposition as you will find by the inclosed copy of a letter to him. He readily undertakes to use it with all the effect he can give it, by writing immediately on the subject to the local authority in New Orleans. I shall write at the same time to Mr Hulings, who will enforce as far as he may have an opportunity the motives for recalling the unwarrantable prohibitions. It is to be hoped that the Intendant will be led to see the error he has committed, and to correct it, before a very great share of its mischief will have happened. Should he prove as obstinate as he has been ignorant or wicked, nothing can temper the irritation and indignation of the Western Country, but a persuasion that the energy of their own Government will obtain from the justice of that of Spain, the most ample redress.

It has long been manifest, that whilst the injuries to the United States, so frequently occurring from the Colonial officers scattered over our hemisphere and in our neighbourhood, can only be repaired by a resort to their respective Sovereigns in Europe, that it will be impossible to guard against the most serious inconveniences. The instance before us strikes with particular force, and presents an occasion on which you may advantageously suggest to the Spanish Government, the expediency of placing in their Minister on the Spot an authority to controul or correct the mischievous proceedings of their Colonial Officers towards our citizens; without which any one of fifteen or twenty individuals, not always among either the wisest or the best of men, may at any time threaten the good understanding of the two Countries. The distance between the United States and the old Continent, and the mortifying delays of explanations and negotiations across the Atlantic, on emergencies and in our neighbourhood, render such a provision indispensable, and it cannot be long before all the Governments of Europe having American Colonies must see the policy of making it.

## 18. Thomas Jefferson's Account of Cabinet Meetings, November 12 and 19, 1805

*West Florida was the missing piece of the Louisiana Purchase. Both France and Spain sought to prevent the United States from possessing it. Here Jefferson and the cabinet agree on an effort to purchase the Floridas.*

Source: Jefferson, *Complete ANAS*, 232–34.

Nov. 12, 1805. Present the four Secretaries, subject Spanish affairs.

The extension of the war in Europe in leaving us without danger of a sudden peace, depriving us of the chance of an ally, I proposed that we should address ourselves to France, informing her that it was a last effort at amicable settlement with Spain, an offer to her or through her; 1. A sum of money for the rights of Spain east of Iberville, say the Floridas. 2. To cede the part of Louisiana from the Rio Bravo to the Guadaloupe. 3. Spain to pay within a certain time spoliations under her own flag agreed to by the convention (which we guess to be 100 vessels worth 2,000,000 dollars) and those subsequent (worth as much more) and to hypothecate to us for those payments the country from Guadaloupe to Rio Bravo.

Armstrong to be employed. The first was to be the exciting motive with France, to whom Spain is in arrears for subsidies, and who will be glad also to secure us from going into the scale of England. The second soothing motive with Spain which France would press bona fide because she claimed to the Rio Bravo. The third to quiet our merchants—it was agreed to unanimously and the sum to be offered fixed not to exceed five million dollars.

Mr. Gallatin did not like purchasing Florida under an apprehension of war, lest we should be thought in fact to purchase peace. We thought this overweighed by taking advantage of the opportunity, which might not occur again, of getting a country essential to our peace, and to the security of the commerce of the Mississippi. It was agreed that Yrujo should be sounded through Dallas as to whether he is not going away, and if not, he should be made to understand that his presence at Washington, will not be agreeable and that his departure is expected.

Casacalvo, Morales and all the Spanish officers at New Orleans are to be desired to depart, with a discretion to Clayborne to let any friendly ones remain who will resign and become citizens; as also women receiving pensions to remain if they choose.

Nov. 19. Present the same.

Since our last meeting we have received a letter from General Armstrong containing Talleyrand's propositions, which are equivalent to ours nearly, except as to the sum, he requiring 7,000,000 dollars.

He advises that we alarm the fears of Spain by a vigorous language and conduct, in order to induce her to join us in appealing to the interference of the Emperor. We now agree to modify our propositions so as to accommodate them to his as much as possible. We agree to pay 5,000,000 dollars for the Floridas as soon as the treaty is ratified by Spain, a vote of credit obtained from Congress and orders delivered us for the surrender of the country.

We agree to his proposition that the Colorado shall be our western boundary, and a belt of 30 leagues on each side of it to be kept unsettled. We agree that joint commissioners shall settle all spoliations and to take payment from Spain by bills on her colonies. We agree to say nothing about the French spoliations in Spanish ports which broke off the former convention. We propose to pay the 5,000,000 dollars after a simple vote of credit, by stock redeemable in three years, within which time we can pay it.

We agree to orders to the commanding officer at Natchitoches to patrol the country on this side the Sabine and all the Red river as being in our possession, except the settlement of Bayou Pierre, which he is not to disturb unless they become aggressive. He is to protect our citizens and repel all invasions of the preceding country by Spanish soldiers, to take all offenders without shedding blood unless his orders cannot otherwise be executed.

## 19. Berlin Decree, November 21, 1806

*At the height of the wars of the French Revolution, Great Britain and France tried to strangle each other to death. Here follows the text of the Berlin Decree, the French response to the British blockade. The Berlin Decree placed the British Isles in a state of blockade, but France was in no position to enforce it.*

Source: *American State Papers*, 3:290.

ART. 1. The British islands are declared in a state of blockade.

ART. 2. All commerce and correspondence with the British islands are prohibited. In consequence, letters or packets addressed either to England, to an Englishman, or in the English language, shall not pass through the post office, and shall be seized.

ART. 3. Every subject of England, of what rank and condition soever, who shall be found in the countries occupied by our troops, or by those of our allies, shall be made a prisoner of war.

ART. 4. All magazines, merchandise, or property whatsoever belonging to a subject of England, shall be declared lawful prize.

ART. 5. The trade in English merchandise is forbidden. All merchandise belonging to England, or coming from its manufactories and colonies, is declared lawful prize.

ART. 6. One-half of the proceeds of the confiscation of the merchandise and property declared good prize by the preceding articles, shall be applied to indemnify the merchants for the losses which they have suffered by the capture of merchant vessels by English cruisers.

ART. 7. No vessel coming directly from England, or from the English colonies, or having been there since the publication of the present decree, shall be received in any port.

ART. 8. Every vessel contravening the above clause, by means of a false declaration, shall be seized, and the vessel and cargo confiscated as if they were English property.

ART. 9. Our tribunal of prizes at Paris is charged with the definitive adjudication of all controversies, which may arise within our empire, or in the countries occupied by the French army, relative to the execution of the present decree. Our tribunal of prizes at Milan shall be charged with the definitive adjudication of the said controversies, which may arise within the extent of our kingdom of Italy.

ART. 10. The present decree shall be communicated by our Minister of Exterior Relations to the Kings of Spain, of Naples, of Holland, of Etruria, and to our allies, whose subjects, like ours, are the victims of the injustice and the barbarism of the English maritime laws.

Our Ministers of Exterior Relations, of War, of Marine, of Finances, of Police, and our Postmasters General, are charged each in what concerns him with the execution of the present decree.

## 20. Order-in-Council, January 7, 1807

*Although the British tinkered with their maritime regulations, they were unwilling to alter their essential nature. The British regarded the Order-in-Council of January 7, 1807, as a concession, replacing the blockade of May 16, 1806, with the normal operation of the Rule of 1756.*

Source: Eli F. Heckscher, *The Continental System: An Economic Interpretation* (Washington: Carnegie Endowment for International Peace, 1922), 389–90.

At the Court at the Queen's Palace, the 7th of January 1807; Present, the King's most excellent Majesty in Council. – Whereas, the French government has issued certain Orders, which, in violation of the usages of war, purport to prohibit the Commerce of all Neutral Nations with his majesty's dominions, and also to prevent such nations from trading with any other country, in any articles, the growth, produce, or manufacture of his majesty's dominions: and whereas the said government has also taken it upon itself to declare all his majesty's dominions to be in a state of blockade, at a time when the fleets of France and her allies are themselves confined within their own ports by the superior valour and discipline of the British navy: and whereas such attempts on the part of the enemy would give to his majesty an unquestionable right of retaliation, and would warrant his majesty in enforcing the same prohibition of all commerce with France, which that power vainly hopes to effect against the commerce of his majesty's subjects; a prohibition which the superiority of his majesty's naval forces might enable him to support, by actually investing the ports and coasts of the enemy with numerous squadrons and cruisers; so as to make the entrance or approach thereto manifestly dangerous: and whereas his majesty, though unwilling to follow the example of his enemies, by proceeding to an extremity so distressing to all nations not engaged in the war, and carrying on their accustomed trade, yet feels himself bound by a due regard to the just defence of the rights and interests of his people, not to suffer such measures to be taken by the enemy, without taking some steps on his part to restrain this violence, and to retort upon him the evils of their own injustice: his majesty is thereupon pleased, by and with the advice of his privy council, to order, and it hereby ordered, That no vessel shall be permitted to trade from one port to another, both which ports shall belong to or be in the possession of France or her allies, or shall be so far under their controul, as that British vessels may not freely trade thereat: and the commanders of his majesty's ships of war and privateers shall be, and are hereby instructed to warn every neutral vessel coming from any such port, and destined to another such port, to discontinue her voyage, and not to proceed to any such port; and any vessel after being so warned, or any vessel coming from any such port, after a reasonable time shall have been afforded for receiving information of this his majesty's Order, which shall be found proceeding to another such port, shall be captured and brought in, and, together with her cargo, shall be condemned as lawful prize: and his majesty's principle secretaries of state, the lords commissioners of the admiralty, and the judges of the high court of admiralty, and courts of vice admiralty, are to take the necessary measures herein as to them shall respectively appertain.

## 21. Milan Decree, December 17, 1807

*The French had no more regard for neutral rights than the British. When the British offered a license trade in the Orders-in-Council of November 11, 1807, Napoleon responded with the Milan Decree.*

Source: *American State Papers*, 3:290–91.

NAPOLEON, *Emperor of the French, King of Italy, and Protector of the Rhenish Confederation*:

Observing the measures adopted by the British Government, on the 11th November last, by which vessels belonging to neutral, friendly, or even Powers the allies of England, are made liable, not only to be searched by English cruisers, but to be compulsorily detained in England, and to have a tax laid on them of so much per cent on the cargo, to be regulated by the British Legislature:

Observing that, by these acts, the British Government denationalizes ships of every nation in Europe; that it is not competent for any Government to detract from its own independence and rights, all the sovereigns of Europe having in trust the sovereignties and independence of the flag; that if by unpardonable weakness, and which in the eyes of posterity would be an indelible stain, if such a tyranny was allowed to be established into principles, and consecrated by usage, the English would avail themselves of it to assert it as a right, as they have availed themselves of the tolerance of Government to establish the infamous principle that the flag of a nation does not cover goods, and have to their right of blockade an arbitrary extension, and which infringes of the sovereignty of every State; we have decreed and do decree as follows:

Art. 1. Every ship, to whatever nation it belong, that shall have submitted to be searched by an English ship, or to a voyage to England, or shall have paid any tax whatsoever to the English government, is hereby and for that alone declared to be denationalized, to have forfeited the protection of its King, and to have become English property.

Art. 2. Whether the ships thus denationalized by the arbitrary measures of the English Government enter into our ports, or those of our allies, or whether they fall into the hands of our ships of war, or of our privateers, they are declared to be good and lawful prize.

Art. 3. The British islands are declared to be in a state of blockade, both by land and sea. Every ship, of whatever nation, or whatsoever the nature of its cargo so may be, that sails from the ports of England, or those of the English colonies, and of the countries occupied by English troops, and proceeding to England, or to the English colonies, or to countries occupied by English troops, is good and lawful prize, as contrary to the present decree, and may be captured by our ships of war, or our privateers, and adjudged to the captor.

Art. 4. These measures, which are resorted to only in just retaliation of the barbarous system adopted by England, which assimilates its legislation to that of Algiers, shall cease to have any effect with respect to all nations who shall have the firmness to compel the English Government to respect their flag. They shall continue to be rigorously in force as long as that Government does not return to the principle of the law of nations, which regulates the relations of civilized States in a state of war. The provisions of the present decree shall be abrogated and null, in fact, as soon as the English abide again by the principles of the law of nations, which are also the principles of justice and honor.

All our ministers are charged with the execution of the present decree, which shall be inserted in the bulletin of the laws.

## 22. James Madison to Thomas Jefferson, April 24, 1809

*Much of Republican foreign policy assumed French friendship, regardless of the form of the French government. Here Madison lays out his expectations of and fears about France.*

Source: Madison, *Papers,* 1:135–36.

I have recd. your favor of the 19th. You will see in the newspapers the result of the Advances made by G.B. Attempts were made to give shapes to the arrangement implying inconsistency and blame on our part. They were however met in a proper manner & readily abandoned; leaving these charges in their full force, as they now bear on the other side. The B. Cabinet must have changed its course under a full conviction that an adjustment with this Country, had become essential; & it is not improbable that this policy may direct the ensuing negociation; mingling with it, at the same time, the hope that it may embroil us with France. To this use it may be expected the Federalists will endeavor to turn what is already done, at the coming session of Congs. The steps deemed proper to give the proceeding a contrary turn will not be omitted. And if France be not bereft of common sense, or be not predetermined on war with us, she will certainly not play into the hand of her Enemy. Besides the general motive to follow the example of G.B. she cannot be insensible of the dangerous tendency of prolonging the commercial sufferings of her Allies, particularly Russia, all of them already weary of such a state of things, after the pretext for enforcing it shall have ceased. She must be equally aware of the importance of our relations to Spanish America, which must now become the great object of Napoleon's pride & Ambition. Should he repeal his decrees with a view to this object, the most probable source of conflict will be in his extending the principle on which he required a *prohibition* of the Trade with St. Domingo, to the case of the Spanish Colonies. Nor is it improbable that he may couple such a requisition with an offer to cede the Floridas, which would present a dilemma not very pleasant.

## 23. Henry Clay's Speech, February 22, 1810

*The War Hawks did not form a coherent body until November 1811. Their leader, Henry Clay, laid out the central argument more than a year in advance. Clay notes the outrages committed by Great Britain, as well as his confidence that the British might easily be opposed.*

Source: Henry Clay, *The Papers of Henry Clay*, James F. Hopkins, Mary M. W. Hargreaves, et al., eds. (Lexington: University Press of Kentucky, 1959–93), 1:448–50.

Sir, have we not been for years contending against the tyranny of the ocean? Has not congress pledged itself to the world not to surrender our rights? Has not the nation, at large, in all its capacities of meetings of the people, state and general governments, resolved to maintain, at all hazards our maritime independence? Your whole circle of commercial restrictions, including the non-importation, embargo, and non-intercourse acts, had in view an opposition to the offensive measures of the belligerents, so justly complained of by us. They presented *resistance*—the *peaceful* resistance of the law. When this is abandoned, without effect, I am for resistance by the *sword.*

No man in the nation desires peace more than I. But I prefer the troubled ocean of war, demanded by the honor and independence of the country, with all its calamities, and desolations, to the tranquil, putrescent pool of ignominious peace. If we can accommodate our differences with one of the belligerents only, I should prefer that one to be Great-Britain. But if with neither, and we are forced into a selection of our enemy, then I am for war with Britain; because I believe her prior in aggression, and her injuries and insults to us were atrocious in character. I shall not attempt to exhibit an account between the belligerents of mercantile spoliations, inflicted and menaced. On that point we have just cause of war with both. Britain stands preeminent, in her outrage on us, by her violations of the sacred personal rights of American freemen, in the arbitrary and lawless impressment of our seamen—the attack on the Chesapeake—the murder, Sir, I will not dwell on the long catalogue of our wrongs & disgraces, which has been repeated until the sensibility of the nation is benumbed by the dishonorable detail.

But we are asked for the means of carrying on War; and those who oppose it triumphantly appeal to the vacant vaults of the treasury. With the unimpaired credit of the government, invigorated by a faithful observance of public engagements, and a rapid extinction of the debt of the revolution; with the boundless territories in the west, presenting a safe pledge for reimbursement of loans to any extent—is it not astonishing that despondency itself should disparage the resources of this country? You have, sir, I am credibly informed in the city & vicinity of New

Orleans alone, public property sufficient to extinguish the celebrated deficit in the Secretary's report. And are we to regard as nothing the patriotic offer so often made by the states to spend their last cent, and risk their last drop of blood in the preservation of our neutral privileges? Or, are we to be governed by the low, groveling parsimony of the counting room, and to cast up the actual pence in the drawer before we assert our inestimable rights? It is said, however, that no object is obtainable by war with Britain. In its fortunes we are to estimate not only the benefit to be derived to ourselves, but the injury to be done the enemy. The conquest of Canada is in your power. I trust I shall not be deemed presumptuous when I state, what I verily believe, that the militia of Kentucky are alone competent to place Montreal and Upper Canada at your feet. Is it nothing to the British nation—is it nothing to the pride of her monarch to have the last of the immense North American possessions held by him in the commencement of his reign, wrested from his dominion? Is it nothing to us to extinguish the torch which lights up savage warfare? Is it nothing to acquire the entire fur trade connected with that country, and to destroy the temptation and the opportunity of violating your revenue and other laws?

## 24. The Cadore Letter (Duc de Cadore to John Armstrong), August 5, 1810

*Madison's acceptance of the Cadore letter as a genuine representation of French policy was a key moment on the road to war with Great Britain. The Cadore letter seemed to promise an eventual repeal of the Berlin and Milan Decrees, although with the caveat that Great Britain must repeal its orders.*

Source: *American State Papers*, 3:336–37.

I have laid before His Majesty, the Emperor and King, the act of Congress of the 1st of May, taken from the Gazette of the United States, which you have sent to me.

His Majesty could have wished that this act, and all the other acts of the Government of the United States, which interest France, had always been officially made known to him. In general, he has only had a knowledge of them indirectly, and after a long interval of time. There have resulted from this delay serious inconveniences, which would not have existed if these acts had been promptly and officially communicated.

The Emperor had applauded the general embargo laid by the United States on all their vessels, because that measure, if it has been prejudicial to France, had in at least nothing offensive to her honor. It has caused her to lose her colonies of Martinique, Guadaloupe, and Cayenne; the Emperor has not complained of it. He has made this sacrifice to the principle which had determined the Americans to lay the embargo, inspiring them with the noble resolution of interdicting to themselves the ocean, rather than to submit to the laws of those who wished to make themselves the tyrants of it.

The act of the 1st March has raised the embargo, and substituted for it a measure the most injurious to the interests of France.

This act, of which the Emperor knew nothing until very lately, interdicted to American vessels the commerce of France, at the time it authorized that to Spain, Naples, and Holland, that is to say, to the countries under French influence, and denounced confiscation against all French vessels which should enter the ports of America. Reprisal was a right, and commanded by the dignity of France, a circumstance on which it was impossible to make a compromise. The sequestration of all the American vessels in France has been the necessary consequence of the measure taken by Congress.

Now Congress retrace their steps, they revoke the act of the 1st of March; the ports of America are now open to French commerce, and France is no longer interdicted to the Americans; in short, Congress engages to oppose itself to that one of the belligerent Powers which should refuse to acknowledge the rights of neutrals.

In this new state of things, I am authorized to declare to you, sir, that the decrees of Berlin and Milan are revoked, and that after the 1st of November they will cease to have effect; it being understood that, in consequence of this declaration, the English shall revoke their orders in council, and renounce the new principles of blockade, which they have wished to establish; or that the United States, conformably to the act you just communicated, shall cause their rights to be respected by the English.

It is with the most particular satisfaction, sir, that I make known to you this determination of the Emperor. His Majesty loves the Americans. Their prosperity and their commerce are within the scope of his policy.

The independence of America is one of the principal titles of glory to France. Since that epoch, the Emperor is pleased in aggrandizing the United States, and, under all circumstances, that which can contribute to the independence, to the prosperity, and the liberty of the Americans, the Emperor will consider as conformable with the interests of his empire.

### 25. John Quincy Adams to John Adams, December 26, 1814

*The Treaty of Ghent was a better treaty for the United States than battlefield results warranted. Here John Quincy Adams explains to his father how the treaty was signed and why he was unable to secure a more explicit guarantee for American access to the fisheries.*

Source: John Quincy Adams, *The Writings of John Quincy Adams*, Worthington C. Ford, ed. (New York: Macmillan, 1913–17), 5:250–53.

We were instructed not to suffer our right to the fisheries to be brought into discussion. We had no authority to admit any discrimination between the first and the last parts of the third article of the treaty of 1783; no power to offer or agree to an equivalent either for the rights or the liberties. I considered both as standing on the same footing, both as the continuance of franchises always enjoyed, and the difference in the expressions only as arising from the operation of our change from the condition of British subjects to that of a sovereign people upon an object in one part of general and in the other of special jurisdiction. The special jurisdiction had been that of our own sovereign; by the Revolution and the treaty of peace it became a foreign, but still remained a special jurisdiction. By the very same instrument in which we thus acknowledged it as a foreign jurisdiction, we reserved to ourselves, with the full assent of its sovereign, and without any limitation of time or of events, the franchise which we have always enjoyed while the jurisdiction had been our own.

It was termed a *liberty*, because it was a freedom to be enjoyed within a special jurisdiction; the fisheries on the Banks were termed rights, because they were to be enjoyed on the ocean, the common jurisdiction of all nations; but there was nothing in the terms themselves, and nothing in the article or in the treaty, implying an intention or expectation of either of the contracting parties that one more than the other should be liable to forfeiture by a subsequent war. On the maturest deliberation I still hold this argument to be sound, and it is to my mind the only *one* by which our claim to the fisheries within British jurisdiction can be maintained. But after the declaration made by the British government it was not to be expected that they would be converted to this opinion without much discussion, which was forbidden to us, and the results of which must have been very doubtful upon minds at all times inclined, and at this time most peculiarly prone, rather to lean upon power than to listen to reason. We stated the general principles in one of our notes to the British plenipotentiaries, as the ground upon which our government deemed no new stipulation necessary to secure the enjoyment of all our rights and liberties in the fisheries. They did not answer that part of our note; but when they came to ask a stipulation for the right of British subjects to navigate the Mississippi, we objected that by our construction of the treaty of 1783 it was unnecessary. If we admitted their construction of that treaty so as to give them a new right to the navigation, they must give us an equivalent for it. We offered an article recognizing the continuance of the rights on both sides; this offer met however with very great opposition among ourselves, for there were two of us against making it, and who thought the navigation of the Mississippi incomparably more valuable than the contested part of the fisheries. Not so did the British government think; for they, instead of accepting it, offered us an article stipulating to negotiate hereafter for an equivalent to be given by Great Britain for the right of navigating the Mississippi, and by the United States for the liberties of the fisheries within British jurisdiction. This was merely to obtain from us the formal admission that both the rights were abrogated by the war. To that admission I was determined not to subscribe. The article was withdrawn last Thursday by the British plenipotentiaries, who accepted our proposal to say nothing in the treaty about either, and to omit the article by which they had agreed that our boundary west from the Lake of the Woods should be the forty-ninth parallel of north latitude. They at the same time referred again to their original declaration that the fisheries within British jurisdiction would not hereafter be granted without an equivalent. It is evident that it must be the subject of a future negotiation; the only thing possible to be done now was to reserve our whole claim unimpaired, and with that I consented to the treaty.

We were also obliged to except from the immediate restitution of territory taken during the war the islands in Passamaquoddy Bay. The British claim them as having been before the peace of 1783 within the limits of Nova Scotia, and insisted upon holding them, not as taken them during the war, but as of right belonging to them. At first they declared their right to be too clear even for discussion; but they finally agreed to refer to commissioners and to a friendly sovereign the title to them, and even to the island of Grant Manan in the Bay of Fundy, which has been since 1724 in their possession. We persisted in demanding that the Passamaquoddy Islands should be included in the general restoration, until they manifested a determination to break off rather than yield the point. Their inflexibility upon two objects exclusively interesting to the state of Massachusetts is a melancholy comment upon that policy by which Massachusetts has arrayed herself against the government of the Union. Had Massachusetts been true to herself and to the Union, Great Britain would not have dared to hinge the question of peace or war upon Moose Island, or upon the privileges of Massachusetts fishermen. As a citizen of Massachusetts I felt it to be most peculiarly my duty not to abandon any one of her rights, and I would have refused to sign the treaty had any of them been abandoned. But it was impossible to force a stipulation in favor of the fisheries; and for a temporary possession of Moose Island, merely until it should be ascertained whether it belongs to her or not, we could not think of continuing the war. . . . I have great satisfaction in saying that our harmony has been as great and constant as perhaps ever existed between five persons employed together upon so important a trust. Upon almost all the important questions we have been unanimous.

# Notes

## Introduction

1. Rodney to Madison, January 10, 1810, in James Madison, *The Papers of James Madison: Presidential Series*, Robert A. Rutland and J. C. A. Stagg et al., eds. (Charlottesville: University of Virginia Press, 1984–), 2:181.

## Chapter 1. The Diplomacy of Independence

1. For the Secret Committee, see Elizabeth Miles Nuxoll, *Congress and the Munitions Merchants: The Secret Committee of Trade during the American Revolution 1775–1777* (New York: Garland, 1985), 42–46.
2. Thomas Paine, "Common Sense," in Thomas Paine, *Collected Writings*, Eric Foner, ed. (New York: Library of America, 1995), 25, 28.
3. Ibid., 22, 24.
4. Debate notes, March–April 1776, in John Adams, *Diary and Autobiography of John Adams*, L. H. Butterfield et al., eds. (Cambridge, MA: Harvard University Press, 1961), 2:236.
5. Samuel Flagg Bemis, *The Diplomacy of the American Revolution*, rev. ed. (Bloomington: Indiana University Press, 1957), 23–27; Orville T. Murphy, *Charles Gravier, Comte de Vergennes: French Diplomacy in the Age of Revolution 1719–1787* (Albany: State University of New York Press, 1982), 235–37.
6. Dickinson speech notes, July 1, 1776, in Paul H. Smith, ed., *Letters of Delegates to Congress, 1774–1789* (Washington: Library of Congress, 1976–2000), 4:354–56.

7. Model Treaty, in John Adams, *Papers of John Adams*, Robert J. Taylor et al., eds. (Cambridge, MA: Harvard University Press, 1977–), 4:265–76.
8. Franklin to Lee, March 21, 1777, in Benjamin Franklin, *The Papers of Benjamin Franklin*, Leonard W. Labaree et al., eds. (New Haven, CT: Yale University Press, 1959–), 23:511.
9. Francis Wharton, *The Revolutionary Diplomatic Correspondence of the United States* (Washington: Government Printing Office, 1889), 1:523.
10. Jonathan R. Dull, *A Diplomatic History of the American Revolution* (New Haven, CT: Yale University Press, 1985), 89–91.
11. Text of treaties in Hunter Miller, ed., *Treaties and Other International Acts of the United States of America* (Washington: Government Printing Office, 1931–1948), 2:4–47.
12. William C. Stinchcombe, *The American Revolution and the French Alliance* (Syracuse, NY: Syracuse University Press, 1969), 25.
13. Quoted in Murphy, *Vergennes*, 329.
14. Franklin to Samuel Huntington, August 9, 1780, in Franklin, *Papers*, 33:162.
15. Adams to the president of Congress, February 1, 1781, in Wharton, *Revolutionary Diplomatic Correspondence*, 4:244.
16. Bemis, *Diplomacy of the American Revolution*, 150–56.
17. Draft treaty in "John Jay to the President of Congress, October 3, 1781," in Wharton, *Revolutionary Diplomatic Correspondence*, 4:738–65.
18. Miller, *Treaties*, 2:58–88.
19. Diary entry, November 5, 1782, in Adams, *Diary*, 3:46–47.
20. Quoted in Richard B. Morris, *The Peacemakers: The Great Powers and American Independence* (New York: Harper & Row, 1965), 382.
21. Diary entry, February 18, 1783, in Adams, *Diary*, 3:108.
22. Jay to Morris, October 13, 1782, in Wharton, *Revolutionary Diplomatic Correspondence*, 5:810.
23. Franklin to Vergennes, December 17, 1782, ibid., 6:144.

### Chapter 2. The Failure of the Confederation

1. Lee to John Adams, March 3, 1783, in Adams, *Papers*, 14:321.

2. Adams to Elbridge Gerry, September 3, 1783, in Wharton, *Revolutionary Diplomatic Correspondence*, 6:670.
3. Jay to Adams, October 14, 1785, in Mary A. Giunta et al., eds., *The Emerging Nation: A Documentary History of the Foreign Relations of the United States under the Articles of Confederation, 1780–1789* (Washington: National Historical Publications and Records Commission, 1996), 2:863.
4. Otto to the Comte de Montmorin, April 10, 1787, ibid., 3:464.
5. Miller, *Treaties*, 2:123–49.
6. Ibid., 2:162–83.
7. Ibid., 2:212–19.
8. Jay to Adams, October 15, 1785, in Giunta et al., eds., *Emerging Nation*, 2:863.
9. Jefferson to Monroe, November 11, 1784, in Thomas Jefferson, *The Papers of Thomas Jefferson*, Julian Boyd et al., eds. (Princeton, NJ: Princeton University Press, 1950–), 7:511–12.
10. Adams to Jefferson, July 31, 1786, in Giunta et al., eds., *Emerging Nation*, 3:245.
11. Adams to Jay, May 5, 1785, ibid., 2:617.
12. Adams to Jay, August 6, 1785, ibid., 2:733.
13. Adams to Cotton Tufts, May 26, 1786, in L. H. Butterfield, Marc Friedlaender, and Richard Allen Ryerson, et al., eds., *Adams Family Correspondence*, 7:207.
14. Adams to Jay, July 19, 1785, in John Adams, *The Works of John Adams*, Charles Francis Adams, ed. (Boston: Little, Brown, 1850–56), 8:282.
15. Adams to Jay, February 26, 1786, ibid., 8:380–81.
16. Vergennes to the Chevalier de la Luzerne, February 15, 1784, in Giunta et al., eds., *Emerging Nation*, 2:301.
17. Merrill D. Peterson, "Thomas Jefferson and Commercial Policy, 1783–1793," *William and Mary Quarterly* 22, 3rd series, no. 4 (October 1965): 592.
18. Luzerne to Vergennes, May 17, 1784, in Giunta et al., eds., *Emerging Nation*, 2:370–71.
19. Jefferson to Vergennes, August 15, 1785, in Jefferson, *Papers*, 8:389.

20. Jacob Price, *France and the Chesapeake: A History of the French Tobacco Monopoly, 1674–1791, and of Its Relationship to the British and American Tobacco Trades* (Ann Arbor: University of Michigan Press, 1973), 2:731–81.
21. Jefferson to the Comte de Montmorin, July 23, 1787, in Jefferson, *Papers*, 11:616.
22. "Observations on the Whale-Fishery," ibid., 14:245, 251–52, 254, 268–69.
23. Thomas Jefferson, *Notes on the State of Virginia* [1787] (Chapel Hill: University of North Carolina Press, 1954), 164–65, 174–75.
24. Quoted in Jon Kukla, *A Wilderness So Immense: The Louisiana Purchase and the Destiny of America* (New York: Knopf, 2003), 53.
25. Jay report, February 25, 1786, in Giunta et al., eds., *Emerging Nation*, 3:106.
26. Jay to the president of Congress, August 3, 1786, ibid., 3:247–55.
27. "Notes on Ancient and Modern Confederacies," in James Madison, *The Papers of James Madison*, William T. Hutchinson, William M. E. Rachal, et al., eds. (Chicago and Charlottesville: University of Chicago Press and University of Virginia Press, 1962–91), 9:4–24.
28. "Vices of the Political System of the United States," ibid., 9:348–58. For the ideological argument, see Robert W. Smith, *Keeping the Republic: Ideology and Early American Diplomacy* (Dekalb: Northern Illinois University Press, 2004), 54–55.
29. David C. Henrickson, *Peace Pact: The Lost World of the American Founding* (Lawrence: University of Kansas Press, 2003); Max M. Edling, *A Revolution in Favor of Government: Origins of the U.S. Constitution and the Making of the American State* (New York: Oxford University Press, 2003).
30. H. James Henderson, *Party Politics in the Continental Congress* (New York: McGraw-Hill, 1974), 312.
31. Max Farrand, ed., *The Records of the Federal Convention of 1787* (New Haven, CT: Yale University Press, 1911–37), 1:462, 465.
32. Ibid., 1:482.
33. Ibid., 1:528, 530–31.
34. Ibid., 1:402.
35. Ibid., 1:466–67.
36. Ibid., 2:318–19.

37. Ibid., 2:306–8.
38. Ibid., 2:361–63.
39. Ibid., 2:449–53.
40. Ibid., 2:297.
41. Ibid., 2:540–41.
42. Ibid., 2:547–50.
43. See Frederick W. Marks III, *Independence on Trial: Foreign Affairs and the Making of the Constitution* (Baton Rouge: Louisiana State University Press, 1973), 200–206.
44. Alexander Hamilton, John Jay, and James Madison, *The Federalist*, Jacob E. Cooke, ed. (Middletown, CT: Wesleyan University Press, 1961), 18–23.
45. Ibid., 64.
46. Ibid., 83, 85.
47. Ibid., 5.
48. Ibid., 28, 31–32.
49. Ibid., 36–39, 43.
50. Herbert J. Storing, ed., *The Anti-Federalist: Writings by the Opponents of the Constitution* (Chicago: University of Chicago Press, 1985), 17, 48, 148–49.
51. Merrill Jensen et al., eds., *The Documentary History of the Ratification of the Constitution* (Madison: State Historical Society of Wisconsin, 1976–), 2:583–84.
52. Ibid., 6:1250, 1288, 1318, 1419.
53. Ibid., 9:929, 1051, 955; 10:1527.
54. Ibid., 9:934–35, 977, 1008–9.
55. Moustier to the Comte de Montmorin, December 25, 1788, in Guinta et al., eds., *Emerging Nation*, 3:903.

### Chapter 3. American Foreign Relations in the Federalist Era

1. Statistics in Charles R. Ritcheson, *Aftermath of Revolution: British Policy toward the United States, 1783–1795* (Dallas: Southern Methodist University Press, 1969), 188.
2. Max M. Edling, "'So Immense a Power in the Affairs of War': Alexander Hamilton and the Restoration of Public Credit," *William and Mary Quarterly* 64, 3rd series, no. 2 (April 2007): 287–326.

3. Jefferson to Madison, August 29, 1789, in Jefferson, *Papers*, 15:366.
4. Hamilton to Lafayette, October 6, 1789, in Alexander Hamilton, *The Papers of Alexander Hamilton*, Harold C. Syrett et al., eds. (New York: Columbia University Press, 1961–1987), 5:425.
5. Quoted in Charles Downer Hazen, *Contemporary American Opinion of the French Revolution* (Baltimore: Johns Hopkins University Press, 1897), 81.
6. Jefferson to Jonathan B. Smith, April 26, 1791, in Jefferson, *Papers*, 20:290.
7. Proclamation of Neutrality, April 22, 1793, in James D. Richardson, ed., *A Compilation of the Messages and Papers of the Presidents 1789–1902* (Washington: Bureau of National Literature and Art, 1905–1906), 1:156–57.
8. Samuel Flagg Bemis, *Jay's Treaty: A Study of Commerce and Diplomacy*, rev. ed. (New Haven, CT: Yale University Press, 1962), 185.
9. "Opinion on the Treaties with France," April 28, 1793, in Jefferson, *Papers*, 25:608–18.
10. Hamilton and Knox to Washington, May 2, 1793, in Hamilton, *Papers*, 14:367–96.
11. Jefferson to Madison, May 19, 1793, in Jefferson, *Papers*, 25:62.
12. Genet to the foreign minister, June 6, 1793, in Frederick J. Turner, ed., "Correspondence of the French Ministers to the United States, 1791–1797," *Annual Report of the American Historical Association for the Year 1903*, vol. 2 (Washington: Government Printing Office, 1904), 217.
13. "Pacificus No. 1," June 29, 1793, in Hamilton, *Papers*, 15:38, 40, 42.
14. "Helvidius No. 1," August 24, 1793, in Madison, *Papers*, 15:66, 69.
15. Quoted in Louis Martin Sears, *George Washington and the French Revolution* (Detroit: Wayne State University Press, 1960), 187.
16. Hamilton to Washington, April 14, 1794, in Hamilton, *Papers*, 16:266–67.
17. Hamilton to Jay, May 6, 1794, ibid., 16:381–85.
18. Miller, *Treaties*, 2:245–64.
19. Turner, ed., "Correspondence of the French Ministers," 451.
20. For the implications for American politics, see Todd Estes, *The Jay Treaty Debate, Public Opinion, and the Evolution of Early American Political Culture* (Amherst: University of Massachusetts Press, 2006).
21. Arthur Preston Whitaker, *The Spanish-American Frontier, 1783–1795: The Westward Movement and the Spanish Retreat in the Mississippi Valley* (Boston:

Houghton Mifflin, 1927), 206–7; Samuel Flagg Bemis, *Pinckney's Treaty: America's Advantage from Europe's Distress, 1783–1800*, rev. ed. (New Haven, CT: Yale University Press, 1960), 234.

22. Miller, *Treaties*, 2:318–38.
23. James Madison, March 7, 1796, *Annals of the Congress of the United States* (Washington: Gales & Seaton, 1834–56), 5:437–38.
24. Albert Gallatin, March 24, 1796, ibid., 5:739–40, 742–43.
25. Daniel Buck, March 24, 1796, ibid., 5:716.
26. Robert Goodloe Harper, March 9, 1796, ibid., 5:463.
27. March 24 and 30, 1796, ibid., 5:759–61.
28. Samuel Lyman, April 15, 1796, ibid., 5:990.
29. Madison, April 15, 1796, ibid., 5:975–86.
30. Lyman, April 15, 1796, ibid., 5:988.
31. Fisher Ames, April 29, 1796, ibid., 5:1139–63.
32. Quoted in Stanley Elkins and Eric McKitrick, *The Age of Federalism: The Early American Republic, 1788–1800* (New York: Oxford University Press, 1993), 510–11.
33. See editorial note, *Papers of Alexander Hamilton*, 20:167–73
34. Farewell Address, in Richardson, ed., *Messages and Papers*, 1:215–16.
35. Ibid., 1:221.
36. Ibid., 1:222.
37. Adams to Abigail Adams, March 5, 1797, in Adams Papers, reel 383, Massachusetts Historical Society.
38. Speech of May 16, 1797, in Richardson, ed., *Messages and Papers*, 1:245–36.
39. Quoted in William C. Stinchcombe, *The XYZ Affair* (Westport, CT: Greenwood, 1980), 58.
40. Barlow to Abraham Baldwin, March 4, 1798, in Thomas Jefferson Papers, Library of Congress.
41. Message of June 21, 1798, in Richardson, ed., *Messages and Papers*, 1:266.
42. Quoted in Alexander DeConde, *The Quasi-War: The Politics and Diplomacy of the Undeclared War with France, 1797–1801* (New York: Charles Scribner's Sons, 1966), 107.
43. Miller, *Treaties*, 2:457–80.

### Chapter 4. The Jeffersonian Revolution in Foreign Affairs

1. First Inaugural Address, March 4, 1801, in Richardson, *Messages and Papers,* 1:323.
2. Miller, *Treaties,* 2:529–35.
3. Joseph J. Ellis, *American Sphinx: The Character of Thomas Jefferson* (New York: Knopf, 1997), 204.
4. Quoted in Tim Matthewson, *A Proslavery Foreign Policy: Haitian-American Relations during the Early Republic* (Westport, CT: Praeger, 2003), 100.
5. Madison to Livingston, September 28, 1801, in James Madison, *The Papers of James Madison: Secretary of State Series,* Robert A. Rutland et al., eds. (Charlottesville: University of Virginia Press, 1986–), 2:144–45.
6. Jefferson to Livingston, April 18, 1802, in Thomas Jefferson, *The Works of Thomas Jefferson*, Paul Leicester, ed. (New York: G. P. Putnam's Sons, 1904–1905), 9:364–65.
7. Livingston to Madison, August 10, 1802, in *American State Papers: Foreign Relations* (Washington: Gales & Seaton, 1833–61), 2:520–24; George Dangerfield, *Chancellor Robert R. Livingston of New York, 1746–1813* (New York: Harcourt, Brace, 1960), 331–35.
8. Quoted in Kukla, *Wilderness,* 249–50.
9. Miller, *Treaties,* 2:498–505.
10. Robert W. Tucker and David C. Hendrickson, *Empire of Liberty: The Statecraft of Thomas Jefferson* (New York: Oxford University Press, 1990), 163.
11. Henry Adams, *History of the United States during the Administrations of Thomas Jefferson and James Madison* (New York: Library of America, 1986), 1:979.
12. Second Annual Message, December 15, 1802, in Richardson, *Messages and Papers,* 1:342.
13. Quoted in Bradford Perkins, *Prologue to War: England and the United States 1805–1812* (Berkeley: University of California Press, 1961), 111–12.
14. Jefferson to Monroe, May 4, 1806, quoted in Henry Adams, *History of the United States,* 1:880–81.
15. Madison to Monroe and Pinkney, May 17, 1806, in *American State Papers,* 3:119–24.

16. Monroe and Pinkney to Madison, September 11, 1806, in ibid., 3:133–35.
17. Monroe and Pinkney to Madison, November 11, 1806, in ibid., 3:137–40.
18. Monroe-Pinkney Treaty, December 31, 1806, in ibid., 3:147–51.
19. Monroe and Pinkney to Madison, January 3, 1807, in ibid., 3:146–47.
20. Madison to Monroe and Pinkney, May 20, 1807, in James Madison, *The Writings of James Madison*, Gaillard Hunt, ed. (New York: G. P. Putnam's Sons, 1900–10), 7:421, 443–45.
21. Monroe to John Taylor of Caroline, September 10, 1810, quoted in Adams, *History of the United States*, 1:887.
22. Perkins, *Prologue to War*, 144.
23. Quoted in Burton Spivak, *Jefferson's English Crisis: Commerce, Embargo and the Republican Revolution* (Charlottesville: University of Virginia Press, 1979), 78.
24. Quoted in Frank E. Melvin, *Napoleon's Navigation System: A Study of Trade Control during the Continental Blockade* (New York: Appleton-Century, 1919), 46–47.
25. Quoted in Perkins, *Prologue to War*, 152.
26. See Smith, *Keeping the Republic*, 128.
27. John A. Logan, Jr., *No Transfer: An American Security Principle* (New Haven, CT: Yale University Press, 1961), 106.
28. Annual Message, November 8, 1808, in Richardson, *Messages and Papers*, 1:452–53.

**Chapter 5. Mr. Madison's Wars**

1. Quoted in Perkins, *Prologue to War*, 242.
2. Cadore letter, August 5, 1810, in *American State Papers*, 3:386–87.
3. Andrew McMichael, *Atlantic Loyalties: Americans in Spanish West Florida, 1785–1810* (Athens: University of Georgia Press, 2008), 157.
4. See J. C. A. Stagg, *Mr. Madison's War: Politics, Diplomacy and Warfare in the Early American Republic, 1783–1830* (Princeton, NJ: Princeton University Press, 1983), 68–69.
5. Third Annual Message, November 5, 1811, in Richardson, *Messages and Papers*, 1:493–94.

6. Donald R. Hickey, *The War of 1812: A Forgotten Conflict* (Urbana: University of Illinois Press, 1989), 33.
7. Message of June 1, 1812, in Richardson, *Messages and Papers*, 1:499–505.
8. Roger H. Brown, *The Republic in Peril: 1812* (New York: Columbia University Press, 1964), 72–73, 78–79, 82–83.
9. On the Late Loyalists, see Alan Taylor, "The Late Loyalists: Northern Reflections of the Early American Republic," *Journal of the Early Republic* 27, no. 1 (Spring 2007): 1–34.
10. Diary entry, October 9, 1810, in John Quincy Adams, *Memoirs of John Quincy Adams*, Charles Francis Adams, ed. (Philadelphia: Lippincott, 1874–77), 2:180.
11. Monroe to the American commissioners, April 15, 1813, in *American State Papers*, 3:695–700.
12. See Hickey, *War of 1812*, 182.
13. Quoted in Adams, *History of the United States*, 2:1186.
14. Miller, *Treaties*, 2:574–82.
15. Ibid., 2:595–99.
16. See James A. Carr, "The Battle of New Orleans and the Treaty of Ghent," *Diplomatic History* 3, no. 3 (Summer 1979): 273–82.
17. Miller, *Treaties*, 2:585–91.

# Selected Bibliography

## Printed Primary Sources

Adams, John. *Diary and Autobiography of John Adams*, 4 vols. Edited by L. H. Butterfield et al. Cambridge, MA: Harvard University Press, 1961.

———. *The Works of John Adams*, 10 vols. Edited by Charles Francis Adams. Boston: Little, Brown, 1850–56.

———. *Papers of John Adams*, 14 vols. to date. Edited by Robert J. Taylor et al. Cambridge, MA: Harvard University Press, 1977–.

Adams, John Quincy. *Memoirs of John Quincy Adams*, 12 vols. Edited by Charles Francis Adams. Philadelphia: Lippincott, 1874–77.

———. *The Writings of John Quincy Adams,* 7 vols. Edited by Worthington C. Ford. New York: Macmillan, 1913–17.

*American State Papers: Foreign Relations*, 6 vols. Washington: Gales & Seaton, 1833–61.

*Annals of the Congress of the United States*, 42 vols. Washington: Gales & Seaton, 1834–56.

Butterfield, L. H., Marc Friedlaender, and Richard Allen Ryerson et al., eds. *Adams Family Correspondence*, 10 vols. to date. Cambridge, MA: Harvard University Press, 1963–.

Clay, Henry. *The Papers of Henry Clay*, 11 vols. Edited by James F. Hopkins, Mary M. W. Hargreaves et al. Lexington: University Press of Kentucky, 1959–93.

Farand, Max, ed. *The Records of the Federal Convention of 1787*, 4 vols. New Haven, CT: Yale University Press, 1911–37.

Ford, Worthington C., ed. *Journals of the Continental Congress, 1774–1789*, 34 vols. Washington: Government Printing Office, 1904–37.

Franklin, Benjamin. *The Papers of Benjamin Franklin*, 39 vols. to date. Edited by Leonard W. Larabee et al. New Haven, CT: Yale University Press, 1959–.

Giunta, Mary A. et al., eds. *The Emerging Nation: A Documentary History of the Foreign Relations of the United States under the Articles of Confederation, 1780–1789*, 3 vols. Washington: National Historical Publications and Records Commission, 1996.

Hamilton, Alexander. *The Papers of Alexander Hamilton*, 27 vols. Edited by Harold C. Syrett et al. New York: Columbia University Press, 1961–87.

———, John Jay, and James Madison. *The Federalist*. Edited by Jacob E. Cooke. Middletown, CT: Wesleyan University Press, 1961.

Jay, John. *The Correspondence and Public Papers of John Jay*, 4 vols. Edited by Henry P. Johnston. New York: G. P. Putnam's Sons, 1890–94.

Jefferson, Thomas. *The Complete ANAS of Thomas Jefferson*. Edited by Franklin B. Sawvel. New York: Roundtable, 1903.

———. *Notes on the State of Virginia*. Edited by William Peden. Chapel Hill: University of North Carolina Press, 1954.

———. *The Papers of Thomas Jefferson*, 35 vols. to date. Edited by Julian P. Boyd et al. Princeton, NJ: Princeton University Press, 1950–.

———. *The Works of Thomas Jefferson*, 12 vols. Edited by Paul Leicester Ford. New York: G. P. Putnam's Sons, 1904–5.

———. *The Writings of Thomas Jefferson*, 20 vols. Edited by Andrew A. Lipscomb and Albert Bergh. Washington: Thomas Jefferson Memorial Association, 1904–5.

Jensen, Merrill et al., eds. *The Documentary History of the Ratification of the Constitution*, 20 vols. to date. Madison: State Historical Society of Wisconsin, 1976–.

Madison, James. *The Papers of James Madison*, 17 vols. Edited by William T. Hutchinson, William M. E. Rachal et al. Chicago and Charlottesville: University of Chicago Press and University of Virginia Press, 1959–91.

———. *The Papers of James Madison: Presidential Series*, 6 vols. to date. Edited by Robert A. Rutland, J. C. A. Stagg et al. Charlottesville: University of Virginia Press, 1984–.

———. *The Papers of James Madison: Secretary of State Series*, 8 vols. to date. Edited by Robert A. Rutland et al. Charlottesville: University of Virginia Press, 1986–.

———. *The Writings of James Madison*, 9 vols. Edited by Gaillard Hunt. New York: G. P. Putnam's Sons, 1900–1910.

Monroe, James. *The Writings of James Monroe*, 7 vols. Edited by Stanislaus Murray Hamilton. New York: G. P. Putnam's Sons, 1898–1903.

Paine, Thomas. *Collected Writings*. Edited by Eric Foner. New York: Library of America, 1995.

Richardson, James D., ed. *A Compilation of the Messages and Papers of the Presidents, 1789–1902*, 10 vols. Washington: Bureau of National Literature and Art, 1905–6.

Smith, Paul H., ed. *Letters of Delegates to Congress, 1774–1789*, 26 vols. Washington: Library of Congress, 1976–98.

Washington, George. *The Papers of George Washington: Presidential Series*, 13 vols. to date. Edited by W. W. Abbott et al. Charlottesville: University of Virginia Press, 1987–.

———. *The Writings of George Washington*, 39 vols. Edited by John C. Fitzpatrick. Washington: Government Printing Office, 1931–44.

Wharton, Francis, ed. *The Revolutionary Diplomatic Correspondence of the United States*, 6 vols. Washington: Government Printing Office, 1889.

## Secondary Sources

Adams, Henry. *History of the United States of America during the Administrations of Thomas Jefferson and James Madison*, 2 vols. New York: Library of America, 1986.

Adams, Henry A. *Prussian-American Relations 1775–1871*. Cleveland: Case Western Reserve University, 1960.

Adams, William Howard. *Gouverneur Morris: An Independent Life*. New Haven, CT: Yale University Press, 2003.

Ammon, Harry. *The Genet Mission*. New York: Norton, 1973.

———. *James Monroe: The Quest for National Identity*. New York: McGraw-Hill, 1971.

Barnby, H. G. *The Prisoners of Algiers: An Account of the Forgotten American-Algerian War, 1785–1797*. New York: Oxford University Press, 1966.

Beirne, Francis J. *The War of 1812*. New York: Dutton, 1949.

Bemis, Samuel Flagg. *The Diplomacy of the American Revolution,* rev. ed. Bloomington: Indiana University Press, 1957.

———. *Jay's Treaty: A Study of Commerce and Diplomacy*, rev. ed. New Haven, CT: Yale University Press, 1962.

———. *John Quincy Adams and the Foundations of American Foreign Policy*. New York: Knopf, 1949.

———. *Pinckney's Treaty: America's Advantage from Europe's Distress, 1783–1800*, rev. ed. New Haven, CT: Yale University Press, 1960.

Ben-Atar, Doron S. *The Origins of Jeffersonian Commercial Policy and Diplomacy*. New York: St. Martin's, 1993.

Bhagat, G. *Americans in India, 1784–1860*. New York: New York University Press, 1970.

Bird, Harrison. *War for the West, 1790–1813*. New York: Oxford University Press, 1971.

Black, Jeremy. *European International Relations, 1648–1815*. New York: Palgrave, 2002.

Bolkhovitinov, Nikolai N. *Russia and the American Revolution*. Translated by C. Jay Smith. Tallahassee, FL: Diplomatic Press, 1976.

Bowman, Albert Hall. *The Struggle for Neutrality: Franco-American Diplomacy during the Federalist Era*. Knoxville: University of Tennessee Press, 1974.

Boyd, Julian P. *Number 7: Alexander Hamilton's Secret Attempts to Control American Foreign Policy*. Princeton, NJ: Princeton University Press, 1964.

Brant, Irving. *James Madison*, 6 vols. Indianapolis, IN: Bobbs-Merrill, 1941–61.

Brecher, Frank W. *Negotiating the Louisiana Purchase: Robert Livingston's Mission to France, 1801–1804*. Jefferson, NC: McFarland, 2006.

———. *Securing American Independence: John Jay and the French Alliance*. Westport, CT: Praeger, 2003.

Brown, Gordon S. *Toussaint's Clause: The Founding Fathers and the Haitian Revolution*. Jackson: University of Mississippi Press, 2005.

Brown, Ralph Adams. *The Presidency of John Adams*. Lawrence: University Press of Kansas, 1975.

Brown, Roger H. *The Republic in Peril: 1812*. New York: Columbia University Press, 1964.

Brown, Weldon A. *Empire or Independence: A Study in the Failure of Reconciliation, 1774–1783*. Baton Rouge: Louisiana State University Press, 1941.

Burt, A. L. *The United States, Great Britain and British North America: From the Revolution to the Establishment of Peace after the War of 1812*. Washington: Carnegie Endowment for International Peace, 1940.

Carroll, Charles Griffin. *The United States and the Disruption of the Spanish Empire 1810–1822: A Study of the Relations of the United States with Spain and with the Rebel Spanish Colonies*. New York: Columbia University Press, 1937.

Casto, William R. *Foreign Affairs and the Constitution in the Age of Fighting Sail*. Columbia: University of South Carolina Press, 2006.

Chavez, Thomas E. *Spain and the Independence of the United States: An Intrinsic Gift*. Albuquerque: University of New Mexico Press, 2002.

Coles, Harry L. *The War of 1812*. Chicago: University of Chicago Press, 1965.

Combs, Jerald A. *The Jay Treaty: Political Battleground of the Founding Fathers*. Berkeley: University of California Press, 1970.

Cusick, James G. *The Other War of 1812: The Patriot War and the American Invasion of Spanish East Florida*. Gainesville: University Press of Florida, 2003.

Dangerfield, George. *Chancellor Robert R. Livingston of New York, 1746–1813*. New York: Harcourt, Brace, 1960.

DeConde, Alexander. *Entangling Alliance: Politics & Diplomacy under George Washington*. Durham, NC: Duke University Press, 1958.

———. *The Quasi-War: The Politics and Diplomacy of the Undeclared War with France, 1797–1801*. New York: Charles Scribner's Sons, 1966.

———. *This Affair of Louisiana*. New York: Charles Scribner's Sons, 1976.

Downs, Jacques M. *The Golden Ghetto: The American Commercial Community at Canton and the Shaping of American China Policy*. Bethlehem, PA: Lehigh University Press, 1997.

Dull, Jonathan R. *A Diplomatic History of the American Revolution*. New Haven, CT: Yale University Press, 1985.

———. *Franklin the Diplomat: The French Mission*. Philadelphia: American Philosophical Society, 1982.

Dulles, Foster Rhea. *The Old China Trade*. Boston: Houghton Mifflin, 1930.

Edling, Max M. "'So Immense a Power in the Affairs of War': Alexander Hamilton and the Restoration of Public Credit." *William and Mary Quarterly* 64, 3rd series, no. 2 (April 2007): 285–326.

Edmunds, R. David. *Tecumseh and the Quest for Indian Leadership*. Boston: Little, Brown, 1984.

Egan, Clifford L. *Neither Peace nor War: Franco-American Relations, 1803–1812*. Baton Rouge: Louisiana State University Press, 1983.

Egnal, Marc. *A Mighty Empire: The Origins of the American Revolution*. Ithaca, NY: Cornell University Press, 1988.

Elkins, Stanley, and Eric McKitrick. *The Age of Federalism: The Early American Republic, 1788–1800*. New York: Oxford University Press, 1993.

Ernst, Robert. *Rufus King: American Federalist*. Chapel Hill: University of North Carolina Press, 1968.

Estes, Todd. *The Jay Treaty Debate, Public Opinion, and the Evolution of Early American Political Culture*. Amherst: University of Massachusetts Press, 2006.

Field, James A., Jr. *America and the Mediterranean World 1776–1882*. Princeton, NJ: Princeton University Press, 1969.

Flexner, James Thomas. *George Washington*, 4 vols. Boston: Little, Brown, 1965–1972.

Freeman, Douglas Southall. *George Washington*, 7 vols. New York: Charles Scribner's Sons, 1948–57.

Furber, Holden. "The Beginnings of American Trade with India, 1784–1812." *New England Quarterly* 11, no. 2 (June 1938): 235–65.

Gilbert, Felix. *To the Farewell Address: Ideas of Early American Foreign Policy*. Princeton, NJ: Princeton University Press, 1961.

Graebner, Norman A. "Isolation and Antifederalism: The Ratification Debates." *Diplomatic History* 11, no. 4 (Fall 1987): 337–53.

Gruber, Ira D. *The Howe Brothers and the American Revolution*. Chapel Hill: University of North Carolina Press, 1972.

Heckscher, Eli F. *The Continental System: An Economic Interpretation*. Washington: Carnegie Endowment for International Peace, 1922.

Henderson, H. James. *Party Politics in the Continental Congress*. New York: McGraw-Hill, 1974.

Hendrickson, David C. *Peace Pact: The Lost World of the American Founding*. Lawrence: University of Kansas Press, 2003.

Hickey, Donald. *The War of 1812: A Forgotten Conflict*. Urbana: University of Illinois Press, 1989.

Hill, Peter P. *Napoleon's Troublesome Americans: Franco-American Relations, 1804–1815*. Washington: Potomac Books, 2005.

Horsman, Reginald. *The Causes of the War of 1812*. Philadelphia: University of Pennsylvania Press, 1962.

———. *The Diplomacy of the New Republic, 1776–1815*. Arlington Heights, IL: Harlan Davidson, 1985.

———. *Expansion and American Indian Policy, 1783–1812*. East Lansing: Michigan State University Press, 1967.

———. *The War of 1812*. New York: Knopf, 1969.

Hutson, James H. *John Adams and the Diplomacy of the American Revolution*. Lexington: University Press of Kentucky, 1980.

Hyneman, Charles S. *The First American Neutrality: A Study of the American Understanding of Neutral Obligations during the Years 1792 to 1815*. Urbana: University of Illinois Press, 1934.

Jensen, Merrill. *The New Nation: A History of the United States during the Confederation, 1781–1789*. New York: Knopf, 1950.

Kaminski, John P. "Honor and Interest: John Jay's Diplomacy during the Confederation." *New York History* 33, no. 3 (Summer 2002): 293–327.

Kammen, Michael G. *A Rope of Sand: The Colonial Agents, British Politics, and the American Revolution*. Ithaca, NY: Cornell University Press, 1968.

Kaplan, Lawrence S. *Alexander Hamilton: Ambivalent Anglophile*. Wilmington, DE: Scholarly Resources, 2002.

———. *Colonies into Nation: American Diplomacy, 1763–1801*. New York: Macmillan, 1972.

———. *Entangling Alliances with None: American Foreign Policy in the Age of Jefferson*. Kent, OH: Kent State University Press, 1987.

———. *Jefferson and France: An Essay on Politics and Political Ideas*. New Haven, CT: Yale University Press, 1967.

———. *Thomas Jefferson: Westward the Course of Empire*. Wilmington, DE: Scholarly Resources, 1999.

Ketcham, Ralph L. *James Madison: A Biography*. New York: Macmillan, 1971.

Kukla, Jon. *A Wilderness So Immense: The Louisiana Purchase and the Destiny of America*. New York: Knopf, 2003.

Lambert, Frank. *The Barbary Wars: American Independence in the Atlantic World*. New York: Hill & Wang, 2005.

Lang, Daniel G. *Foreign Policy in the Early Republic: The Law of Nations and the Balance of Power*. Baton Rouge: Louisiana State University Press, 1985.

Latimer, Jon. *1812: War with America*. Cambridge, MA: Harvard University Press, 2007.

Leiner, Frederick C. *The End of Barbary Terror: America's 1815 War against the Pirates of North Africa*. New York: Oxford University Press, 2006.

Lewis, James E., Jr. *The American Union and the Problem of Neighborhood: The United States and the Collapse of the Spanish Empire, 1783–1829*. Chapel Hill: University of North Carolina Press, 1998.

Logan, John A., Jr. *No Transfer: An American Security Principle*. New Haven, CT: Yale University Press, 1961.

Lycan, Gilbert L. *Alexander Hamilton and American Foreign Policy*. Norman: University of Oklahoma Press, 1970.

Lyon, E. Wilson. *Louisiana in French Diplomacy*. Norman: University of Oklahoma Press, 1974.

Mahon, John K. *The War of 1812*. Gainesville: University Press of Florida, 1972.

Malone, Dumas. *Jefferson and His Time*, 6 vols. Boston: Little, Brown, 1948–81.

Marks, Frederick W., III. *Independence on Trial: Foreign Affairs and the Making of the Constitution*. Baton Rouge: Louisiana State University Press, 1973.

———. "Power, Pride, and Purse: Diplomatic Origins of the Constitution." *Diplomatic History* 11, no. 4 (Fall 1987): 303–19.

Masterson, William H. *Tories and Democrats: British Diplomats in Pre-Jacksonian America*. College Station: Texas A&M University Press, 1985.

Matthews, Marty D. *Forgotten Founder: The Life and Times of Charles Pinckney*. Columbia: University of South Carolina Press, 2004.

Matthewson, Tim. *A Proslavery Foreign Policy: Haitian-American Relations during the Early Republic*. Westport, CT: Praeger, 2003.

McKay, Derek, and H. M. Scott. *The Rise of the Great Powers, 1648–1815*. New York: Longman, 1983.

McMichael, Andrew. *Atlantic Loyalties: Americans in Spanish West Florida, 1785–1810*. Athens: University of Georgia Press, 2008.

Melvin, Frank E. *Napoleon's Navigation System: A Study of Trade Control during the Continental Blockade*. New York: Appleton-Century, 1919.

Miller, Melanie Randolph. *Envoy to the Terror: Gouverneur Morris and the French Revolution*. Washington: Potomac Books, 2005.

Monaghan, Frank. *John Jay: Defender of Liberty against Kings and Peoples*. New York: Bobbs-Merrill, 1935.

Morris, Richard B. *The Peacemakers: The Great Powers and American Independence*. New York: Harper & Row, 1965.

Murphy, Charles T. *Charles Gravier, Compte de Vergennes: French Diplomacy in the Age of Revolution, 1719–1787*. Albany: State University of New York Press, 1982.

Nuxoll, Elizabeth Miles. *Congress and the Munitions Merchants: The Secret Committee of Trade during the American Revolution, 1775–1777*. New York: Garland, 1985.

Onuf, Peter, and Nicholas Onuf. *Federal Union, Modern World: The Law of Nations in an Age of Revolution, 1776–1814*. Madison, WI: Madison House, 1993.

Ott, Thomas O. *The Haitian Revolution, 1789–1804*. Knoxville: University of Tennessee Press, 1973.

Owsley, Frank Lawrence Jr., and Gene A. Smith. *Filibusters and Expansionists: Jeffersonian Manifest Destiny, 1800–1821*. Tuscaloosa: University of Alabama Press, 1997.

Pares, Richard. *Colonial Blockade and Neutral Rights, 1739–1763*. London: Oxford University Press, 1938.

Parker, Richard B. *Uncle Sam in Barbary: A Diplomatic History*. Gainesville: University Press of Florida, 2004.

Patrick, Rembert W. *Florida Fiasco: Rampant Rebels on the Georgia-Florida Border*. Athens: University of Georgia Press, 1954.

Perkins, Bradford. *Castlereagh and Adams: England and the United States, 1812–1823*. Berkeley: University of California Press, 1964.

———. *The First Rapprochement: England and the United States, 1795–1805.* Berkeley: University of California Press, 1955.

———. *Prologue to War: England and the United States, 1805–1812.* Berkeley: University of California Press, 1961.

Peterson, Merrill D. "Thomas Jefferson and Commercial Policy, 1783–1793." *William and Mary Quarterly* 23, 3rd series, no. 4 (October 1965): 584–610.

———. *Thomas Jefferson and the New Nation: A Biography.* New York: Oxford University Press, 1970.

Potts, Louis W. *Arthur Lee: A Virtuous Revolutionary.* Baton Rouge: Louisiana State University Press, 1981.

Pratt, Julius W. *Expansionists of 1812.* New York: Macmillan, 1925.

Price, Jacob M. *France and the Chesapeake: A History of the French Tobacco Monopoly, 1674–1791, and of Its Relationship to the British and American Tobacco Trades*, 2 vols. Ann Arbor: University of Michigan Press, 1973.

Rakove, Jack M. *The Beginning of National Politics: An Interpretive History of the Continental Congress.* New York: Knopf, 1979.

Remini, Robert V. *Henry Clay: Statesman for the Union.* New York: Norton, 1991.

Ritcheson, Charles R. *Aftermath of Revolution: British Policy toward the United States, 1783–1795.* Dallas: Southern Methodist University Press, 1969.

———. *British Politics and the American Revolution.* Norman: University of Oklahoma Press, 1954.

Rutland, Robert Allen. *The Presidency of James Madison.* Lawrence: University Press of Kansas, 1990.

Saul, Norman. *Distant Friends: The United States and Russia, 1763–1867.* Lawrence: University Press of Kansas, 1991.

Savelle, Max. *The Origins of American Diplomacy.* New York: Macmillan, 1967.

Schiff, Stacy. *A Great Improvisation: Franklin, France, and the Birth of America.* New York: Holt, 2005.

Schulte Nordholt, Jan Willem. *The Dutch Republic and American Independence.* Translated by Herbert H. Rowen. Chapel Hill: University of North Carolina Press, 1982.

Sears, Louis Martin. *George Washington and the French Revolution.* Detroit: Wayne State University Press, 1960.

Setser, Vernon G. *The Commercial Reciprocity Policy of the United States, 1774–1829*. Philadelphia: University of Pennsylvania Press, 1937.

Shackleford, George Green. *Jefferson's Adopted Son: The Life of William Short, 1759–1848*. Lexington: University Press of Kentucky, 1993.

Skeen, C. Edward. *John Armstrong, Jr., 1758–1843: A Biography*. Syracuse, NY: Syracuse University Press, 1981.

Smith, Page. *John Adams*, 2 vols. Garden City, NY: Doubleday, 1962.

Smith, Robert W. *Keeping the Republic: Ideology and Early American Diplomacy*. DeKalb: Northern Illinois University Press, 2004.

Spalding, Matthew, and Patrick J. Garraty. *A Sacred Union of Citizens: George Washington's Farewell Address and the American Character*. Lanham, MD: Rowman & Littlefield, 1996.

Spivak, Burton. *Jefferson's English Crisis: Commerce, Embargo, and the Republican Revolution*. Charlottesville: University of Virginia Press, 1979.

Stagg, J. C. A. *Borderlines in Borderlands: James Madison and the Spanish American Frontier, 1776–1821*. New Haven, CT: Yale University Press, 2009.

———. *Mr. Madison's War: Politics, Diplomacy and Warfare in the Early American Republic, 1783–1830*. Princeton, NJ: Princeton University Press, 1983.

Stahr, Walter. *John Jay: Founding Father*. New York: Hambledon & London, 2005.

Stinchcombe, William C. *The American Revolution and the French Alliance*. Syracuse, NY: Syracuse University Press, 1969.

———. *The XYZ Affair*. Westport, CT: Greenwood, 1980.

Stockley, Andrew. *Britain and France at the Birth of America: The European Powers and the Peace Negotiations of 1782–83*. Exeter, UK: University of Exeter Press, 2001.

Stourzh, Gerald. *Benjamin Franklin and American Foreign Policy*. Chicago: University of Chicago Press, 1969.

Stover, John F. "Franco-American Trade during the Confederation, 1781–1789." *North Carolina Historical Review* 25, no. 4 (October 1958): 399–414.

Sword, Wiley. *President Washington's Indian War: The Struggle for the Old Northwest, 1790–1795*. Norman: University of Oklahoma Press, 1985.

Tucker, Robert W., and David C. Hendrickson. *Empire of Liberty: The Statecraft of Thomas Jefferson*. New York: Oxford University Press, 1990.

———. *The Fall of the First British Empire*. Baltimore: Johns Hopkins University Press, 1982.

Tucker, Spencer C. *The Jeffersonian Gunboat Navy*. Columbia: University of South Carolina Press, 1993.

———, and Frank T. Reuter. *Injured Honor: The* Chesapeake-Leopard *Affair, June 22, 1807*. Annapolis, MD: Naval Institute Press, 1996.

Van Doren, Carl. *Benjamin Franklin*. New York: Viking, 1938.

Varg, Paul A. *Foreign Policies of the Founding Fathers*. East Lansing: Michigan State University Press, 1963.

Waciuma, Wanjohi. *Intervention in Spanish Floridas, 1801–1813: A Study in Jeffersonian Foreign Policy*. Boston: Branden Press, 1976.

Watson, J. Steven. *The Reign of George III, 1760–1815*. London: Oxford University Press, 1960.

Webster, Charles K. *Foreign Policy of Castlereagh, 1812–1815: Britain and the Reconstruction of Europe*. London: G. Bell & Sons, 1931.

Whitaker, Arthur Preston. *The Mississippi Question, 1795–1803: A Study in Trade, Politics, and Diplomacy*. Washington: American Historical Society, 1934.

———. *The Spanish-American Frontier, 1783–1795: The Westward Movement and the Spanish Retreat in the Mississippi Valley*. Boston: Houghton Mifflin, 1927.

———. *The United States and the Independence of Latin America, 1800–1830*. Baltimore: Johns Hopkins University Press, 1941.

White, David Hart. *Vicente Folch, Governor in Spanish East Florida, 1787–1811*. Washington: University Press of America, 1981.

Woodress, James. *A Yankee's Odyssey: The Life of Joel Barlow*. Philadelphia: Lippincott, 1958.

Wright, J. Leitch, Jr. *Britain and the American Frontier, 1783–1815*. Athens: University of Georgia Press, 1975.

Wright, Louis B., and Julia H. MacLeod. *The First Americans in North Africa: William Eaton's Struggle for a Vigorous Foreign Policy against the Barbary Pirates, 1799–1805*. Princeton, NJ: Princeton University Press, 1945.

Zimmerman, James F. *Impressment of American Seamen*. New York: Columbia University Press, 1925.

# Index

# About the Author

Robert W. Smith is assistant professor of history at Worcester State University, where he teaches the history of American foreign relations. He is the author of *Keeping the Republic: Ideology and Early American Diplomacy* and is a contributing editor of the online edition of *American Foreign Relations since 1600: A Guide to the Literature*. He lives in Marshfield, Massachusetts.